Erne:

The Uniqueness of Knowledge Management in Small Companies

Ernesto Villalba

The Uniqueness of Knowledge Management in Small Companies

Managing Knowledge as an Employer Strategy for Lifelong Learning

VDM Verlag Dr. Müller

Imprint

Bibliographic information by the German National Library: The German National Library lists this publication at the German National Bibliography; detailed bibliographic information is available on the Internet at http://dnb.d-nb.de.

Cover image: www.purestockx.com

Publisher:
VDM Verlag Dr. Müller Aktiengesellschaft & Co. KG , Dudweiler Landstr. 125 a, 66123 Saarbrücken, Germany,
Phone +49 681 9100-698, Fax +49 681 9100-988,
Email: info@vdm-verlag.de

Zugl.: Stockholm, Stockholm University, Dissertation 2006

Produced in USA and UK by:
Lightning Source Inc., La Vergne, Tennessee, USA
Lightning Source UK Ltd., Milton Keynes, UK
BookSurge LLC, 5341 Dorchester Road, Suite 16, North Charleston, SC 29418, USA

ISBN: 978-3-8364-5717-0

ABSTRACT

The present study explores the relationship between the 'knowledge-enabling environment' and the demand for training using a sample of 18 small private companies providing educational and consultancy services in Sweden. In this way, the dissertation is an exploration of the ways Swedish knowledge-intensive companies manage their knowledge. The 18 companies have participated in a European program for developing employee competence, financed by the European Social Fund. As part of this European-financed program companies have evaluated their business activity and determined their training needs in order to remain competitive. The 18 companies, thus, provide a rare opportunity to explore aspects of the demand for training in small enterprises.

Knowledge is understood here as both the structure and the content of mental schemas. It is embodied in individuals; it differs from information and data; and it can be tacit or explicit. Knowledge is a dynamic entity that is in a constant dialectic process with the reality it represents. It is through this dialectic process that people learn. This conceptualization of knowledge implies that when looking at organizational processes for managing knowledge, it is important to consider formal organized activities for learning, but also informal learning activities, which constitute the main source for tacit knowledge as well as the conditions in place for knowledge creation, what is here called the 'knowledge-enabling environment'. It is argued that through knowledge management, companies are indeed implementing strategies for the promotion of lifelong learning. Lifelong learning has been used in policy arenas as a guiding principle for educational policies and reforms.

Each company in the sample is rather unique in organization and promotion of knowledge intensiveness in their ordinary business activities, and, there is no consistent set of actions for managing knowledge in the individual companies. In both the education and consultancy companies in the study, the different aspects of the equally heterogeneous 'knowledge-enabling environment' do not present strong relationships.

The exploration of the demand for training shows that the selected companies invest only less than half their perceived training needs. The companies mainly provide training for professional purposes and the subjects of interest are usually associated with the company profile, though the expressed training needs are non-specific. Education and consultancy do not present major differences in terms of educational needs, though they differ in training costs : consultancy has higher direct costs and education pays higher labor costs per course. Educational companies tend to plan for longer courses with more employees involved.

In both sectors the working-environment characteristics that according to the theories reviewed, should promote learning, do not necessarily foster a higher demand for learning, with the exception of information technology. Finally, Also interesting is that employees demand more training if their engagement in informal learning is low.

Keywords: Knowledge management, lifelong learning, European Social Fund, SME, adult education, training, knowledge, Sweden.

TABLE OF CONTENTS

ANNOTATED TABLE OF CONTENTS

LIST OF TABLES AND FIGURES

List of Figures

List of tables

LIST OF ABBREVIATIONS

General Abbreviations

ANOVA	Analysis of Variance
BES	Business Enterprise Sector
BSC	Balanced Score Card
CCI	Collaborative Climate Index
CEDEFOP	The European center for the development of vocational training
CIS3	Continuing Innovation Survey (Third round)
CoP	Communities of Practices
CORDIS	Community Research and Development Information Service
CSF	Community Support Framework
CVT	Continuing Vocational Training
CVTS	Continuing Vocational Training Survey
DfEE	Department for Education and Employment, UK
EAGGF	European Agricultural Guidance and Guarantee Fund
EEA	European Economic Area[1]
EIB	European Investment Bank
EPO	European Patent Office
ERDF	European Regional Development Fund
ESF	European Social Fund
EU 15	European Union, 15 members previous to May 1st 2004
EU25	EU members after May 1st 2004.
EUROSTAT	Statistical office of the European Communities
EURYDICE	The information network on education in Europe
FIFG	Financial Instrument for Fisheries Guidance
HR	Human Resources
HRM	Human Resource Management
HRDC	Human Resource Development Canada
GBAORD	Government budget appropriations or outlays on R&D
IALS	International Adult Literacy Survey
IC	Intellectual Capital
ISIC Rev. 3	International Standard Industrial Classification of all economic activities (Third revision)
ISCED	International Standard Classification of EDucation
IT	Information Technologies
KBS	Knowledge-Based Systems
KIBS	Knowledge Intensive Business Services
KM	Knowledge Management
LFS	Labor Force Survey
MSEK	Thousands of Swedish crowns
NACE	General industrial classification of economic activities within the European Communities
OECD	Organization for Economic Cooperation and Development
OP	Operational Program

---

[1] For this research, the EEA does not include data on Liechtenstein, but includes Candidate Countries: Bulgaria, Croatia and Romania.

R&D	Research and Development
SEK	Swedish crowns
SECI	Socialization, Externalization, Combination and Internalization
SME	Small and Medium Enterprises
SNI	International Sector Number
SPD	Single Programming Document
Std. dev.	Standard deviation
UNESCO	United Nations Educational, Scientific and Cultural Organization
USPTO	United States Patent and Trademark Office
XML	Extensible Markup Language

Country Abbreviations

EU 15 includes:

BE	Belgium
DK	Denmark
DE	Germany
EL	Greece
ES	Spain
FR	France
IE	Ireland
IT	Italy
LU	Luxembourg
NL	Netherlands
AT	Austria
PT	Portugal
FI	Finland
SE	Sweden

EU25: includes EU 15 and:

CZ	Czech Republic
EE	Estonia
CY	Cyprus
LV	Latvia
LT	Lithuania
HU	Hungary
MT	Malta
PL	Poland
SI	Slovenia
SK	Slovak Republic

Other countries:

BG	Bulgaria
RO	Romania
TR	Turkey
CA	Canada
CH	Switzerland
IS	Iceland
JP	Japan
NO	Norway
US	United States

ACKNOWLEDGEMENTS

The process of doing this Ph.D. has provided me with the opportunity to meet many interesting people who in one way or another have contributed to the development of this monograph. Some of them have directly read and made valuable comments on the manuscript, others have allowed me to bore them with my research topic, listening patiently and providing feedback, and others have simply been there to support me in many different ways. Here, I want to take the opportunity of thanking them all. I might not be able to mention everybody, but I hope, that whoever reads this acknowledgement knows that I am talking about him or her.

First I want to express my gratitude to all companies that agreed to participate in the study. I would like to thank my Supervisor, Professor Ingemar Fägerlind who helped me in many different ways through the course of this research. He gave me this great opportunity and I am deeply grateful for his help. Also my gratitude goes to Professor Holger Daun for always helping in any matters when needed; in particular, I want to thank him for his engagement at the end of the dissertation, making a space in his busy schedule to read and make comments on the manuscript. I am also thankful to Professor Albert Tuijnman who was always helpful and open for discussion. He played a crucial role in getting access to the companies. The rest of the members of the Institute of International Education, staff, students and visiting scholars, all have provided me with great support over the years. Through seminars, courses and informal meetings I have had the opportunity to learn from different cultures and research approaches, and to receive feedback on my unfolding research approach. I do not have the space to mention all the people I have met and who create an incredible atmosphere at the IIE. To all of you, thank you. Special mention to Zenia Hellström, Marika Ljungdahl, Gunn-Britt Norberg, Theo Radich and Görel Strömqvist, for always helping in administrative maters and providing interesting conversations; to Reza Arjmand for being more than a colleague in the infinite hours of work, to my numerous roommates along the way: Ann-Kristin, Dinah, Shawn, Nuzzly, Chad and Christelle.

I want to thank Ph.D. Richard Desjardins for reading some chapters of the manuscript and making valuable comments; Ph.D. Margarita Limón, from Autonomous University of Madrid, for providing excellent feedback on chapter 2. She also helped me a lot at the initial stage of my research career. She was the person to whom I owe my interest in doing research. Marga, you are an example to follow in conducting good research. Also, thank you to Viviann Pettersson who made my English readable in a very efficient manner and to Veera Lumme for translating the documents and helping in some of the interviews.

The first part of this research was financed and framed within the European Funded TMR-network PRESTiGE. It was a precious experience, where I had the opportunity to meet great academics that I have come to know and admire. I am especially thankful to Ph.D. Hubert Ertl who devoted some of his busy time to read and comment on my manuscript. Thank you for helping me in difficult times.

The European Social Fund Council provided the access to the companies and financial support for data collection. I am especially thankful to Christer Florman, who helped in different matters relating to the ESF.

I also want to thank all those friends who without knowing anything about my research have always believed more than myself that I could do it; it won't be "año y medio" anymore! Thank you to my mother in Sweden, Gunilla Petersson, who showed me the beauty of Sweden. Thanks to my Family på lapis and the people I meet in my ERASMUS, when you were here and away, the ones who stayed and the ones who left, I am so happy I met you; to my colleagues at Autonoma in Madrid; to my soccer mates, especially Robert and the

Sporting troop, Jacob, Kalle, and the Caprice team and Per and Spoon; they provided me with infinite opportunities to release my stress and helped me to survive in Sweden. To my Lieber Austrian freund, who always brought a smile to my face with his emails, to my "cuatro magníficos, que son 6", for things I can't even mention. Thank you to my family, who has always provided me with the right environment and support to do whatever I have desired, especially to my father, who is not among us anymore and to my mother, a truly giving person, an example to follow. No puedo expresar con palabras lo agardecido que estoy, Gracias, Mamá. They both were examples of hard workers.

Also to mi hijo, Gabriel, who gave me new perspective in life. And last but not least, to my wonderful wife, incredible woman. Knowing her has been the best thing that ever happened to me. I am the luckiest man in the world, and it is only thanks to you that I am finishing this Ph.D. Soon your turn, my love.

PART I   INTRODUCTION

CHAPTER 1: INTRODUCTION

1.1 Introduction

The service sector employed some 46% of the Swedish workforce in 1963 and by 2005 it accounted for more than 75% of the nations employment (www.scb.se). Meanwhile, the distinction between services and products is getting blurred, and many manufacturing companies are selling not only a product but also the service associated with it (Drejer, 2001; Ernst and Young Center for Business Innovation and OECD, 1997). There is a shift from product-centered production to a customer-oriented production (Wiig, 1997, Malhotra, 2000); like an old tailor the company takes the "measures" of the customer and creates a "suit" that fits perfectly. In other words, firms have to be prepared to rapidly adapt to swiftly changing demands with innovation being a necessity in order to remain competitive. In addition, physical capital accounts for very little of the book value of a company (Sveiby, 1997). The most valuable assets are no longer buildings, furniture, and products; but image, people and services. This is especially true in the case of professional service firms (Hurwitz *et al.*, 2002, p. 60). Two such services are consultancy and education. Both sectors rely heavily on their employee's expertise to deliver quality services. In this vein, they can be considered knowledge-intensive businesses and they, more than other services, need to keep their employees' knowledge current and on the cutting edge.

Training and competence development are critical for maintaining and renewing knowledge, and hence competitiveness. At the political level, the European Union is making efforts to establish a European area of lifelong learning; promoting initiatives towards skills and competence development (see e.g. European Commission 2005a). Member states such as the United Kigdom (DfEE 1998), Sweden (The Swedish National Board for Education 2000), or the Netherlands (Dutch Ministry of Education, Culture and Science 1998) have placed lifelong learning at the center of their educational debates (see e.g. Field 2000, CEDEFOP and EURYDICE 2001, Leader 2003). The basic principle in lifelong learning is that knowledge, skills and competencies need to be constantly updated through out life. The knowledge and skills acquired at one point in time are no longer sufficient for an entire working live (Tuijnman, 1999; Lundvall, 2000). Thus workers must be autonomous lifelong learners, with higher levels of multiple skills and increased flexibility.

The concept of lifelong learning implies not only that learning occurs along the whole life span, but also that learning occurs in different settings and in various ways. This includes formal, non-formal and informal forms of learning. Private as well as public institutions have to create opportunities for individuals to develop their competencies, both through planned training activities as well as through the design of working conditions that promote learning while on the job (Hasan, 1996; Rubenson, 2003). Thus organizations have to become learning organizations, defined as those "that encourage learning at all levels (individually and collectively) and continually transform [themselves] as a result" (European Commission 2001a, p. 33).

One mechanism the European Commission has at its disposal to promote policies in support of lifelong learning is the European Structural Funds (European Commission, 2001b). Objective 3 of these funds, financed entirely by the European Social Fund (ESF), has as its main objective "supporting the adaptation and modernization of education, training and employment policies and systems". This dissertation studies companies in knowledge intensive services that have received support from this fund in order to develop their employee's competencies and skills in Sweden.

1

1.2 Background of the study

The importance of education and learning in fostering sustainable development is not only found in policy documents (OECD, 1996, 1997, 1998, 2000; European Commission, 2000a, 2000b, 2001a, 2001c, 2002a, 2005); management and economic literature also place a high value on learning and the creation of knowledge. In the last few years many different fields have contributed to expanding the body of knowledge in the area of management and competence and skills development in organizations; however, there has been little direct communication among these endeavors. Studies on learning organizations and organizational learning have been geared toward providing managers with tools to build an adequate environment for learning and experimentation (see e.g. Argyris and Schon, 1974; Hedberg, 1981; Senge, 1990). Important contributions have been made by studies on innovation processes at a micro level; that is to say, how to develop new products. Studies in this area cover the management of research and development (R&D) groups (Harryson, 2000; Liebowitz, 2000), managing creative people (Johannessen *et al.* 1999) and creating conditions for innovation (Nonaka, 1991; Nonaka and Takeuchi, 1995; von Krough *et al.*, 2000, Takeuchi and Nonaka, 2004a). Human resource management (HRM) has likewise claimed an important role in the study of knowledge management in organizations (Gloet and Berrel, 2003; Rodriguez *et al.* 2003; Oltra, 2005). Skills and competencies have also been examined from the intellectual capital perspective. These studies have focused on providing information on non-financial capital, that is to say, the intangibles of the companies (see e.g. Sveiby, 1997 Edvinsson and Malone, 1998; Guthrie *et al.*, 2001; Marr, 2005a). Additionally, important contributions to the study of knowledge in organizations have been made within the framework of human capital theory. Since the 1960s human capital theory has approached, from an economic perspective, the interests of states, companies and individuals in investing in education and training (see for example: Schultz, 1961; Becker, 1962). In addition it has provided a conceptual structure to explore factors that influence the demand and supply of training (Tuijnman 1989; Boudard, 2000, 2001; Desjardins, 2004).

This dissertation proposes and defends the idea that these different fields can be brought together within the framework of knowledge management (see e.g. Wei Choo and Bontis, 2002a; McElroy, 2003; Villalba, 2004; Stankosky, 2005a). Assumptions and findings from the fields of human capital theory, intellectual capital, organizational learning, the knowledge-creating company and human resource development are brought together to create a holistic framework to study knowledge management in small companies in Sweden.

From the early 1980s knowledge management was typically associated with the use of information technologies (IT), knowledge based systems (KBS), search engines, portals and data-repositories in companies. But starting around the year 2000, knowledge management has grown to become an integral part of basic management, especially in knowledge-intensive organizations and in non IT related organizational processes. In this incarnation, knowledge management integrates all organizational processes that are directed towards knowledge creation and use, and information distribution and storage. Despite the central role that knowledge creation plays in knowledge management, few references to educational science and learning can be found. Therefore, exploring how knowledge management is related to training activities in organizations is an interesting and useful endeavor. Further, as Wong and Aspinwall (2004) point out, the study of knowledge management has primarily been concerned with large corporations and little attention has been paid to Small and Medium Enterprises (SME). However, studies within the area of human capital theory have found that small companies face more problems in providing training opportunities to their employees than large firms. In addition, it has been found that certain company and work characteristics, such as size of the company and literacy practices at work, are associated with higher levels of training participation (Boudard, 2000, 2001). Thus, it seems particularly interesting to explore the relationship between the way small organizations manage their knowledge and their demand for training.

In this dissertation it is hypothesized that small knowledge intensive organizations foster knowledge creation, distribution, storage and use processes through strategic actions directed towards the management of knowledge. These actions, which constitute the knowledge management approach of each company, have been grouped into three main areas: the knowledge-enabling environment, learning arenas and knowledge use. The knowledge-enabling environment refers to the organization of a company, its working methods and the facilities provided employees in order to both deliver services and constantly upgrade their knowledge. Learning arenas refer mainly to activities directed specifically towards the creation of knowledge, such as training. Finally, the use of knowledge refers to the outcomes of the knowledge-enabling environment and learning activities.

1.3 Purpose of the study

The aim of this study is to explore the management of knowledge in relation to the demand for training in small, private knowledge intensive organizations. The specific objectives are:

- Explore through analysis and comparison the knowledge-enabling environment in selected companies in education and consultancy.
- Explore through analysis and comparison the companies' perceived needs for continuous competence development, which constitute the companies' demand for training in selected companies in education and consultancy.
- Explore and analyze the relationship between the knowledge-enabling environment and the demand for training in selected small knowledge intensive companies in education and consultancy.

This study is mainly exploratory, and as such, its aim is to develop questions rather than find answers. The study explores 18 small knowledge intensive companies in education and consultancy that have received funding from the ESF to provide training to their employees. These companies have evaluated their business activities and determined their training needs in order to remain competitive. They, thus, provide a unique opportunity for the study of the demand for training.

1.4 Limitations of the study

The study is limited to 18 private companies that provide a rich amount of information and constitute interesting cases for the purpose of the dissertation. They are small private Swedish companies that work within two services that can be considered "knowledge-intensive", namely, consultancy and education. The companies are a self-selected sample of a very particular kind; all the companies have applied and received grants from the Structural Social Fund of the European Union under Objective 3 (see Chapter 5) for competence development. This provided an opportunity to gain access to specific information on the demand for training that would be very difficult to obtain in any other sample. However, despite their involvement in Objective 3, very few companies, from an initial group of 119, agreed to participate in this study. In the end only 18 companies provided a satisfactory amount of information for the case study. Thus, it is important to note that the results of this study can only be generalized with caution to other small knowledge-intensive enterprises. The two services under study present different gender balances, which might affect the way companies approach knowledge management, although this has not been taken up in the study.

Within the limitations of the research it is important to acknowledge that the subject of knowledge, that has been the center of epistemology for more than 2000 years, has an endless number of perspectives. Studying the management of such a "slippery" entity is basically endless and thus any study, almost by definition, is incomplete. In the present work, knowledge is understood both as the structure and the content of mental schemas. It is, therefore a dynamic entity that is in a constant dialectic process with the reality it represents. It is through this dialectic process that people learn.

This study makes an inquiry into the companies' promotion of learning activities, but it is not clear if the promotion of these activities, such as training, is actually producing changes to individual knowledge. This is not measured here and a different approach would be required in order to study changes in personal knowledge levels. This study can only identify if certain characteristics, that theoretically improve the learning possibilities of employees, are in place or not.

The study uses methodological and data triangulation. Data are from documents, interviews and questionnaires analyzed. This permits the study of the same phenomena from different perspectives. However, it is important to mention that the data sources placed certain limitations on the research. The documents analyzed, for example, were created to fulfill the requirements stipulated by the European Social Council in Sweden in order to gain access to financial aid. Thus it is likely that this limited the type of information that the companies provided. In order to complement information from the documents, an interview was conducted with a person from the company in charge of the ESF program. The interviews lasted between 45-90 minutes and only a restricted amount of information can be collected in this period of time. Finally it was not possible to collect questionnaires from all company employees. Thus, the information from the questionnaires represents, in some cases, only a small fraction of a company's workforce. It is also important to keep in mind that the study provides only a static picture of a company at a given moment in time.

1.5 Structure of the thesis

This dissertation is divided into five parts. The first part is the introduction. The second part is the theoretical framework and includes Chapters 2 through 4. Chapter 2 presents the author's vision of knowledge. Chapter 3 presents the different disciplines that have been used in order to build the theoretical model that is then presented in Chapter 4. The third part presents the context and methodology of the study and includes chapters five and six. Chapter 5 gives a brief historical review of the European Social Fund. It also presents the way the funds work, in order to explain how the companies under study obtained funding for competence development. Chapter 5 also presents different aggregate indicators at the national level on knowledge creation and innovation in order to present the Swedish context for knowledge management in comparison with other European countries. It also presents specific characteristics of the sectors in the study, namely consultancy and education. Chapter 6 presents the methodological rationale of the thesis and its research procedures. Chapter 7 and 8 constitute the fourth part of the study, which presents the empirical illustration. Chapter 7 is centered on the organizational processes, what are referred to here as the knowledge-enabling environment. Chapter 8 presents the findings on the learning arenas. Chapter 9, the fifth and final part of the study, presents a summary of the findings and major implications of the research.

PART II THEORETICAL FRAMEWORK

CHAPTER 2: FROM KNOWLEDGE TO LEARNING

2.1 Introduction

Knowledge and how people acquire knowledge has fascinated human beings from the ancient Greeks to our day. With the emergence of the so-called knowledge economy, knowledge has become one of the most fashionable terms in the political and managerial sphere. As Weiler (2001, p. 36) put it: "The politics of knowledge become less and less separable from the politics of production and profit, arguably the most powerful political dynamics in today's world". Halal's (1998, p. 2) enthusiastic words show this central role of knowledge in the new way of looking at organizations: "We see now that knowledge is the most strategic asset in enterprise, the source of all creativity, innovation and economic value". In a dissertation about knowledge management and training it is important first to define what is understood as knowledge. The conceptualization of knowledge determines any further steps taken in the study, since positions differ depending on what is understood by knowledge.

First a brief introduction on epistemological ideas is presented. Three main approaches to epistemology are proposed in a broad sense: innatist/introspection, empiricism/behaviorism and critical philosophy/constructivism. Special emphasis is placed on constructivism since it is the main approach proposed. Afterwards, knowledge is conceptualized from a managerial perspective. The chapter ends with a brief summary of the characteristics of knowledge and the relation between knowledge, action and learning.

2.2 Epistemological approaches and the psychology of knowledge

2.2.1 Three main epistemological approaches

There are countless studies of philosophy and the history of philosophy. It is not the intention of this section to present a long, comprehensive view of the different theories, but to present the bases for the position defended in this dissertation.

One could argue that there are three main approaches in traditional epistemology. The first has its origins in Plato and is based on the idea that knowledge exists independently of empirical reality (see e.g. O'connor and Carr, 1982; Kenny 2001). Descartes would be in line with this position too (see e.g. Markie, 1998; Garber, 1998). The second is referred to as the empiricist approach. Here Aristotle is the main figure and he contends that knowledge is created through experience (see e.g. Smith and Rose, 1908; Lear, 1988). And finally a third approach, mainly represented by Kant, which would be placed between the two previous ones, holds that knowledge is a combination of experience and inner capacities (see e.g. Kant, 1781/2003; Stegmüller, 1977). This is obviously an oversimplification of the approaches, reducing them to some specific characteristics that make them similar. A deeper analysis would be needed in order to fully understand the work of the different authors.

More recently, the field of psychology has made some interesting contributions to the field of epistemology. Three main approaches have been proposed in classical epistemology, and similarly, three main approaches to psychology are presented: (1) psychology of the inner mental world, corresponding to the epistemology of Plato and Descartes; (2) behaviorist psychology, corresponding to traditional empiricism; and, (3) constructivist psychology, related to the third approach to epistemological thought: critical rationalism. The first approach in psychology combines contributions from quite diverse authors: Wundt, Köhler and Freud. It is argued, however, that all of them share the conviction that the inner mental world is crucial in understanding the nature of knowledge. For them, knowledge is in one way or another generated mainly from the inside out. This approach to psychology, therefore, considers an inner world that is partially (if not totally) independent of empirical reality. Knowledge is mainly produced inside our heads from our own resources.

Behaviorism is a psychology tradition rooted in physiology. Behaviorism has its basis in Pavlov's work on classical conditioning (see e.g. Pavlov, 1904 or 1928). For Watson (1924, p. 5), "...behavioristic psychology attempts to formulate, through systematic observation and experimentation, the generalizations, laws and principles which underlie man's behavior".

Behaviorism is, therefore, not so much concerned with knowledge as it is with behavior. However, learning has a central role in these theories, since learning is the result of a successful training process in which a behaviour has been modified. Skinner, in his work with animals, especially pigeons, managed to "teach" them to get food by pressing a button. This "intelligent" behavior elicited the correct reinforcements – giving food – when the pigeon produced the correct response – pressing the button. Skinner (1953, p. 153) argues:

> The whole process of becoming competent in any field must be divided into a very large number of small steps, and reinforcement must be contingent upon the accomplishment of each step... By making each successive step as small as possible, the frequency of reinforcement can be raised to maximum, while the possible aversive consequences of being wrong are reduced to a minimum.

Behaviorists claim that the human mind cannot be studied; only its consequences, behavior, can be empirically studied (Saettler, 1990, p. 13). The different types of reinforcements that we receive shapes our behavior. Thinking is for the behaviorists "sub-vocal talking", just one type of "implicit habit responses" (Watson, 1924, p.15). Knowledge is therefore external to the human mind; it occurs "from the outside-in"; it is the association of stimulus and responses (Shuell and Moran, 1996, p. 3340). Complex learning occurs through the operant conditioning of different sequences of responses.

2.2.2 Constructivism

The third approach to psychology noted above, constructivism, consists of an intermediate paradigm between the two previous approaches. It is the one that inspired the approach used in this thesis, and it is, therefore, presented in more detail. Piaget is probably the most prominent exponent of this approach. He is one of the writers on education who is most frequently cited. His genetic epistemology has had, and still has, a great deal of influence on curriculum design, educational theory and development psychology (Perner, 1996). Goldman (1967/ 1971, p. 15) argues that Piaget's ideas are based on Kant's epistemological framework. As Saettler (1990, p. 73) notes, according to Piaget cognition develops through the continuous interaction between learner and environment. For Piaget, the mind operates with schemas, certain patterns of behavior, a "script" that guides our actions in a given context. The adaptation of our schemas to different realities constitutes the process of learning (see e.g. Piaget, 1977). The schema will guide the person's behavior within a given context (for example, how to behave in a restaurant). When confronting a new object or situation the script will assimilate or accommodate the new object or situation. Piaget defines assimilation as "the incorporation of objects into patterns of behavior" (Piaget, 1950, p. 9); this means that the script grows, adding a new object (or situation). For example, assimilation occurs when a child is confronted with a pencil. The child can use the schema "grab and thrust" that s/he has already used with other similar objects. Using the schema will be successful, and therefore, the object "pencil" will be incorporated into the functional schema of "grab and thrust". Accommodation, on the other hand, occurs when the application of previously known schema to a given object is not successful; for example, the child cannot use the schema "grab and thrust" with a big ball. In this case, it is the "script" that changes, and the child will accommodate his/her schemata to the ball (see e.g. Flavel, 1963/ 1973; Boeree, 2002). For Piaget (1950, pp. 9-10) this process of accommodation and assimilation is the process of adaptation and further, the process of learning:

> We can define adaptation as an equilibrium between assimilation and accommodation, which amounts to the same as an equilibrium of iteration between subject and object... Psychological life... begins ... with functional interaction, that is to say, from the point at which assimilation no longer alters assimilated objects in a physico-chemical manner but simply incorporates them in its own forms of activity (and when accommodation only modifies this activity). The whole development of mental activity ... is thus a function of this gradually increasing distance of interaction, and hence of the equilibrium between an assimilation of realities further and further removed from the action itself and an accommodation of the latter [action] to the former [realities].

Piaget proposes a human mind developed through an interactive process between the representation of the reality and the "response" of the reality when we act. Mental development implies that the "scripts", the schemas, the representation of the reality that guides our actions, become more abstract and less fixed in the specific action.

Shute (1996, p. 3322) defines schemas as an "interconnected set of propositions and concepts representing a situation". Schemas compound mental models that are "a highly organized set of propositions, concepts, and rules for relating them to one another" (Shute, 1996, p. 3323). Some authors have referred to these mental models as implicit theories (see Chi, Glaser and Farr, 1988). Implicit theories constitute a representation of the world, a map where the different concepts are placed; in fact, they guide how we confront reality.

When we act, new information is processed and will produce some kind of disequilibrium or cognitive conflict in the schema or theory. The process of adaptation (assimilation or accommodation) will tend to restore the equilibrium. Piaget (1975) maintains that adapted responses to this disequilibrium can be of three types: *alfa*, *beta* or *gamma*. Limón (2001, p. 359) explains the three responses as follows:

> Alpha answers involve individuals who ignore or do not take into account the conflicting data. Beta answers are characterized by producing partial modifications in the learner's theory, through generalization and differentiation (generating an "ad hoc" explanation). Finally, gamma answers involve the modification of the central core of the theory.

The *beta* and *gamma* types of learning relate to what Ausubel and Robinson (1969, p. 57) called meaningful learning, which refers to learning of "materials that can be *meaningfully* incorporated into cognitive structure" (emphasis added). The change in this cognitive structure has also been called "conceptual change" (see e.g. Vosniadou, 1996).

Piaget's theories have usually been criticized for not taking into account the social context where learning takes place (Hagström, 2003, p. 4). In this sense, Vygotski is the other main figure in constructivism. His view of child development has usually been referred to as social constructivism. For him, the child builds her/his high mental processes with the help of an adult. In fact, as Ardichvili (2001, p. 35) maintains,

> ...in Vygotski's view, mental functioning in the individual can be understood only by going outside the individual and examining the social and cultural processes from which it derives.

For Vygotski, learning occurs first in an interpersonal manner and then it is internalized. His theory of the mind follows a stratified system of development where the concept of a "Zone of Proximal Development" becomes central; he defines it as:

> actual developmental level as determined by independent problem solving and the
> level of potential development as determined through problem solving under adult
> guidance or in collaboration with more capable peers (Vygotski, 1978, pp. 85-86).

Therefore, in Vygotski's view, mental development is the result of interaction with the environment, but is mainly mediated by social agents. In this way, language becomes the main tool in constructing the mental structure. Thus language and thinking are co-constructed (Riviere, 1997).

2.3 Understanding knowledge from a knowledge management perspective

The previous section presented three epistemological approaches. This section presents the position business administration literature has taken towards knowledge. In recent years almost every book or article about knowledge management begins by referring to knowledge. It is necessary to inquire how knowledge management theorists and practitioners, who will be referred to in later chapters, regard the nature of knowledge. Before discussing the conceptualization of knowledge it is important to make certain distinctions that are recurrent in the field. In order to understand the definition of knowledge that will be used throughout this thesis, it is important to differentiate it from the type of knowledge implied by other related terms such as information and data, and to explain different types of knowledge that must be managed through different strategies.

2.3.1 Data, information, knowledge and expertise

The first distinction addressed in the literature is between knowledge, information, data and expertise. It is important to make a clear distinction between them, otherwise knowledge management would be confused with systems for information processing. Figure 2.1 shows the classical hierarchical positions of the concepts. Data constitute the bricks from which the pyramid of knowledge is built. Davenport *et al.* (1998, p. 2) define data as "a set of discrete, objective facts about events". Most of the knowledge management literature agrees with this

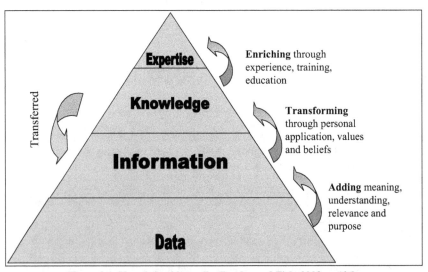

Figure 2.1: Knowledge hierarchy (Bender and Fish, 2000, p. 126).

definition (see Tuomi 1999, p. 104-105 for a review). Data constitute all the empirical reality that is presented to us in our daily experience, the "ocean of impressions" in Kant's terms. In managerial terms, data are that which are available without much restriction in the knowledge society, on the Internet, in databases, and in daily activities. Bender and Fish (2000, p. 126) point out that data become information only when they have been imbued with meaning, understanding, relevance and purpose. Wiig (1993, p. 81-82) maintains that information is the "full or partial description of the state or condition of a situation" and he agrees with Cleveland (1985, p. 24), who says: "information is organized data – organized by someone else, not by me". For Drucker (1988, p. 46) "information is data endowed with relevance and purpose. Converting data into information thus requires knowledge". Mårtensson (2000, p. 208) makes the distinction between general information and contextual information. While general information is data that are organized and structured, contextual information is created by filtering and organizing general information to meet the requirements of a specific community of users.

Information is transformed into knowledge when the individual processes it and internalizes it. New information has to be integrated into the individual's existing knowledge structure in order to produce learning. In Piaget's terms, the new information can be either accommodated or assimilated. If the new information is assimilated there is a change in the content of the schema. We add the information into our schema, but the schema does not change dramatically. If accommodation occurs, the new information triggers a change in the structure of the schema. A new schema means that the reality that the information refers to is looked upon in a different way. In this way, schemas "form the basis for comparing and interpreting incoming data" (Shute, 1996, p. 3322).

Finally, if one masters a certain subject or area of knowledge, one becomes an expert. Alexander (2003, p. 3), in her review of psychology research on expertise, maintains that experts:

- possess extensive and highly integrated bodies of domain knowledge;
- are effective at recognizing the underlying structure of domain problems;
- select and apply appropriate problem-solving procedures for the problem at hand; and,
- can retrieve relevant domain knowledge and strategies with minimal cognitive effort.

Wiig (1993, p. 163) refers to the proficiency dimension to explain levels of expertise with regard to knowledge. He proposes seven different categories from beginner to "grand master". He differentiates between expertise and wisdom. Expertise refers to "specialized knowledge and skills in a particular area" (Wiig, 1993, p. 84) whereas wisdom involves, in addition to a high level of knowledge in a specific area, certain personal characteristics such as the willingness to learn or to be flexible (Wiig, 1993, p. 85).

Tuomi (1999) criticizes this classical hierarchical conception of knowledge and information. He argues that all these models consider knowledge as a "higher form of information" (Tuomi 1999, 104). For Tuomi (1999, p. 107), "data emerge last – only after knowledge and information are available. There are no 'isolated peaces of simple facts'". He turns the pyramid upside-down. Once knowledge is articulated, verbalized and structured, it is transformed into information. Information is transformed into data when it is placed within certain predefined structures (see Figure 2.2). Curry (1997) arrived at a similar conclusion through the analysis of management literature of knowledge using a Marxist rationale.

In this dissertation, the relationship between information and knowledge travels in both directions: knowledge is made explicit and becomes information, while information is internalized and becomes knowledge. Thus, Tuomi's view does not exclude the classical hierarchy model, but complements it (Tuomi, 2002).

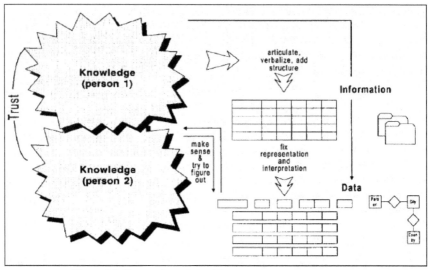

Figure 2.2: Reverse knowledge hierarchy (Tuomi, 1999, p. 112).

2.3.2 Explicit and tacit knowledge, the public and the private

Tuomi's (1999, 2002) arguments are based on a highly influential dichotomy of tacit versus explicit knowledge. The distinction between tacit and explicit is probably the one most frequently referred to in the knowledge management literature. The work of Polanyi (1962, 1967, 1969) is extensively quoted and referred to in this matter (See e.g. Hislop 2002 or Jasmuddin *et al.* 2005 for a review). For Polanyi (1967, p. 4) "people know more than they can tell". In this simple way Polanyi defines what he calls tacit knowledge as opposed to explicit knowledge that can be expressed (see also Polanyi, 1969). For Polanyi (1962, p. 601-602, emphasis in the original) any activity has two dimensions of knowledge:

> (1) knowing a thing *by attending to it,* in the way we attend to an entity as a whole and (2) knowing a thing *by relying on our awareness of it for the purpose of attending to an entity to which it contributes.* The latter knowledge can be said to be *tacit...* We may call "knowing by attending to" a *focal* knowing, and "knowing by relying on" a *subsidiary* knowing...What is subsidiarily known is tacitly known; but it seems appropriate to extend the meaning of "tacit knowing" to include the integration of subsidiary to focal knowing... [A]ll knowing ultimately relies on a tacit process of knowing.

Sveiby (1997) defines focal and tacit knowledge more clearly. Focal knowledge is knowledge of a specific thing, while tacit knowledge is "the knowledge that is used as a tool to handle what is being focused on" (Sveiby, 1997, p. 30). Nonaka is probably the first to promote the importance of tacit knowledge (see e.g. Nonaka, 1991, 1994). As will be presented in the next chapter, tacit knowledge is crucial in fostering innovation in Nonaka's model. The spiral of knowledge creation that he proposes is based on the transfer from tacit to explicit knowledge and from explicit to tacit (see e.g. Nonaka, 1991; Nonaka and Takeuchi, 1995; Nonaka *et al.* 1996). For Li and Gao (2003, p. 8), however, Nonaka's model is more concerned with the implicitness of knowledge than with the "tacitness" of it. For them,

> tacit knowing is such elusive and subjective "awareness" of individual that cannot be articulated in words ... [while] implicitness ... implies that one can articulate it but is unwilling to do that because of specific reasons under certain settings (such as intrinsic behavior in perception, cultural custom, or organizational style).

From the point of view of this study, Li and Gao fail to understand that the tacit dimension in Nonaka's work is referring not only to a set of routines that are not, or do not want to be, expressed, but is also referring to schemas that framed the action in Piaget's terms.

Karmilof-Smith and Inhelder (1974) use the term theory-in-action in psychology to refer to the schemas that are guiding the action in certain situations without our being conscious of them. In organizational theory, Argyris and Schon (1974) used the same term for the theories that guide our interpersonal behavior and influence our ways of learning. Later, Argyris (1993, 1999) referred to governing values as the principles that guide judgments and actions. Senge (1990) refers to "mental models" as the conceptual structures that drive cognitive processes. Dweck (1999, p. ix) talks about self-theories as a set of meaning systems: "people develop beliefs that organize their world and give meaning to their experiences". This is similar to what Wood (2001) refers to as implicit theories of managers. What is proposed here is that the governing values, theory-in-use, implicit theories and Piaget's schema are all referring to the same thing: tacit knowledge. What these terms have in common is that they constitute certain structures of the mind; they constitute our ways of understanding the world. Further, these schemas guide our actions and the manner in which we look at data. These schemas are not only cognitive, but they also have an important motivational and sentimental component (Pintrich and De Groot, 1990; Pintrich et al., 1993; Mezirow, 2003). People feel attached to their theories-in-use since they are an important part of their ways of being.

Tacit knowledge is not public but private in the sense that only the individual possesses it. It belongs to the individual and only the individual can fully use it (Leonard and Sensiper, 1998). Mayo (2000) maintains that all knowledge always has certain private components. In a similar vein, Bender and Fish (2000) maintain that the transfer of expertise always implies a transfer of the expert her/himself since it is never possible to totally articulate all knowledge. Nonaka and Takeuchi (1995, p. 64) call the process of making implicit knowledge explicit "externalization". For them, "tacit knowledge becomes explicit taking the shape of metaphors, analogies, concepts, hypotheses or models". They maintain that there is always certain knowledge that cannot be articulated:

> Yet expressions are often inadequate, inconsistent and insufficient. Such discrepancies and gaps between images and expressions, however, help promote "reflection" and interaction between individuals (Nonaka and Takeuchi, 1995, p. 64).

In similar terms, Sveiby (1997, p. 34) maintains "because we always know more than we can tell, it follows that what has been articulated and formalized is less than what we tacitly know". Wiig (1993, p. 74) refers to internal and external knowledge as tacit and explicit knowledge respectively.

In his review of the literature on knowledge management, Spender (2002, p. 151) proposes two approaches to viewing knowledge within the field:

> One in which knowledge is conceived to be ultimately objectifiable, understandable in a scientific sense, and a second, less explored domain wherein the term knowledge is considered to extend beyond that which can ever be objectified or otherwise made explicit.

Using the above distinctions of tacit and explicit knowledge, in the first approach knowledge and information would be seen if not as the same, then as interchangeable. Knowledge can always be translated into information and all knowledge can be made explicit. In the second approach, knowledge cannot be totally explicit, since there is always a subjective component. Although Spender (2002) argues that the distinction between tacit and explicit knowledge is different than the distinction between the two approaches, it seems clear that these two approaches correspond to the emphasis on explicit knowledge versus the emphasis on tacit knowledge, respectively. An emphasis on explicit knowledge will very likely assume that all knowledge is ultimately objectifiable, or that at least the important knowledge is.

Hislop (2002) divides knowledge management approaches into "objectivist" and "practice-based" philosophies of knowledge that would correspond to Spender's first and second approaches, respectively. In Hislop (2002) these two philosophies of knowledge recognize a different relationship between tacit and explicit knowledge. The objectivists argue that knowledge equals information, while practice-based philosophy makes a clear distinction. Jasimuddin *et al.* (2005) maintain that objectivist theorists consider tacit and explicit knowledge to be two different categories, while practice-based philosophy perceives knowledge as a continuum. Jasimuddin *et al.* (2005, p. 104) position themselves within the second tradition; for them, all knowledge "has both tacit and explicit components", which would be in line with Polanyi's assumptions (see e.g. Polanyi, 1962, 1967).

It seems therefore that there are two clearly defined groups in the literature: one where knowledge is perfectly translated into information, and another where there is always a tacit component in knowledge. These two domains correspond roughly with the behaviorist/empiricist and the innatist/rationalist approaches. The former sees knowledge as objective while the latter sees it as subjective. In this study, however, the main bulk of literature was published after 1995, when tacit knowledge has become relatively widely accepted and fewer contributions to the objectivist theory are presented.

For this dissertation, tacit and explicit knowledge are seen as necessarily different and they cannot be regarded as poles in a similar dimension. All knowledge is tacit at some point in time (it is not being expressed) and certain components of this knowledge cannot be expressed. However, once this tacit knowledge is made explicit, it is transformed into explicit knowledge, that is, information to the listener/reader or whomever can understand the code under which the knowledge is codified. Thus, tacit and explicit knowledge are exclusive categories. Specific knowledge at one point in time is either tacit or explicit. Using Piaget's perspective, knowledge is understood as both the schema and the content of the schema. The content of the schema will be easier to make explicit in some instances since it is declarative knowledge, and by definition it is easy to declare. The schemata, on the other hand, posses certain aspects that cannot be expressed properly, and further, we are not aware of some parts of the schemata. Hislop (2002) views this perspective as pertaining to the objectivist theory. However, from the point of view of this author, Hislop fails to understand that the knowledge expressed is by definition explicit knowledge. It does not have tacit components; it comes from tacit knowledge, but in expressing, writing or even drawing a picture of it, one is making the tacit knowledge explicit. This author agrees with Hislop that this knowledge expressed is not and cannot be a perfect replica of one's tacit knowledge. It is true that the knowledge one expresses has tacit components, but only to the person in question, and not to anyone else. For anyone else, this "explicit knowledge" is information. Thus this thesis agrees with Hislop's (2002, p. 167) statement about the objectivist theory that: "tacit knowledge and explicit knowledge are argued to possess completely different characteristics and are shared in completely different ways as well", despite the fact that this thesis is not at all within an objectivist tradition.

Two main characteristics are apparent from the above conceptualization of knowledge. First, knowledge is *embodied in the individual* and secondly, as a consequence, knowledge must be studied in a *particular context*. The individual processes the data, the information, and adds to the information her/his own previous knowledge, beliefs, values, etc. In Piaget's terms, the schemas are in the human mind, and it is in the human mind that the schemas have to adapt to new realities. Knowledge is something that one constructs by one in an interaction with the environment and with others.

Articulated explicit knowledge is, therefore, public in the sense that it is accessible to anyone who can understand the code in which it is written, as opposed to knowledge that is private (such as tacit knowledge), which is only inside one's head. In other words, knowledge becomes information when it is made explicit. Explicit knowledge and specific information, as defined by Mårtensson (2000), are two sides of the same coin. When I am writing, or talking, I articulate my knowledge; that is, I am "externalizing" tacit knowledge into explicit knowledge. However, the receptor of my explicit knowledge, in this case the patient reader, is reading information, and only if s/he adapts (assimilates or accommodates) this information into his/her schemata or theory will the information become knowledge.

This knowledge acquisition process is, therefore, an individual process, since it is the reader who will or will not process the information read. Knowledge, by definition, is in someone's head, and when it is not in someone's head it is information or data (see Figure 2.3). Further, it is important to note that the information can never be a perfect replica of the knowledge the individual has, and different individuals will have different ways of approaching the same information.

However, as already mentioned, certain meanings have to be shared in order for people to understand each other. Vygotski's theory maintains that knowledge is interpersonal before being individualized knowledge. Linguistic theorists, such as Saussure and Pierce, maintain that communication is only possible because the transmitter and receptor share the code and the context, where certain implicit meanings are shared (see e.g. Buchler, 1955; Hookway, 1995). It is therefore debatable to what extent knowledge is individualized. Demarest (1997) maintains that there is a "shared knowledge" that all people in each organization share and understand. Likewise, Wiig (1993) talks about organizational knowledge or embedded knowledge. Von Krogh and Roos (1995) refer to organizational knowledge socialized as the knowledge of the social system per se (see also von Krogh and Roos, 1995; von Krogh *et al.* 1996).

This dissertation defends that knowledge is always private in the sense that it belongs to the individual. Some authors believe that there is knowledge independent of the individual; this is called collective knowledge or organizational knowledge (see e.g. von Krog et al. 1996). The present work maintains that knowledge is never outside of an individual; what is outside is information. Collective knowledge is therefore defined here as similar knowledge in different people's heads; there is no supra-individual knowledge. If knowledge is shared, what is being shared is information. In the present work, "shared knowledge" is understood as knowledge that is inside the individual, but is similar to the knowledge of other individuals. It is argued here that the more communication that exists between the different individuals within an organization, the more likely it is that their tacit knowledge is similar. Communication intensiveness is therefore regarded as an important factor in creating common understandings. Nonaka maintains that knowledge can be tacitly shared when, for example, two persons work together. This tacit-tacit sharing is recognized and acknowledged here. However, it is important to note that it is only possible to share tacit knowledge because acting is a way of providing information (see Boisot, 2002; pp. 67-8). In this way, people teach each other tacitly by working together, but they do not share tacit knowledge; they share the information created through the process of acting.

Because knowledge is individual and in many cases tacit, knowledge should be studied in a particular context (Whitaker, 1998; Mårtensson, 2000). It is important, therefore, to be aware of the surroundings influencing the knowledge a specific person creates and uses. As such, knowledge cannot be considered in isolation. For this reason cultural practices are important in understanding knowledge and furthering the knowledge management approach. Culture, without going into too much detail, is understood here as a set of routines and behaviors that certain groups share. The culture will determine the context in which both knowledge and information will be created, transferred and shared.

2.3.3 Knowledge content

A third distinction commonly referred to in the literature, both in knowledge management and in epistemology, relates to the content of knowledge. O'Connor and Carr (1982, p. 61) maintain that there are two widely accepted types of knowledge: know-what and know-how, the first referring to "knowing that a proposition is true" and the second to knowing how to do something. Shute (1996), on the other hand, refers to declarative knowledge and procedural knowledge. Declarative knowledge corresponds to know-what and it is "knowledge *about* something", while procedural knowledge refers to "knowledge of *how to do* something" (Shute, 1996, p. 3323, emphasis in original). Wiig (1993, p. 12) refers to four conceptual levels of knowledge: idealistic knowledge, systematic knowledge, pragmatic knowledge and automatic knowledge. The first two correspond to declarative knowledge and the last two correspond to know-how. Quinn *et al.* (1998) maintain that there are four levels of professional knowledge held by employees: (1) cognitive knowledge (corresponding to know-what), (2) advanced skills (know-how), (3) system understanding (know-why) and (4) self-motivated creativity. The OECD (2000), in its monograph on knowledge management, adds knowing-who. These different types of knowledge are briefly explained below.

Know-what

Know-what refers to the knowledge of something: knowing a date, a phone number or a name. The OECD maintains that this type of knowledge is "what is usually called information" (OECD, 2000, p. 14). As it is defined here, know-what cannot be identified as information; information is external to the individual, while know-what is within the individual. Know-what can be divided into factual knowledge and conceptual knowledge. Factual knowledge refers to the knowledge of dates, names or specific events. Conceptual knowledge refers to the knowledge of concepts, such as the knowledge of what a mammal is. In this way, conceptual knowledge has a higher level of abstraction than factual knowledge does. To a certain degree, there is a correspondence between conceptual knowledge and information as well as between factual knowledge and data. Factual knowledge could be considered the data of the brain, the bricks that form the mind. Conceptual knowledge, however, is formed of organized facts to which certain meanings have been added. Pozo (2003) has pointed out that factual knowledge is important in order to be able to build certain kinds of expertise or to create a theory.

In the so-called knowledge society, gaining factual knowledge is relatively easy: dates, names and facts are available on the Internet, in books, on the television, etc. Knowledge management must be designed to channel and control the information flow in order to increase the efficiency of information processing, which will in turn increase the efficiency of creating useful knowledge.

Know-why

Know-why has been defined by the OECD (2000, p. 14) as knowledge "about principles and laws of motion in nature, in the human mind and in society". It refers therefore to the explanation of realities, in other words, theories. The term theory is used here to "refer to a complex, relational framework, which includes explanations of phenomena, and not necessarily to a well-informed scientific theory" (Vosniadou, 1996, p. 3153). As has been shown, these theories are in many instances tacit. Further, know-why will likely guide our behavior. Know-why thus refers mainly to the schema in Piaget's terms.

This theory or schema serves as a framework in which to place the facts and concepts. Studies of novices and experts have shown that the types of theories that individuals hold differ not only quantitatively, in the number of facts or concepts (what could be call the richness of the theory), but also qualitatively, in how the different concepts are organized. Studies of experts and novices have shown that experts solve problems guided by these theories-in-use based on their extensive experience. Know-how is therefore related to know-why.

Know-how

In recent years, especially in management literature, know-how has received a lot of attention. Sveiby (1997) refers to it as the key to the "new organizational wealth". It has also been called procedural knowledge; it refers to the knowledge of how to do something. As in the case of know-what, two levels of abstraction can be defined: know-how can be divided into techniques and strategies. Techniques refer to ways of doing things in a specific context, such as the technique of the "drive" in tennis. Through practice, techniques become automatic and they are executed with no, or very little, participation on the part of the conscious mind. Shulte (1996, p. 3323) has referred to this know-how as skills that might be cognitive, motor or social. Strategies, however, refer to a higher level of abstraction. They are also ways of doing things, but imply a broader scope. Strategies might become automatic, but no strategic action can be taken without a certain consciousness of the situation and the problem. In this sense, strategic knowledge implies that at some level (either explicit or implicit) there is a certain amount of know-why since the strategic action is based on the schema we put into use.

Knowing-how is usually acquired through experience, or as Senge (1990), borrowing from Dewey's work, puts it: "learning by doing". It is by doing that our technical skills and our strategic know-how improve. Through experimentation and trial and error we create a theory-in-action that has different degrees of explicitness, but in most cases is, in fact, totally impossible to articulate. In order to promote know-how, therefore, it is important to have some opportunity for experimentation and self-learning. But further, a certain level of reflective thinking must always follow any action since it is thus that theories can be evaluated and improved. It is also important to note that these theories-in-action are attached to the context in which they are used; they are, in most cases, context-specific.

Know-who

Finally, the OECD (2000) refers to another type of knowledge: know-who. Although this type of knowledge is little discussed in traditional epistemological theories, for knowledge management it is a crucial type of knowledge in terms of content. It refers to knowing who possesses certain kinds of knowledge or expertise. Know-who implies knowing who is an expert in a specific subject and being able to consult her/him if necessary for help in a specific area.

Know-who is therefore related to the social relationships that a person has. As such, these relationships allow the person to engage in a learning process with others. Face-to-face interactions will provide richer information than reading organizational documents or memos. Knowing-who is therefore connected with the idea of networking, of being part of a group and knowing the members of that group. In knowledge management literature, these groups have been referred to as communities of practice (CoP). Lesser and Stork (2001, p. 831) define CoP as: "a group whose members regularly engage in sharing and learning, based on their common interests". This group does not necessarily include only people within the organization, but may also include customers and competitors as well as other relevant people outside the organization (see e.g. Plaskoff, 2003).

2.4 Knowledge, action and learning

The different terms and differentiations that knowledge management literature has provided in the conceptualization of knowledge have been presented. Knowledge is in people's heads, it differs from information or data, it is individual, and in some instances it can be made public or shared as information. In addition, the difference between various types of knowledge has been explained in terms of content. Andriessen (2006, p. 97) identifies six different metaphors in his analysis of the treatment of knowledge in key publications of the knowledge management field: knowledge as something physical, as a wave, as a living organism, as thought and feelings, as a process and as a structure.

In the present work, knowledge is understood both as the structure and the content of the mental schemas. Therefore, this study uses knowledge as "something physical" and "as a structure" as defined by Andriessen. It also includes the idea of knowledge as feelings since the schemas have important emotional components. Further, it includes knowledge as a process, as a wave and as a living organism, since these three elements refer to the idea that knowledge is in a constant dialectic process with the reality it represents. The frame and the content are reinforced or change in each action that we perform. It is through action that we test our schema in the real world. This action will inform us about the schema that in turn will or will not change. In this way, action develops our knowledge, and knowledge is therefore a *dynamic entity*. Knowledge as a static entity never changes. The positivistic view of science maintains that scientific inquiry looks for objective and universal knowledge, what traditionally has been called Truth with a capital T. However, post-positivistic views criticize the idea of a universal truth and propose the existence of different truths. Thus there is not a unique, invariant knowledge but different types of knowledge viewed from different perspectives.

In the management literature, as Demarest (1997, p. 375) has pointed out, interest is focused on commercial knowledge, as in the following:

> The goal of commercial knowledge is not truth, but effective performance: not 'what is right' but 'what works' or even 'what works better' where better is defined in competitive and financial contexts.

In a similar vein, Spender (2002, p. 151) has indicated that:

> We need to keep a careful eye on the utility of theorizing [about knowledge], whether our conclusions can ever be reattached to our discipline's established empirical work in economics, strategy, competition, institutionalized theorizing, management and so forth.

The dynamic feature of knowledge is thus related to the idea that knowledge must be translated into and associated with action (Blacker, 1995; Elkjaer, 2003; Hunt, 2003). Further, the action uses knowledge but does not "consume" the knowledge that can be re-used in its modified form. Thus it is important to mention that "knowledge is *not 'consumed'* in a process, it sometimes increases through use" (Wiig *et al.* 1997, p. 16, emphasis added; Halal, 1998, p. 13). Through this process of adaptation, or equilibrium in Piaget's terms, knowledge, action and learning are closely linked together.

To conclude, it is important to note that knowledge is related to learning. Lim *et al.* (2003, p. 17) argue: "learning and knowledge mutually reinforce each other in a cycle. The act of learning provides knowledge and understanding, which in turn feed further learning". As has been argued already (see 2.3.1), learning can be regarded as the adaptation of mental structures to the specific realities that an individual confronts. Knowledge, understood both as content and as schema, will therefore be constructed during this process of adaptation through its interaction with the environment. When we are presented with data (facts, impressions), we will examine that specific information (which has some meaning and structure for us) with the knowledge that we already have. In fact, the previous knowledge will guide the type of data that we seek, or beyond that, the information we seek and are capable of understanding. If that specific information content (either know-what, why, how or who) appears in adequate conditions of motivation, interest and attention, the content will be "absorbed" into the mental model (or theory) that we are applying to that specific context. The new content might not produce much change in the structure of the mental model (*alpha* answer), it might produce partial modification (*beta* answer) or it might result in a critical modification (*gamma* answer, significant learning or conceptual change). These changes in our schema constitute, in fact, learning. Figure 2.3 shows that learning is the process of transforming data into knowledge, making something public (information) into something private (knowledge).

The process of transforming knowledge into data is the process of teaching, understood broadly. The information that starts the process of learning is usually the articulation of

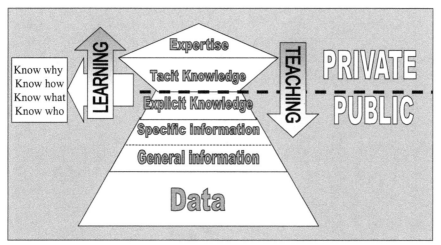

Figure 2.3: The conceptualization of knowledge in this dissertation.

someone's knowledge that served to codify and externalize her/his knowledge. If the students (or any listener or reader) incorporate the data that has been externalized, then there is learning.

Finally, it is important to mention that knowledge can acquired through different means. Knowledge is not only created through theoretical means (such as reading or analyzing information); learning also occurs by doing. Thus when we act, our acts "teach" us, providing us with information on our performance. This process of learning is not necessarily a conscious one, and can occur implicitly without the individual realizing it; in this way we acquire tacit knowledge.

To sum up, this dissertation considers learning and knowledge to be totally interrelated, since learning is the process of creating knowledge and knowledge guides the process of learning. Learning occurs constantly and throughout the entire life span, and in this sense the concept of lifelong learning becomes useful and interesting to analyze. In the next chapter lifelong learning and knowledge management are related to each other, and chapter 4 presents a combination of both fields in a proposed theoretical model.

CHAPTER 3: FROM LIFELONG LEARNING TO KNOWLEDGE MANAGEMENT

3.1 Introduction

The previous chapter presented an overview of the concept of knowledge. It concludes that knowledge and learning have an intricate relationship. Learning is the process of creating knowledge and knowledge guides the process of learning. Our knowledge is constantly changing; in other words we are continually learning throughout our entire life span and in all different kinds of settings. The concept of lifelong learning seems useful in this context. It has been used mainly by intergovernmental organizations as a guiding principle for educational policies.

This chapter takes the author's conceptualization of lifelong learning and shows how knowledge management is integrated into it (see also Villalba, 2004). The chapter starts with a brief historical overview of the development of lifelong learning before the author's conceptualization of lifelong learning is presented. This is followed by an explanation of the relationship between lifelong learning and knowledge management. The chapter then presents different fields involved in the development of knowledge management as a scientific discipline. Knowledge management is related to various aspects of a number of different fields such as: human capital theory, organizational learning, the learning organization, intellectual capital and the knowledge creating company. The chapter finishes with a short review of propositions of knowledge management as integrated with these different disciplines. The holistic model of lifelong learning and knowledge management defended in this dissertation is presented in Chapter 4.

3.2 Lifelong learning

3.2.1 Historical development

The origin of lifelong learning lies in terms such as lifelong education, recurrent education or continuing education (Hasan 1996). Rubenson (2001a, p. 30-31) argues that the concept of lifelong learning has evolved over three generations. The first generation started at the end of the 1960s and has a humanistic rationale (Rubenson 1997). It was promoted mainly within UNESCO and led to the publication, edited by Faure (1972), *Learning To Be*. At this stage, the term "lifelong education" was used instead of "lifelong learning". While some authors have used these terms interchangeably they are generally seen as having different meanings. Aspin and Chapman (2001, p. 10) argue that lifelong education is concerned mainly with the provision of education within institutional boundaries while lifelong learning takes into account other types of education. Hasan (1996, p. 35) maintains that in the 1960s lifelong education was mainly referred to within the context of adult education. In contrast Davé (1976, p. 51) sees lifelong education as seeking vertical articulation, that is to say, it looks for continuity in all stages of education, from compulsory school, upper secondary school and post-secondary stages and as well as adult education.

Lifelong education cohabitated with the concept of recurrent education which was mainly promoted by OECD (1973, p. 16) and defined as:

> a comprehensive educational strategy for all post-compulsory or post-basic education, the essential characteristic of which is the distribution of education over the total-life span of the individual in a recurrent way, i.e. in alternation with other activities, principally with work, but also with leisure and retirement.

Kallen (1979, p. 46) has pointed out that while lifelong education and recurrent education are conceptually different they can be seen as equivalent in policy terms. Tuijnman (1996, p. 100) argues that recurrent education is "more utilitarian" than lifelong education and that, in fact, it constitutes a planning strategy for lifelong education.

In the 1980s the concept of lifelong education lost some of its strength. It reappeared in the political arena in the beginning of the 1990s. During this second stage there is a shift from lifelong education to lifelong learning and an emphasis on the differences between education and learning (Rubenson 2001b). The business sector played a major role at this stage with the predominant idea being an "economistic worldview" (Rubenson 2001a, p. 32). The focus is on development of human capital in order to promote productivity and competitiveness. Jarvis (2002, p. 22) puts it: "People have become human capital who need to be developed so that they can play their role in the work force more effectively". In addition, Field (2001, p. 8) maintains that during this second generation the intergovernmental agencies that promoted lifelong learning, such as OECD and specially the European Commission, gained power and thus increased the impact of the concept in policy arenas. It was in this way that lifelong learning was absorbed into national policy debates.

By the third generation lifelong learning does not only have an 'economistic' rationale but also a equalitarian and participatory approach. For Rubenson (2001a, p. 30) this new shift for lifelong learning can be observed in the publication of the European Commission (2000b) *Memorandum on Lifelong Learning*. It could be argued that the OECD (2001a) would follow a similar shift with the publication *The Well Being of Nations*, and its emphasis on social capital instead of human capital.

The three stages of lifelong learning presented above could correspond with what Aspin and Chapman (2001, p. 29) call the triadic nature of lifelong learning. They argue that lifelong learning has three components: (1) personal development and fulfillment; (2) economic progress and development; and, (3) social inclusion and democratic understanding and activity. The first generation explained above can be seen as emphasizing the personal development component, the second generation economic progress and the third generation adding social inclusion and democratic understanding. Aspin and Chapman (2000, p. 16) place the concept in the third generation: "There is a complex interplay between all three, that makes education for a more highly-skilled work-force at the same time an education for better democracy and a more rewarding life".

The three stages of lifelong learning show the development of the concept from an emphasis on education towards an emphasis on learning. But it is important to clarify the concept in order to better place knowledge management within this framework. The next section presents the perspective on lifelong learning maintained in this dissertation.

3.2.2 Understanding lifelong learning

The concept of lifelong learning has been promoted mainly by intergovernmental organizations (Field 2000, 2001; Edwards *et al.* 2002). It "has evaded precise definition" (Tuijnman and Boström 2002, p. 103) in order to be adaptable to different contexts and cultures (Tuijnman 1999, p. 5). However, certain common characteristics can be found. Tuijnman (1999, p. 6), for example, states that lifelong learning statements,

> ...are based on the belief that everyone is able to learn, all must become motivated to learn and should be actively encouraged to do so throughout the whole life span, whether this occurs in formal institutions of education and training or informally – at home, at work or in the wider community.

Hasan (1996, p. 34) maintains that we can find four common characteristics in lifelong learning: (1) the belief in the intrinsic value of education; (2) the desire for universal access to learning opportunities; (3) the importance of non-formal learning; and, (4) the emphasis on "learning to learn". For Leader (2003, p. 361) "lifelong learning is a multi-faceted, intricate arrangement of trends and developments". Gustavsson (2002, p. 18), in a more philosophical tradition, defines it as: "A dialectic movement of constant excursions and returns, from one's own always constrained horizon to the continuous meeting with what is foreign and different". In other words, different definitions of lifelong learning refer to its variety of characteristics.

In this thesis, following Rubenson (1999, 2001a), three main attributes associated with the concept of lifelong learning are considered: lifelong, life-wide and the focus on learning. The lifelong attribute refers to the idea that learning takes place through the whole life span. Lifelong learning is thus concerned with learning activities from early childhood education through retirement. Illeris (2003a, p. 57) argues that learning at different stages in life demand very different approaches and learning conditions. In addition, as Husén (1999, p. 40) maintains, the lifelong attribute implies that skills and competencies have to be constantly updated (see also Husén. 1968). Education at an early age is not sufficient to cope with the pace of change. In this way, educational certificates are not dead ends and people have to have the possibility of re-directing their careers towards new areas in later stages of life.

Rubensson (2001a, p. 33) argues, however, that the central attribute in the second and third stages of lifelong learning, is not "lifelong" but rather "its focus on learning". The emphasis on learning gives a central role to the individual who becomes responsible for updating her/his own knowledge and skills (Illeris 2003b). As Rubenson (2001a, p. 32) building on Marginson (1997) puts it, life becomes "the enterprise of oneself" where individuals have to take care of the investment in their own human capital. In a similar line, Tuijnman and Boström (2002, p.103) maintain that "... the realization of lifelong learning depends to a large degree on the capacity and motivation of individuals to take care of their own learning".

The emphasis on learning implies the third attribute of lifelong learning, namely 'life-wide'. The conceptualization of the life-wide perspective is important for a better understanding of the relationship between lifelong learning and knowledge management. Thus a fuller discussion of this attribute is needed.

The life-wide perspective of learning

In the first generation of lifelong learning, the life-wide attribute appears as the "horizontal integration" (see e.g. Davé 1976, p. 51). Formal education (at this stage the term used was education and not learning) refers to traditional institutionalized schooling. Non-formal was introduced by Coombs (1973) to refer to organized, systematic education outside the formal system (Carr-Hill *et al.* 2001, p. 331). And finally, informal education as Coombs and Ahmed (1974, p. 8) defined it, is "the life-wide process by which every person acquires and accumulates knowledge, skills, attitudes and insights from daily experiences and exposure to the environment". According to Tuijnman and Boström (2002, p. 97), formal and non-formal education differ, in Coombs and Ahmed's view, with respect to sponsorship, the manner in which they are arranged and the objectives towards which they aim. They, however, have similar pedagogical forms and methods. In contrast, informal learning is qualitatively different since it is not systematically planned.

In the mid 1990s the debate on lifelong learning shifted emphasis from education to learning and placed more attention on informal learning and the life-wide perspective. Livingstone (2001, p. 21) distinguishes between four forms of learning: initial formal schooling; further non-formal adult education; informal training; and, non-taught informal learning. Using these distinctions, Livingstone emphasizes the intentionality of the learning processes. The three first forms of education occur in an intentional continuous process of acquiring "understanding, knowledge or skill" in different institutionally organized settings or outside of institutions providing educational programs (Livingstone 2001, p. 22). Non-taught informal learning occurs "individually or collectively without direct reliance" while coping with our changing environment (Livingstone 2001, p. 22). In this way, learning can be acquired without us being conscious of it, in a tacit way.

Boström (2002, 2003) on the other hand, saw the life-wide perspective as a continuum of norms, from hierarchical to spontaneously generated. Using Fukuyama's (2000) ideas on social capital, Boström (2002, p. 519) argues that the hierarchical generated norms correspond with a more formal mode of learning, whereas "norms that are spontaneously generated tend to be more informal". Life-wide, clearly becomes a dimension where the structure of learning activities enters as a crucial element.

The task force on measuring lifelong learning created by the European Commission in EUROSTAT (2001) presented eight criteria to distinguish between the different types of learning: formal, non-formal and informal (see Table 3.1). These criteria include: (1) intentionality; (2) organization; (3) institutional framework and location; (4) hierarchy level-grade structure; (5) admission requirements; (6) registration; (7) predetermined teaching/learning methods; and, (8) scheduling. For them, formal learning would fulfill all the criteria. Non-formal learning would be intentional, organized and would have a certain institutionalized framework and, to different degrees, it could have the other criteria, but not all of them. Informal learning, on the other hand, would only fulfill the intentionality criteria.

Table 3.1: Criteria for distinguishing different types of learning.

	Criterion	Formal	Non-Formal	Informal
(1)	Intentionality	x	x	x
(2)	Organization	x	x	
(3)	Institutional framework and location	x	x	
(4)	Hierarchy level-grade structure	x		
(5)	Admission requirements	x		
(6)	Registration	x		
(7)	Teaching and learning methods (predetermined)	x		
(8)	Scheduling	x		

Source: EUROSTAT (2001, p.11).

3.2.3 The rhetoric on lifelong learning and its implications

Lifelong learning is an underlying principle that has guided educational reforms for the past 20 years. Three main attributes define lifelong learning: (1) it refers to the whole life span (lifelong); (2) it takes into account different forms of learning (life-wide): and, (3) it places major emphasis on learning which in turn emphasizes the importance of individual involvement in her/his own learning. As indicated in Aspin *et al.* (2001, p. xx-xxi) lifelong learning has an economic justification in that it is instrumental in maintaining competitiveness and innovation. In addition, the discourse on lifelong learning defends learning as an "intrinsically valuable activity". Finally, lifelong learning is seen as a "pre-requisite for informed and effective participation in society". This triadic nature provides a robust framework within which nation states can place their policies.

Despite its vagueness, lifelong learning shows certain directions and general guidelines that still make the concept interesting. First, lifelong learning entails a systemic approach both to education and learning. The lifelong attribute implies that changes in earlier parts of the educational system will affect subsequent educational levels. For example, expansion in primary level education enrolment will necessarily affect the secondary level. The life-wide attribute extends this systemic approach to other non-educational institutions. In this way, educational policies are necessarily inter-connected to labor market policies.

Secondly, lifelong learning places a central role on the motivation of learners to learn. This refers to the demand for learning. Individuals are "condemned" to constantly demand training courses, participate in workshops and seminars, and look for information to solve problems. They are condemned to lifelong learning in order to be able to function in society, at work and even in their personal life. This constant demand for learning, however, has to be met not only by formal educational institutions but also by other institutions within the life-wide perspective. The European Commission (2001a, p. 11), for example, stresses the importance of partnerships between public authorities, employers, trade unions, and community and voluntary groups: "All actors share responsibility to work together on lifelong learning and to support individuals in taking responsibility for their own learning". Learning opportunities are not restricted to formalized education. Lifelong learning emphasizes the importance of informal learning, as Rubensson (2003, p. 30) puts it:

> The very core of lifelong learning is the informal learning or "everyday" learning …
> Here the issue is the nature and structure of everyday experiences, and their
> consequences for a person's learning processes, ways of thinking and competences.

The state, thus, is left as a coordinating body of lifelong learning opportunities (Daun, 2003). As Brown (2001, p. 11) puts it: "The role of the welfare state should be limited to encouraging individual enterprise and incentives for people to invest in their human capital and to find employment". The rest of the actors, such an employers or voluntary associations, can provide structures and "everyday experiences" that foster learning and motivation to learn. This is especially true in the area of adult education where employers play a major role in the providing opportunities for learning. Tuijnman and Boudard (2001) using data from the International Adult Literacy Survey (IALS), found that in 15 OECD countries the main sponsor of adult training is the employer. On average 63.2 percent of the population between the ages of 25 and 60 who participated in training activities said they had received employer support, while only 10.1 percent said they had received support from the state.

Rubensson and Xu (1997, p. 93) in their comparative study of six countries (Canada, the Netherlands, Poland, Sweden, Switzerland and the United States) have shown that there is a higher likelihood of receiving employer support for training when there are higher demands for reading, writing and numerical skills at work. In a similar way, Boudard (2001, p. 94) in his study of ten OECD countries has shown that literacy practice at work and firm size are two important predictors of participation in adult training. These often rate higher than other factors such as educational attainment or labor force status. In addition, Boudard and Rubenson (2003) have shown that certain characteristics associated with work conditions, such as labor force status, work experience, firm size, literacy practices at work and individual earning, are mediating the effects of certain family characteristics, such as parent's education or educational attainment, in predicting adult participation in training. More recent data from the second Continuous Vocational Training Survey (CVTS2) shows that firm size is associated with higher participation rates in vocational courses (European Commission, 2002b). Table 3.2 shows that larger companies tend to offer training more than smaller ones;

Table 3.2. Supply and demand of training according to CVTS2 in the EU-15

	Enterprises offering training as percentage of all enterprises	Participants in CVT courses as a percentage of employees in all enterprises	Participants in CVT courses as a percentage of employees in enterprises providing CVTS
10 to 19	49	19	46
20 to 49	67	25	42
50 to 249	81	33	42
250 to 499	94	39	42
500 to 999	96	44	48
1000 and more	99	50	50
Total	62	40	47

Source: European Commission (2002b), data 1999.

however, if small companies offer training the percentage of participants in small and large companies are not so different (46 against 50). This seems to show that size of the firm might play a role in the supply of training but does not play such a big role in the demand for learning. In other words, if a worker belongs to a company that offers training it seems more likely that s/he will go to training irrespective of the size of the organization where s/he is working.

Knowledge management as a strategy for lifelong learning

These different findings have been referred to as the "long-arm of the job" (see Murnane *et al.* 1995, Rubenson and Schuetze 2000). Its basic proposition is that certain working conditions are associated with higher participation in lifelong learning activities, e.g. adult training; but even further, those working conditions are indeed opportunities for skill development and therefore for informal learning. Studies with the IALS have shown that the use of literacy at work actually improves the real literacy skills of workers (see, e.g. OECD and HRDC 1997, pp. 82-84, OECD and Statistics Canada 2000, pp. 38-41). This is, in fact, why it is important to promote "learning while working and working while learning" (Hasan 1996, p. 35) or as the European Commission (2002a, p. 103) puts it "facilitating enterprises to become learning organizations" or organizations "that encourage learning at all levels (individually and collectively) and continually transform [themselves] as a result" (European Commission 2001a, p. 33). Zuboff (1988, p. 395) observed in her study on the introduction of computer-based technologies in a range of work settings that, "The behavior that defines learning and the behavior that defines being productive are one and the same... to put it simply, learning is the new form of labor".

The assumption of this dissertation is that knowledge management is indeed an employer strategy for lifelong learning through structuring "everyday activities" in a way that promotes constant knowledge creation. Knowledge management, as will be defined later, refers to the different business activities directed toward the creation, storage, distribution and use of knowledge and information. Knowledge management creates an environment for constant skills formation and learning, what von Krogh *et al.* (2000) call "the knowledge-enabling environment". On the one hand, knowledge management strategies enforce a lifelong perspective of learning through the continuous emphasis on the creation of knowledge and skills upgrading. On the other hand, knowledge management strategies promote constant opportunities for skill development and learning, both formal and informal. As shown in Figure 3.1, knowledge management includes formal learning activities, such as employee's training at universities that leads to a specific certification within the state educational system. It also includes, non-formal learning activities, structured or semi-structured such as seminars, workshops or other organized learning activities. And finally it includes the working routines that are directed towards not only the improvement of productivity and innovation but also informal learning.

Before presenting the model for knowledge management defended in this dissertation, it is important to acknowledge where knowledge management comes from and the contribution of other fields in the study of training and skill development in organizations. The next sections will discuss different management approaches to the promotion of learning at work, such as human capital theory, organizational learning and intellectual capital. It will also show the connection between these different fields and knowledge management as well as why knowledge management was chosen as the main field within this thesis.

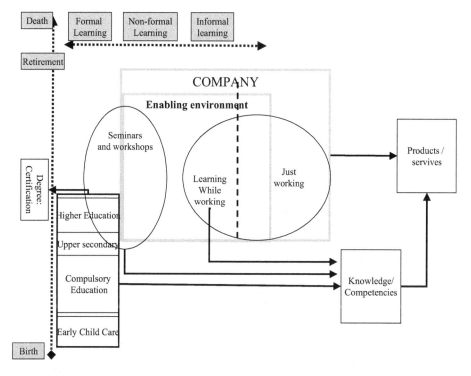

Figure 3.1: Knowledge management and lifelong learning

3.3 Different disciplines contributing to the field of knowledge management

3.3.1 Introduction

As we have seen, knowledge management is related to lifelong learning as an employer strategy for constant upgrading of skills and knowledge. Within the last fifteen years the recognition of knowledge management has increased tremendously in the business and research communities (see e.g. Desouza, 2003, p. 25; Quintas, 2003, p. 30). KPMG (1998) conducted a survey in 1998 of 100 leading United Kigdom companies and found that around 43 percent already had in place a knowledge management strategy. A similar survey conducted in 1999 found the number had increased to 61%. The Garnet Group in a survey including 811 companies in North America and Europe found that 90 percent of the companies where aware of knowledge management and were going to put in place a strategy for it within the next two years (Harris *et al.* 1999). Without going into details of the methodological problems that could be attributed to these surveys (see Foray and Gault, 2003), it seems clear that knowledge management is receiving increasing attention.

Chavuel and Despres (2002) analyzed 59 surveys in the field of knowledge management conducted between 1997 and 2001. They conclude that the field is in its adolescence and that there is no homogeneous definition for knowledge management. Wiig (2000) argues that the field of knowledge management has a long way to go in its development. For him, it will be integrated into management tools and, in this way, will eventually disappear as a separate effort. Winkelen *et al.* (2004, p. 32), in their study of 116 organizations, argue that knowledge management "is evolving from a separate discipline into one that is integrated into business practice".

Quintas (2003, p. 31) has pointed out that knowledge management has existed informally since the "earliest incarnations of organizations". Wiig (1997, p. 2) puts it this way:

> Clearly, knowledge has been managed implicitly as long as people have thought seriously about their work... Nevertheless, systematic knowledge management for business purposes ... did not become explicit until about a decade ago.

DiMattia and Oder (1997, p. 33) trace the beginnings of knowledge management to the 1980s when downsizing was a popular business strategy that resulted in the loss of existing company expertise. Moody and Duff (2000, p. 21) maintain that in order to retain expertise, companies looked for ways of storing employee knowledge. A second origin can be found, according to Wiig (1997, p. 6), when some American companies began to use Knowledge-Based Systems (KBS) to increase their competitiveness in the market. Aguirre *et al.* (2001, p. 1) maintain that the origin of knowledge management can be traced to the extensive research on Artificial Intelligence (AI) from the 1960s before companies were using KBS. Quintas (2003), on the other hand, associates knowledge management with the development of human capital theory and its focus on knowledge. Thus it is clear that knowledge management is nurtured by many different disciplines emphasizing different aspects of the same phenomena: knowledge in organizations and its use.

McElroy (2000, p. 200) argues that knowledge management has two distinct stages. The first generation, as he calls it, concentrated on the "supply" of *existing* knowledge rather than on the demand for *new* knowledge. Tuomi (2002, p. 69-75) maintains that in the time period between 1993 to 1996 knowledge management developed from four different disciplines: organizational information processing; business intelligence; organizational cognition; and, organizational development. The two first would be in line with McElroy's first generation of knowledge management or what Mårtensson (2000, p. 210) refers to as knowledge management as an information-handling tool, whereas the last two are the basis for the second generation. This first generation knowledge management is mainly interested in using information technology in the workplace, creating knowledge-based systems or other so-called knowledge management software. As understood in this thesis (see Chapter 2) and as some authors have indicated, the first generation of knowledge management mainly deals with information and not with knowledge (Fulmer and Keys, 1998). According to McElroy (2000) the main promoters of knowledge management within this line are software development companies which create databases, research engines or KBS to assist decision-making.

In the second generation of knowledge management, which would start around the 1995, the field evolves into a broader perspective where it is seen as a management strategy (Mårtensson 2000, p. 209). The distinction between knowledge and information becomes central (see Chapter 2). The emphasis is placed particularly on tacit knowledge. Nonaka (1991, p. 97) argues that the centerpiece of knowledge intensive companies approach:

> ...is the recognition that creating new knowledge is not simply a matter of "processing" objective information. Rather, it depends on tapping the tacit and often highly subjective insights, intuitions and hunches of individual employees and making those insights available for testing and use of the company as a whole.

In this second generation, thus, the assumption is that knowledge is owned and controlled by individuals. Hence, knowledge management centers on people rather than on technology. In this generation, information technologies are viewed as an enabler of the knowledge management process (Martiny, 1998, p. 76; Alavi and Tiwana, 2003; Rao, 2005a). Information technologies are directed towards group activities as well as allowing for a certain degree of personal communication, taking into account the tacit nature of knowledge.

In addition further development of knowledge management emphasizes the role of collaboration and culture. Chase (1997a) concluded after a survey of different knowledge management initiatives in 143 organizations that a successfully implemented knowledge management system "is mainly linked with 'soft' issues" such as organizational culture and people (Chase 1997a, p. 49; see also, Hauschild *et al.,* 2001). Bixler (2005, p. 61) includes as necessary requirements for building up a knowledge management system conditions such as leadership involvement, developing a sharing culture among employees, and continuous training of employees. Davenport*, et al.* (1998) found that culture was a key factor for success in their study of 31 knowledge management projects (see also Davenport and Prusack 1998, pp. 151-153). They define a culture with positive orientation toward knowledge as "one that highly values learning on and off the job and one in which experience, expertise and rapid innovation supersede hierarchy" (Davenport *et al.* 1998, p. 52). Svensson *et al.* (2002, p. 15) concluded after their study of learning environments in knowledge intensive companies in Sweden, Denmark, the Netherlands, the United Kigdom and Ireland that "the most critical aspects could be called the learning culture of the teams and projects. One aspect of the learning culture is the valuing of learning and the support given to each others space for learning" (see also Svensson, 2005). In a similar way, Ahmed *et al.* (2002) in their review of knowledge management initiatives in 17 international companies found that successful knowledge management initiatives are always related to a knowledge-sharing culture: "Knowledge management requires organization culture that constantly guides organizational members to strive for knowledge and a climate that is conductive to it" (Ahmed *et al.* 2002, p. 48).

One could argue that the field is still in a maturation process. Tuomi (2002, p. 76) maintains that knowledge management is living its third generation. He characterizes it as software that takes into account the dynamic nature of knowledge and the importance of collaboration. For the present work, Tuomi's characterization does not truly differentiate between second and third generation knowledge management. It is argued here that the main feature in the current knowledge management field is that the different disciplines are coming together and being integrated (see e.g. Wei Choo and Bontis, 2002a; Easter-Smith and Lyles 2003b; McElroy 2003; Diakoulakis *et al.*, 2004; Butler and Grace, 2005). Chapter 4 will present the model for knowledge management used in this dissertation. Before presenting the model, however, it is important to review briefly each of the different perspectives that have contributed to its construction.

3.3.2 Human capital theory

Quintas (2003, p. 31) maintains that knowledge viewed from an economic and organizational perspective "has a rather longer history that [the] 'KM' phenomenon suggest". He quotes Penrose (1959, p. 77) as follows:

> Economists have, of course, always recognized the dominant role that increasing knowledge plays in economic processes but have, for the most part, found the whole subject of knowledge too slippery to handle.

Human capital theory could be considered the first economic approach that specifically deals with knowledge and skills. For the last 50 years or so the theory has been used to study the impact of knowledge and skills formation in productivity, both at the macro and micro level and has influenced company training activities.

According to Evans *et al.* (2000, p. 29), "Human capital is defined as the potential and capability of people to add value to the goods and services they produce in the workplace". Moreover, they address the importance of seeing the concept as an individual one: "Human capital belongs to individuals, not to business organizations" (Evans *et al.*, 2000, p.29). OECD (2001a, p.18) defines human capital as: "The knowledge, skills, competences and other attributes embodied in individuals that confer personal, economic and social benefits".

One can conclude therefore that human capital refers to the human characteristics that promote productivity and well-being.

Human capital theory has its origins in Adam Smith's ideas (Robinson-Kaluzny, 2000, p. 5, Sweetland, 1996). Already in 1776 Smith pointed out that "the skill, dexterity and judgment" of human beings is an important part of labor inputs (1776/1952, p.1). According to Sweetland (1996, p. 343), Smith based human capital theory on two fundamental principles: (1) labor inputs are not merely quantitative, and (2) ability acquired through education always has a real cost.

In the 1960s, Theodore Schultz and Gary Becker developed Smith's ideas thereby establishing the field of the human capital theory (Robinson-Kaluzny, 2000, Desjardins, 2003). Shultz (1961, p. 9) in his initial development of the theory attempts to understand the following discrepancy:

> The income of the United States has been increasing at much higher rate than the combined amount of land, man-hours worked and the stock over reproducible capital used to produce income.

Schultz (1961, p. 6) says that the "unexplained large increase in real earnings of workers ... represents ... a return to the investment that has been made in human beings". He maintains that "most of what we call consumption constitutes investment in human capital" (Schultz, 1961, p. 1). His analysis of this investment is concentrated on five major categories that improve human capital capabilities: (1) health; (2) on-the-job training; (3) formally organized education; (4) study programs for adults; and, (5) migration. Another important point in Schultz's analysis is that "human capital, like other forms of reproducible capital, depreciates, becomes obsolete, and entails maintenance" (Schultz, 1961, p. 13).

Becker, on the other hand, studies the rates of return of different investments of human capital. He divides the investments into four categories: (1) on- the-job training; (2) schooling; (3) other knowledge (for example, acquiring information of the economic system); and, (4) improving emotional and physical health (see Becker, 1962). Becker's arguments are based on the study of rates of return of on-the-job training and the distinction he makes between general and specific training. In the following paragraph he tries to summarize his view:

> General training is useful in many firms in addition to the firm providing it. Most of on-the-job training presumably increases the future marginal product of workers in the firm providing it,(...) "Perfectly general" training would be equally useful in many firms and marginal products would rise by the same extent in all of them. (...)[F]irms would provide general training only if they did not have to pay any of the cost. Persons receiving general training would be willing to pay these costs since training raises their future wages. Hence, the cost as well as the return from general training would be borne by trainees, not by firms (Becker, 1962, p. 12-13).

Using this as a point of departure, human capital theory has produced an important amount of literature studying different aspects of the same issue, namely: investment in human capital, including education but not exclusively education, increases wealth both at the societal and the individual level (Sweetland, 1996, p. 351). This has been a catalyst for the promotion of education at a national level under the premise that investment in human capital is a tool for enhancing economic growth (see e.g. Psacharopoulos, 1994; OECD, 1998). For Fägerlind and Saha (1989, p.18) "human capital theory postulates that the most efficient path to the national development of any society lies in the improvement of its population, that is, its human capital". Mincer (1989, p. 27) maintains that human capital theory is "the economist's approach to the analysis of skills, or labor quality". Desjardins (2004, p. 101) adds that the core premise of human capital theory is that "those with more human capital, holding all other variables constant, should be more productive". Evans et al. (2000) argue that there are two approaches in the study of human capital, one focused on quantifying human capital and another focused on growing human capital. The former is related to the study of costs, and the latter is more closely related to training and development.

Human capital theory and knowledge management

Especially important for this dissertation is the measurement of human capital and how companies justify investment in it. In most of the cases, as Desjardins (2004) points out, studies of human capital have been measured in terms of educational attainment. Experience has also been considered a proxy for human capital: the more experience one has the more human capital that one is suppose to have. Post-school training activities are usually considered the main vehicle for human capital formation in adult life (see e.g. Mincer 1997). Theoretically, following Becker's (1962, 1993) assumptions, companies would pay for specific training but not general training.

Human capital theory is not exempt from criticism, especially in terms of how and what to measure. As Desjardins (2004, p. 9) points out, "while the theory has been influential, there is growing concern and dissatisfaction with its treatment". He maintains that not all potential sources of human capital investment are considered in empirical applications. In particular informal learning as a form of human capital formation remains unexplored.

Brown (2001, pp. 13-29) summarizes the criticism to human capital theory in four different categories relating to: (1) the supply side; (2) the demand side; (3) skills measurement; and, (4) the global labor market. Firstly, within the supply side, Brown (2001, pp. 13-16) maintains that human capital theory treats investment in human capital as any other form of capital. In this way, the individual worker is reduced to a "bundle of technical skills that are fed into the economy". It fails to account for "soft issues" such as social relationships, corporate culture or the transfer of tacit knowledge that might play a role in investments in human capital (see also Nonaka and Takeuchi 1995). On the demand side, Brown (2001, pp. 16-23) shows how the model of technological progression defended by human capital theorists is not empirically supported. For him, the model ignores factors such as existing management practices, attitudes toward women, and industrial relations. In relation to measuring skills, Brown (2001, pp. 23- 26) defends the disinterest of human capital theorists with certain skills that are difficult to teach formally, such as creativity or social skills, but that might play a crucial role in increasing productivity. In addition, human capital theory assumes "wages to reflect the productivity of labour" which is difficult to explain in a global context without taking into account domestic issues and the power of individuals and occupations. Another criticism of skills measurement in human capital theory is the emphasis on measurement of outcomes, thereby ignoring the *process* of skill formation. Finally, in relation to the global market, Brown (2001, pp. 26-29) maintains that human capital theory considers a global market and this is an oversimplification of the reality that most workers face in their everyday life.

In conclusion, human capital theory is of crucial importance to understanding investment in activities for knowledge creation, such as training. However, it fails to look into the process in which this human capital formation takes place. In a similar way, it does not take into account the concept that working involves constant learning, which is especially relevant in knowledge-intensive companies. Knowledge management provides a framework to construct and study this process of learning while working. Traditionally, the study of the process of learning at work has been found in the literature on organizational learning. This will be presented briefly in the next section.

3.3.3 Organizational learning and the learning organization

Organizational learning

According to Tuomi (2002, p. 74) second-generation knowledge management has roots in the work of Argyris and Schön on organizational learning (see e.g. Argyris and Schön, 1974, 1978; Argyris, 1991, 1993, 1999, 2004) and in Peter Senge's work about the learning organization (Senge 1990, see also Senge, *et al.* 1994, Senge *et al.* 1999). Easter-Smith and Lyles (2003a: 9-10) maintain that Cyert and March (1963) were the first to articulate the concept of organizational learning. Afterwards, Argyris and Schön (1974, 1978) popularized the concept and clearly defined the field. They used organizational learning to distinguish between organizations that engage in significant learning (Model O-I) and those that do not (Model O-II). Significant learning refers to the change of governing values, the underlying principles that guide organizational behavior, or in Piaget's terms, the gamma change (see Chapter 2).

Argyris (1991, p. 100) argues that "well-educated, high-powered, high-commitment professionals who occupied key leadership positions" do not know how to learn from failure. He argues that they are frequently very good at "single-loop learning", which consists of learning through making small adjustments to their knowledge (what in Chapter 2 is referred as *alpha* or *beta* changes of the theory). They rarely evaluate the underlying principles of their behavior which then might allow them to have "double-loop learning" (that would correspond with *gamma* changes as defined in Chapter 2). In fact, organizations and individuals avoid this type of learning and instead create "defensive routines". Argyris (1993, p. 102) defines these routines as:

> Any action or policy that prevents human beings from experiencing negative surprises, embarrassment, or threat, and simultaneously ... prevents the organization from reducing or eliminating the causes of surprise, embarrassment and threat.

In order for an organization to change, it has to change its theory-in-action or have "double-loop learning", that is to say, the leaders need to change the guiding principles of their behavior. Double-loop learning can create a new set of governing values that impact the routines and framework of action of the company as a whole (Kim, 1998, p. 52). Organizational learning refers, therefore, "to the study of the learning processes of and within organizations" (Easter-Smith and Lyles 2003, p. 2). In other words, it is the study of a knowledge-enabling environment as will be defined later (see Chapter 4).

The learning organization

The term learning organization denotes an ideal type of organization "which has the capacity to learn effectively" (Easter-Smith and Lyles, 2003, p. 2). As Leitch *et al.* (1996, p. 43) concludes in their conceptualization of learning companies:

> It must be emphasized that it is more productive to consider the learning company as an orientation, not an activity, as a purpose and process not an outcome, as becoming not being and as a journey not an archetypical destination.

Tsang (1997: 75) maintains that "there is a simple relation between [organizational learning and learning organization] – a learning organization is the one which is good at organizational learning". Burnes *et al.* (2003) maintains that the literature in the learning organization is mainly prescriptive; it is concerned with telling practitioners what to do in order to make organizations learn. Argyris (1999, p. 1) agrees and goes on to differentiate between the practice-oriented literature on "the learning organization" and the more "skeptical scholarly literature of 'organizational learning'".

Peter Senge's book *The Fifth Discipline* is the corner stone in the field of the learning organization (Flood, 1999). In this book, Senge (1990, p. 3) defines the learning organizations as:

> Organizations where people continually expand their capacity to create results they truly desire, where new and expansive patterns of thinking are nurtured, where collective aspiration is set free, and where people are continually learning how to learn together.

This definition is based on the five pillars of a learning organization: (1) system thinking; (2) personal mastery; (3) mental models; (4) shared vision; and, (5) team learning.

Garvin (1993, p. 80), in a slightly different approach defines the learning organization as: "An organization skilled at creating, acquiring, and transferring knowledge, and at modifying its behavior to reflect new knowledge and insights". Based on Senge's five pillars for a learning organization, Garvin (1993, p. 81- 89) argues that the learning organization is based in five main activities: "systematic problem solving, experimentation with new approaches, learning from their own experience and past history, learning from experience and best practices of others, and transferring knowledge quickly and efficiently". Garvin (1993, p. 89-90) maintains that organizational learning will only be useful if learning is measured. In this sense, contributions from the field of intellectual capital, as presented in the next section, are significant. However, accounting for knowledge as Garvin proposes refers mainly to explicit knowledge and therefore touches only one aspect of the whole knowledge management idea proposed in this thesis.

Organizational learning, the learning organization and knowledge management

The field of organizational learning and the learning organization provide interesting insights into the development of a culture that fosters innovation and constant learning. Many authors refer to organizational learning within the framework of knowledge management and consider it as a strategy for knowledge management (See, e.g. Wiig *et al.* 1997). Others, as McELroy (2000), maintain that knowledge management is an implementation strategy for organizational learning. Bontis *et al.* (2002) believe organizational learning introduces behavioral variables into the study of knowledge within organizations. Easterby-Smith and Lyes (2003, p. 4) argue that knowledge management is more concerned with "the stuff that organizations posses", in other words knowledge, whereas organizational learning is more interested in the process of knowing. In addition, they argue that practitioners are the main promoters of knowledge management while organizational learning has a more theoretical basis (see also, Vera and Crossan, 2003). Butler and Grace (2005, p. 56-57) argue that knowledge management and organizational learning "complement each other, in that the learning process is of no value without an outcome, while knowledge is too intangible, dynamic and contextual to allow it to be managed as a tangible resource". They are advocates of a learning management system which combines organizational learning theories with knowledge management.

In line with Butler and Grace (2005), the present thesis integrates organizational learning and the learning organization within the broader framework of knowledge management. As indicated in Chapter 2, knowledge and learning are so interrelated that a strategy for managing knowledge necessarily has to take into account learning. Further, while knowledge management has a holistic view of company processes, organizational learning and learning organization literature does not include certain important aspects of the these processes such as the role of information technologies and certain key aspects of recruitment.

Organizational learning ideas mainly point toward the importance of constant evaluation of organizational routines or, in other words, the continual monitoring of the organizational processes that allow for constant improvement. However, although these ideas provide guidelines for individual and managerial actions, they do not provide a clear way of assessing and monitoring learning processes and actions. To help fill this gap, contributions from the field of intellectual capital offer additional insight for knowledge management.

3.3.4 Intellectual capital

Studies of intellectual capital were originally focused on providing information about non-financial capital to investors (Mavricknac and Siesfeld, 1997; Johanson, *et al.* 2001). In the 1990s, it was observed that, "Particularly in non-traditional industries, book values of assets tend to correlate poorly with market capitalization" (Guthrie et al., 2001, p. 365). That is to say, the sum of the shares of a company (market capitalization) is very different from the cost of replacing its assets (financial capital). This difference between the total value of a firm and its financial value is defined as the Intellectual Capital (IC) of the company (Edvinsson, 1997, p. 367).

Marr (2005b) presents an overview of the historical development of the field of intellectual capital. He argues that it has evolved from many different disciplines, such as economics, marketing and accounting, without major connections among them. He points to Nassau William Senior in 1835 as one of the first to acknowledge the importance of intellectual capital as a production factor. In his presentation of the field he includes studies on human capital (as described above), the resource-based theory of the firm (Penrose, 1959; Barney, 1991) and new growth theory (Romer, 1990) as important milestones in the evolution of the field.

Johanson et al. (2001, pp. 413-414) argue that the study of intellectual capital comes from the study of "intangibles" in companies (see also Johanson, 1999). Johanson (1999) found four different types of classifications of intangibles in the literature: (1) a dichotomized classification, basically differentiating between legal and non legal ownership (Brooking and Motta, 1996; Brooking 1997), externally or internally purchased (Mortensen et al. 1997) and people dependent or independent (Hall, 1992); (2) classification of intangible investments including R&D activities, software, marketing and organization (Statistics Netherlands and EUROSTAT, 1999); (3) the third classification, which comes from most of the practitioners, consists of a three-way classification of human, market and structure capital (Sveaiby, 1997, Edvinsson and Malone, 1998); and, (4) finally, from the mid 1990s literature on intangibles, a classification which includes not only static states but also recognizes business practices as the intangible of most importance (see, e.g. Hammerer, 1996; Lowendahl, 1997).

For the purpose of this thesis, the main interest resides in the last two types of classifications, since they show company efforts in measuring and, usually, managing their intangible assets where knowledge would be included. Further, as will be shown below, studies that Johanson (1999) classifies as coming from practitioners have evolved into the fourth category. They have become proposals on how to manage, not only how to measure, the intangible assets of the company which includes but is not limited to knowledge.

The influential work of Edvinsson and Malone (1998) at Skandia, a Swedish insurance company, in developing a system to measure intangibles constitute one of the foundational works within the field of intellectual capital accounting. Edvinsson (1997, p. 367) maintains that there are two major investments streams in companies nowadays: (1) investment in knowledge upgrading or competence development leading to human capital; and, (2) investment in the development of information technologies. He continues: "This is something that is invisible in the corporate balance sheet" and while, investing in them reduces the short-term value of the company they actually constitute the main investment for sustainable competitiveness (Edvinsson, 1997, p. 367). Thus, in 1991 Skandia formed an intellectual capital function to "grow and develop intellectual capital as a visible, lasting value, complementary to traditional balance sheet" (Edvinsson, 1997, p. 368). It resulted in a supplement to the company's 1994 financial report.

Edvinsson and Malone (1998) maintain that the market value of a company is the sum of its financial capital and its intellectual capital. Intellectual capital is divided into human capital and structural capital. Structural capital is further divided into organizational capital and customer capital (see Figure 3.2). Sveiby (1997, 2001) followed a similar rationale and simplifies the model to three main families of intangible assets: external structure, internal structure and individual competence (see Figure 3.3). Roos and Roos (1997) divide intellectual capital into human, customer and organizational capital.

The human capital component in Edvinsson and Malone's (1998, p. 34) model is defined in a similar way as that used by OECD (1996, p. 9), that is, as the competencies, capabilities, skills and experiences of the company's employees and managers. This is also how Sveiby

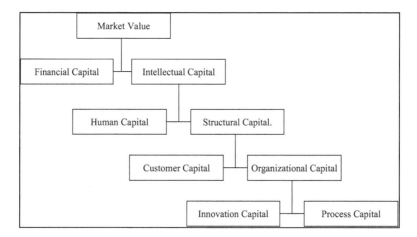

Figure 3.2: Skandia's division of intellectual capital (Edvinsson and Malone, 1998, p. 52).

(2001, p. 346) refers to individual competences. Edvinsson and Malone (1998, p. 35) go on to include creativity and innovativeness of the organization within human capital. In general, human capital is always considered an individual construct.

Structural capital deals with the mechanisms and structures of the company that "can support employees in their quest for optimal intellectual performance" (Edvisson and Åberg 2001, p. 4). As Bontis (1998, p. 66) has noted, structural capital is a company level construct and, as such, it allows intellectual capital to be measured at a company level. Structural capital is divided into customer and organizational capital. Sveiby (1997), however, does not employ this distinction but rather refers to structural capital only as the internal structure which would be equivalent to the organizational capital in Edvinsson and Malone. Structural capital is the main focus of the present dissertation.

Customer capital refers to the different aspects of client relationships such as loyalty,

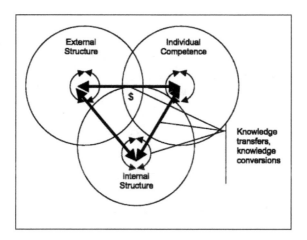

Figure 3.3: Sveiby's model for intellectual capital (Sveiby, 2001, p. 345).

knowledge of marketing or company image. Sveiby (2001, p. 346) refers to external structure as the "relationships with customers, suppliers and reputation of the firm". For the Skandia supplement (The Skandia Group, 1994), customer capital was a part of structural capital, but Edvinsson and Malone (1998, p. 36) acknowledge it as a separate form of capital.

Organizational capital refers to the internal routines and ways of working. Edvinsson and Malone (1998) divide these into process capital and innovation capital. The former refers to operational capacity, including organizational structure, management practices and computer system infrastructure. Innovation capital is divided into intellectual properties and intangible assets. Intellectual properties are defined as "information to which a company has rights against all the world" (Drake, 1997, p.12). Intangible assets refer to the value of the positive culture of the company, assets that do not have physical presence. Roos and Roos (1997) divide organizational capital into business process capital and business renewal capital. The former includes activities directed towards the production process, while the latter includes activities directed towards creating new products or developing new forms of cooperation. Sveiby (1997) includes all these types of capital in his "internal structure" family.

Edvinsson and Malone's classification of intellectual capital led to the creation of Skandia's Navigator (see Figure 3.4) as a tool for monitoring and managing intellectual capital. The tool has three sections relating to the past, present and future of the company and five different focus areas, financial, customer, human, process and renewal. The Skandia navigator became the main tool used to manage Skandia's intangible assets. Shophie Roy (2003, p. 78) in her study on the navigator describe it as follows:

> In the financial focus the outcome of yesterday's performance is shown. Customer, human and process focus visualize what the organization is currently doing to make the financial numbers positive tomorrow as well. Finally, renewal focus and the development focus in which the innovation capital was placed represented investment made today to ensure quality and profitability of tomorrow's performance.

For Edvisson (1997, p. 372) intellectual capital management "is leveraging human capital and structural capital together". For him intellectual capital value emerges out of the relationships between the different components of human and organizational capital. This is also the case in Sveiby's model (Seviby, 2001). In this model value is created through the interaction between different families of intangibles (Sveiby, 2001).

Sveiby's model acknowledges the difference between tacit and explicit knowledge

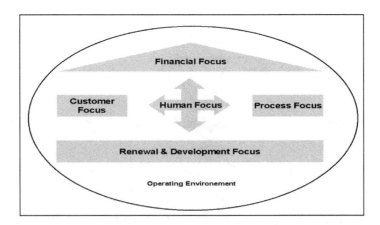

Figure 3.2: Skandia's Navigator (adapted from Roy, 2003, p. 78).

(Sveiby 1997, 2001), while this is not the case in Edvinsson's conceptualization of intellectual capital. One could argue that Edvinsson's proposal is a system to identify the influence of the tacit knowledge in financial terms since it tries to measure the intangible assets that cannot be "seen" or expressed in figures. But Edvinsson and Malone (1998) do not specifically treat the tacit/explicit dichotomy of knowledge. Sveiby (2001, p. 347) proposes that: "The value creation is primarily determined by the tacit/explicit transfer of knowledge between individuals and in the conversion of knowledge from one type to another". In this way, he proposes ten groups of knowledge-enabling strategies to transfer knowledge, one for each of the possible interactions (e.g. between individuals, from individuals to internal structure or from individuals to external structure) plus a tenth one that unifies all the previous nine strategies. For Sveiby, these strategies maximize the capacity-to-act of people both inside and outside the organization. They include many different actions such as, for example, communication between individuals, R&D alliances, building integrated systems of IT, or creating an organizational data-repository (see Sveiby, 2001; Sveiby et al., 2002).

Also interesting in Sveiby's model is the distinction he makes between the different actors in a knowledge organization or what he calls the know-how company (see Figure 3.5). He distinguishes four archetypical actors depending on the level of professional and managerial knowledge they have: the professional; the leader; the support staff; and, the manager (Sveiby, 1992, 1997). For Sveiby the professionals are the employees who possess the knowledge from which the company receives its revenues, such as law, consultant or engineering knowledge. Sveiby (1997, p. 57) points out that in addition to this professional knowledge, the company also needs managerial know-how which he defines as: "marketing, administration, accounting and the art of management itself". These two types of knowledge determine the types of employees (see Figure 3.5). In knowledge-intensive firms professionals make up the majority of the staff.

| | | Professional Knowledge | |
		Low	High
Managerial Knowledge	Low	The support staff	The professional
	High	The manager	The leader

Figure 3.3: Sveiby's worker's categories (Sveiby, 1997, p. 53).

Roy (2003, p. 75) maintains that Edvinsson's work is inspired by Kaplan and Norton's "Balanced Scorecard" (see e.g. Kaplan and Norton, 1992, 1996). Kaplan and Norton (1992, p. 71) define the balanced scorecard as follows:

> The balanced scorecard includes financial measures that tell the results of actions already taken. And it complements the financial measures with operational measures on customer satisfaction, internal processes, and the organization's innovation and improvement activities –operational measures that are the drivers for future financial performance.

Their model translates strategy and vision into indicators in four different perspectives each of which addresses one question. These are:
1. Financial perspective: How do we look the share holders?
2. Customer perspective: How do customers see us?

3. Internal perspective: What can we excel at?
4. Innovation and learning perspective: Can we continue to improve and create value?

Kaplan and Norton (1996) propose four main management processes to be used with the balanced scorecard: (1) translating the vision; (2) communicating and linking; (3) business planning; and, (4) feedback and learning. Finally, Kaplan and Norton (2000, 2004) propose the "strategic map" defined as a framework for linking intangible assets to shareholder value creation. The strategic map provides a tool to determine what intangible assets are necessary for creating value in line with the company strategy. For Kaplan and Norton (2000, p. 175) "[t]he foundation of any strategy map is the learning and growth perspective" which has three categories of intangibles, human, information and organizational capital. Human capital refers to knowledge and skills as in previous measurement models described above. Information capital has two main components, transaction-processing applications and analytic applications. The former refers to repetitive routines, while the latter refers to interpretation and sharing of information. In Edvinsson and Malone's model information capital is part of the structural capital of the company, more concretely it is part of the process capital of the company. Finally, organizational capital refers to culture, leadership, teamwork and other similar aspects of the organization. This would be the intangible asset in Edvinsson and Malone's model.

The balanced scorecard constitutes, therefore, a tool for managing the entire company, not only knowledge or intellectual capital. Interesting for managing knowledge is the fact that application of the balanced scorecard presupposes consensus in the vision and strategy of the company. Thus it is a tool for reflecting upon a company's processes and objectives, as was the case in Argyris' model for organizational learning (see e.g. Argyris, 1993). It also, as Kaplan and Norton (1992) have pointed out, reduces the information flow by reducing the amount of indicators needed since it only considers indicators that are relevant for the vision and strategy of the company.

Knowledge management and intellectual capital

Recent reviews of intellectual capital point out that there is a certain awareness of the importance of intangibles in companies, although there is not a clear consensus on what intellectual capital is (Lev, 2003; Marr and Chatzkel, 2004, Marr, 2005b). Kaufman and Schenider (2004, p. 385), after analyzing 36 key publications on intellectual capital, conclude that "the field lacks the standard definition for intangibles or IC, and that the classification of intangibles in three categories is not sufficient". Sveiby (2002) presents 28 different measurement models of intangibles developed from the 1950s. He classifies them into: (1) direct intellectual capital methods; (2) market capitalization methods; (3) returns on assets methods; and, (4) scorecard methods. The first three estimate monetary value of the intangible assets while the scorecard methods identify intangible components but do not estimate their monetary value (see also Andriessen, 2004a, b).

In a similar way, Bontis et al. (1999) and Bontis (2001) analyze different intellectual capital measurement tools and agree with Marr and Chatzkel (2004) that the intellectual capital field has to be developed further in order to create a greater degree of consensus. However, Bontis (2001) points out that there is a certain consensus emerging despite the different terms used. In this way, three areas of intellectual capital are relatively widely accepted:

1. Human Capital: This usually refers to the employee's competencies. Human capital belongs to individuals. The company rents human capital to produce goods or services.
2. Organizational capital: This second area refers mainly to the company processes and ways of working, or the organizational routines. It also includes infrastructure, such as physical spaces or IT systems.

3. Customer capital: This third area refers to relationships with customers and the image of the company.

Also widely accepted in the field is that intellectual capital creates value for the company. The importance of intangibles for creating value at the organization level has been empirically shown in Hurwitz et al. (2002). In a study with more than a hundred companies, they found that "a value stream based on intangibles performance is the most significant driver for stock returns". In addition they found a significant relationship between a firm's management of human and organizational capital and the growth in the intangible performance, and thus to stock return (Hurwitz et al., 2002, p. 58). Edvinsson and Åberg (2001) found in a study of 43 Swedish IT companies that their measurement of intellectual capital (using IC-rating ™) correlates with efficiency of the company. In a similar way, they found that human capital indicators are the main generator of value. Bontis et al. (2002) also found that learning, and thus the stock of knowledge, affects the overall performance of the company in a study of 32 mutual fund companies. Another study of 25 companies in the financial services industry reported that variables such as leadership, employee satisfaction and commitment are related to business performance (Bontis and Fitz-enz, 2002).

Comparison between different studies is complicated since each study uses a different method to measure intangibles. In addition intellectual capital indicators tend to be specific for each company, making comparison between companies difficult (Johanson, et al. 1999). And further, as Bontis (2001, p. 57) has pointed out, "most researchers have conducted case-based reviews of organizations that have established intellectual capital initiatives already" which makes generalizations exceedingly complex .

However, it is interesting to note, as Johanson et al. (2001b) have addressed, that normally intellectual capital measurement routines are used both as a strategic and an information-handling tool for the companies that have them. In this way, intellectual capital and knowledge management can be seen as similar (see also Chase, 1997b). For Wiig (1997b) knowledge management is more detailed and includes operational and tactic strategies which intellectual capital management does not include. Bontis et al. (2002) maintain that knowledge management is concerned with the processes that nurture intellectual capital. For them intellectual capital is basically the stock of knowledge and intangibles of the company.

There is also a certain consensus in understanding that intellectual capital value is created through the interaction among different categories of intellectual capital, as for example occurs through the value added that the transfer from organizational capital to customer capital might produce. Knowledge management deals mainly with the transformation from human to structural capital. In this way individual competencies and expertise can remain in the company even when the person has left the company. This transformation refers mainly to the transfer from tacit knowledge to explicit knowledge which is what Nonaka and Takeuchi (1995) call externalization (see Chapter 2). In this thesis, however, it is argued that there is also an important transfer of tacit knowledge into tacit knowledge through organizational routines. This is based on the knowledge creating company approach which is presented in the next section (Nonaka 1991, Nonaka and Takeuchi, 1995).

3.3.5 The knowledge creating company and the SECI model

The knowledge creating company approach was originally developed to explain the success of Japanese companies in creating innovation in the 1980s (Hedlund and Nonaka, 1991; Nonaka, 1991; Nonaka and Takeuchi, 1995). Later, it was developed into a broader model to foster innovation within companies. The key characteristic of the model is that the main source for innovation is tacit knowledge (see Chapter 2). For Nonaka and Takeuchi (1995, p. 70):

> Organizational knowledge creation is a continuous and dynamic interaction between tacit and explicit knowledge. This interaction is shaped by shifts between different modes of knowledge conversion.

Therefore, innovation is produced through the interaction between tacit and explicit knowledge. This interaction is referred to as knowledge conversion and has four modes: Socialization, Externalization, Combination and Internalization (SECI). These four modes produce a spiral of knowledge that is at the core of a knowledge-creating company. This is referred to as the SECI model (see Figure 3.6).

Socialization refers to the conversion from tacit to tacit knowledge. This conversion occurs in the process of sharing experiences, images, ideas or mental models with others. One clear example would be the apprentice who learns as s/he is guided by a mentor through observation, imitation and practice (see Nonaka, 1991, p. 98). Informal learning, as defined in Section 3.2, often occurs through socialization. It includes actions such as learning by doing but can also be a broader concept. Externalization occurs when tacit knowledge is made explicit; this is the 'quintessential' of the knowledge creating process. Combination refers to the transfer between explicit forms of knowledge; it is "reconfiguration of existing information" (Noanaka and Takeuchi, 1995, p. 67). Diakoulakis et al. (2004, p. 34) divide this knowledge conversion process in two parts, codification and dissemination of information. Codification constitutes the organization and categorization of externalized information. Dissemination of information involves the transfer of the result of the externalization process in the form of documents, expressions or images. Finally, internalization occurs when explicit knowledge is embodied into tacit knowledge: "When experiences through socialization, externalization and combination are internalized into individual's tacit knowledge bases in the form shared mental models or technical know-how, they become valuable assets"(Nonaka and Takeuchi, 1995, p. 69).

The ideal knowledge creating process is described as occurring in five phases (Nonaka and Takeuchi, 1995, pp. 83-88 and Figure 3.7): (1) sharing tacit knowledge; (2) creating concepts; (3) justifying concepts; (4) building an archetype; and, (5) cross-leveling knowledge. The process starts with the sharing of tacit knowledge, this is the socialization conversion of knowledge. In this phase, according to Nonaka and Takeuchi (1995), it is important to have face-to-face interaction among organizational members where they can share their mental models and feelings, in other words, their tacit knowledge. Through this interaction the process of creating concepts takes place. Within this interaction, because explicit is never as complete as tacit knowledge, there is a gap between the expression of an idea and the idea inside one's head. Such a gap allows for reflection and interaction between

Figure 3.4: Nonaka's spiral of knowledge (adapted from Nonaka and Takeuchi, 1995, p.71).

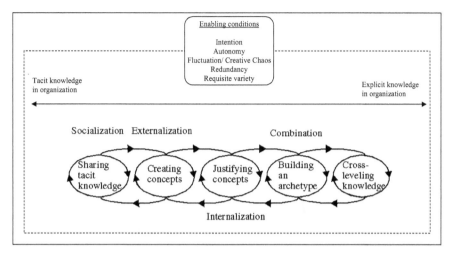

Figure 3.5: Five-Phase model of organizational knowledge-creation process (adapted from Nonaka and Takeuchi, 1995, p.84).

individuals in order to agree on what is understood by the expression. This is the process of "justifying concepts". According to Nonaka and Takeuchi (1995, p. 87), the top management level of an organization has to set the justification criteria "in the form of organizational intention, which is expressed in terms of strategy or vision". These criteria can also be set at lower organizational levels but they have to be "redundant" to the overall vision of the company. The redundancy of information helps to facilitate the justification process.

Once the concept is justified, it has to be converted into something tangible, namely, an "archetype". An archetype can be seen as a new product or as a "model of operating mechanism" in the case of services. Here, they argue, it is important to bring together multi-functional teams, from different parts of the organization with different expertise, that can put together and implement a new model or product. Finally, the fifth phase consists of cross-leveling knowledge. This means that the knowledge creation process can trigger another knowledge-creating spiral in another section of the company or in other affiliated companies.

Nonaka and Takeuchi (1995, p. 225) maintain that it is the individual who performs the transfer between explicit and tacit knowledge; however the individual has to share the knowledge in order to create the knowledge-creating spiral at an organizational level. In this way, the core of knowledge creation occurs at the group level, when individuals discuss and share their knowledge. Or, in other words, as noted in Chapter 2, people have to teach each other. Thus, in the knowledge-creating company, the context should be designed to foster the exchange of ideas that in turn will create new knowledge. This is what Nonaka, in a book written with von Krogh and Ichijo, calls the knowledge-enabling environment (see von Krogh *et al.*, 2000; von Krogh and Grand, 2002; Ichijo, 2004). Nonaka also refers to it as *ba* (see Nonaka and Konno, 1998; Nonaka, *et al.* 2000; Nonaka and Toyama, 2002; Nonaka and Toyama, 2004). *Ba* is a Japanese word that can be roughly translated as "place". The Japanese philosopher Nishida proposed the concept and it was developed by Shimizu (Nonaka *et al.*, 2000, p. 14). For the knowledge creating company it is defined as "a shared context in motion, in which knowledge is shared, created and utilized" (Nonaka and Toyama 2002, p. 1001). For them *ba* can be a physical, a virtual or a mental space. The key differentiation with any other human interaction is that *ba* "is a context which harbors meaning" (Nonaka and Konno, 1998, p. 40). Nonaka and Toyama (2004, pp. 102-103, emphasis in the original) maintain that,

Ba should be understood as *interactions* that occur at a specific time and space... *Ba* is a *way* to organize meaning creation, rather than a form of organization, such as hierarchy or network. A firm can be viewed as an organic configuration of various *ba* where people interact with each other and the environment, based on the knowledge they have and the meaning they create.

Thus, for the knowledge creating process "The role of the organization ... is to provide the proper context for facilitating group activities as well as the creation and accumulation of knowledge at the individual level" (Nonaka and Takeuchi, 1995, p. 73-74). Von Krogh *et al.* (2000) propose five general enablers for knowledge creation: (1) instill a knowledge vision; (2) manage conversation; (3) mobilize knowledge activists; (4) create the right context; and, (5) globalize local knowledge. The first enabler, "instill a knowledge vision", refers to the need for the top of the organization to make knowledge creation a core process within the organizational strategy. This knowledge vision drives the organizational intention (Nonaka and Takeuchi, 1995, p. 74). It is important that this strategy is internalized by those members of the company whose job consists on executing the vision (Ichijo, 2004, p. 138).

The second enabler is "manage conversation". As stated above, externalization of tacit knowledge into explicit knowledge includes a certain gap between the idea in one's head and the expression of the idea that is available to anyone. In the knowledge-creating company, the organization of work is such that it allows for discussion of different views of an idea. This discussion and reflection fosters innovation through the justification of the expression of knowledge and the subsequent use of such a concept as an archetype. This archetype is then shared at different levels of the organization in order to create a final product. "Therefore, finding how to facilitate communication with regard to organizational activities ... is a key enabler for knowledge creation" (Ichijo, 2004, p. 139).

The third enabler, "mobilize knowledge activists", refers to maximizing the efficiency of talented employees. Nonaka and Takeuchi (1995, p. 252) believe employees can "accumulate, generate, and update both tacit and explicit knowledge, acting almost as 'walking archives', on day-to-day basis". Nonaka and Takeuchi (1995) divide knowledge practitioners into knowledge operators and knowledge specialists. The knowledge operator accumulates tacit knowledge through experience, learning by doing. Some examples are sales people, skilled workers and supervisors in the production line or line managers. The knowledge specialists accumulate, generate and update mainly explicit, well-structured knowledge. An example of a specialist is the scientist from the R&D department. In addition to these two types of knowledge practitioners Nonaka and Takeuchi (1995, p. 154) refer to the knowledge engineer. This is the middle manager whose objective is to facilitate the spiral of knowledge at the epistemological level (within knowledge conversion) and ontological level (across different organizational levels). A middle manager mediates between what is and what should be.

The fourth enabler consists of "creating the right context" for knowledge creation. This "involves organizational structures that foster solid relationships and effective collaboration... those that facilitate cross-functional and cross-business unit activities" (Ichijo, 2004, p. 143). In such a context there ought to be five enabling conditions (Nonaka and Takeuchi, 1995, pp. 73-83): (1) intention; (2) autonomy; (3) fluctuation and creative chaos; (4) redundancy; and, (5) requisite variety. Intention refers to having all sections of the company dedicated to knowledge creation using the same vision. The top of the organization is supposed to create a vision that is vague enough so everybody can fit into it. Autonomy refers to empowering the people and different departments to take their own decisions and thus create their own views within the overall vision. This creates discrepancies, what Nonaka refers to as certain degree of chaos or uncertainty. For Nonaka (1988, p. 68) the more chaos an organization has inside its built-in structure, the more innovation can be promoted. An important component of this creative chaos is redundancy. For Nonaka (1991, p. 102) "redundancy is important because it encourages frequent dialogue and communication. This helps to create a 'common cognitive ground' among employees and thus facilitates the transfer of tacit knowledge". Finally, companies are required to have a variety of approaches to the same problem in order to survive in a constantly changing environment. A variety of approaches contributes towards the creative chaos also, creating discrepancies that have to be analyzed and treated.

The fifth enabler, "globalize local knowledge", refers to making the ideas and insights gained from the tacit knowledge within a specific unit of an organization available to the entire organization. Middle managers and IT are crucial to disseminating these insights.

The knowledge creating company and knowledge management

The knowledge creating approach has been most commonly referenced within the knowledge management literature (Wei Choo and Bontis, 2002b). The SECI model proposes a new way of understanding the organization where knowledge creation is central to all business activities. The knowledge creating approach is also tremendously important because it emphasizes the importance of tacit knowledge in innovation as well as the necessity of fostering communication among organizational members. The different characteristics of the knowledge-enabling environment constitute a clear picture of how companies are meant to create the *ba*, the virtual place, physical or mental, where employees interact to create new knowledge. The SECI model constitutes a way of organizing every-day experiences in order to foster knowledge creation or in other words, to encourage constant learning. Thus, the knowledge creating approach acknowledges the necessity of taking into account informal learning activities. In fact, it places informal learning through socialization as one of the key premises of the model.

Formalized training activities as well as intentional informal learning through, for example reading manuals, are not explicitly addressed in the SECI model. However, it is easy to relate socialization and externalization processes to formalized courses. The process of internalization would indeed be the process of learning, of incorporating information into our own mental models.

Also interesting to note is that the SECI model presents a company that has to operate while synthesizing different paradoxes, such as tacit vs. explicit, top-down vs. bottom-up, etc. (see Takeuchi and Nonaka, 2004b). Management of knowledge involves being able to cope with a certain degree of uncertainty. Further, a certain amount of chaos and redundancy has to be fostered. Thus, the SECI modelers proposed a flat structure as the best possible configuration for an organization (see also Drucker, 1988; Sveiby, 1997).

The knowledge creating approach, however, fails to incorporate the latest developments in the area of intellectual capital which deal with controlling and improving the management of knowledge. In this way, Nonaka's approach lacks a certain element of monitoring and evaluation. Although he maintains that any idea will have to pass a process of justification which implies a certain evaluation process, it is not clear how the spiral of knowledge is monitored in order to know if it is or is not working in the desired direction.

Also important to notice is the fact that Nonaka's model is mainly designed for large corporations. It is a model developed mainly for manufacturing companies, which create tangible products. Thus, it is only partially useful for service companies, although it in indubitable that it has had a strong influence in the management of knowledge intensive services.

Nonaka's model is also naive in the sense that it assumes certain good will in all the employees within the organization. Despite conferring great importance to the personal nature of knowledge, it does not discuss in detail the issue of relationships. It basically assumes that everybody will be willing to share knowledge without acknowledging that knowledge is a form of power and that employees might not feel inclined to share their knowledge.

To sum up, one could argue that the knowledge creating approach presents a very interesting way of looking at the organization, placing informal learning through socialization at the core of a business strategy. It involves and acknowledges many different parts of the organization. Thus it is more holistic than intellectual capital approaches and ideas related to organizational learning. However, the knowledge creating approach does not make an effort to integrate these different points of view. It is necessary, thus, to try to build a holistic model of knowledge management, where all these fields are integrated and "working together" in order to create a "best picture" of what constitutes a knowledge intensive company.

3.4 Integrated models of knowledge management

The different terms presented such as organizational learning, intellectual capital accounting, etc., point to different perspectives within the same arena: how to treat people's knowledge at the work place. Despite the different definitions and terms, what is proposed here is that new developments in knowledge management are working towards integrating these different fields (see e.g. Wei Choo and Bontis 2002a, Easter-Smith and Lyles 2003b, McElroy 2003; Stankosky, 2005a). Within these new developments, what Tuomi (2002, p. 76) calls the third generation, knowledge is a dynamic entity constructed through social interaction. Therefore, information technologies are used only as enablers and are therefore only a small part of the knowledge management effort. Knowledge is linked with action within the overall strategy of a company. Knowledge management is not a specific small part of the organization, but a way of organizing the whole business. This can be referred to as increasing the knowledge intensiveness of the firm (See e.g. Starbuck, 1992). In a knowledge-intensive company, the organization of work has to maximize the use of its main source of revenue, the employees' knowledge. The company has to find strategies to make each employee share her/his knowledge with co-workers, both tacitly and explicitly. The company has to assure that the distribution of information is creating new insights in the mind of its employees. And finally, the company has to promote the translation of these new insights into new services or products.

Wiig (1993, 1994, 1995, 1997a, 2000) presents a fairly big picture of what he believes knowledge management encompasses. Wiig (1997) divides knowledge management into four main areas of focus: (1) top-down monitoring and facilitation of knowledge related activities; (2) creation and maintenance of knowledge infrastructure, including but not exclusively information technologies; (3) create, renew, build and organize knowledge assets; and, finally (4) distribute and apply knowledge effectively. Figure 3.8 shows his view of different processes integrated within knowledge management. Wiig (2000) shows how human resource functions, information technology functions as well as research and development functions are integrated with knowledge management. Knowledge management is therefore a conglomerate of different business functions related to knowledge, from creating an information technology infrastructure to determining knowledge strategies within the vision of a company. Wiig (1997a; 2000) includes organizational learning within the frame of knowledge management (Wiig et al. 1997) and maintains that intellectual capital and knowledge management complement each other. For Wiig (1997b) intellectual capital is mainly focused on strategy and governance, while knowledge management is more focused on tactical and operational perspectives.

Wei Choo and Bontis (2002a) present yet another integrated picture of intellectual capital, knowledge management and organizational learning. In their introductory chapter of a 41 article volume, they state the basis for their model. For them, companies generate value from the knowledge that a company possesses through its organizational processes of knowledge creation, knowledge distribution and knowledge utilization (Wei Choo and Bontis, 2002b, p. 16). Through these processes, the firm acquires knowledge and capabilities that are unique and thus develop a competitive advantage. These constitute a firm's intellectual capital. The stock of intellectual capital has to grow and be refreshed through new learning at different levels: the individual, the work-group, and the organizational and networking levels. Wei Choo and Bontis base the knowledge creation process on Nonaka's model. Formal training activities and other types of human resource development strategies are not explicitly considered although they could be part of this process. Organizational learning approaches could be included within the study of knowledge creation processes at different levels. The

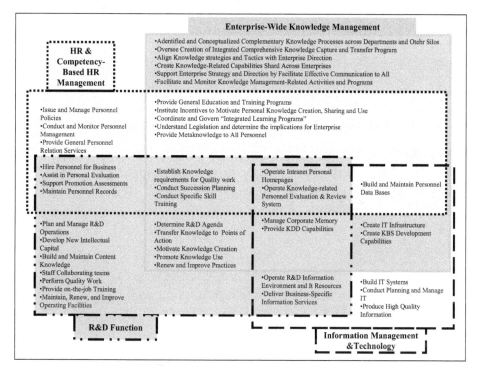

Figure 3.6: Knowledge management activities (adapted from, Wiig, 2000 , p. 12).

management of intellectual capital could be within the knowledge utilization process. Information technology developments, although not really included in their model, could be included within the knowledge transfer process.

Diakoulakis *et al.* (2004) divide their holistic knowledge management approach into three areas: knowledge management measures; knowledge management processes; and, business objectives. Knowledge management measures include strategic management, organizational measures, human resource management (HRM) measurements and technical measures. These different organizational aspects influence the knowledge management processes which include: (1) exploration of the external and internal environment for knowledge; (2) combination, retention/systematization and sharing of knowledge; and, (3) quality and quantity of knowledge used. The quantity and quality of knowledge used has an influence on the business objectives in that they separate typical management objectives (such as productivity, cost reduction, innovation, competitiveness or quality of decision making) from intellectual capital objectives that are associated with different components of intellectual capital.

This chapter presented various views and definitions related lifelong learning and knowledge management and their evolution. These theoretical and empirical findings from a variety of fields provide a platform for the development of the knowledge management model presented in the next chapter. Each field has a different perspectives on the management of knowledge. Only the field of human capital theory has been interested in studying the demand for training, while the rest have few references to training activities. In the next chapter, thus, these different fields are integrated into a framework where training plays an important role in knowledge management.

CHAPTER 4: TOWARDS A MODEL FOR KNOWLEDGE MANAGEMENT

4.1 Introduction: Towards a holistic model for knowledge management

Chapter 3 revealed the complexity of the knowledge management field. As Quintas *et al.* (1997, p. 387) have pointed out the field is at the crossroads of several different disciplines, such as strategic management, information technology and human resource development (see also Liebowitz, 1999; Wei Choo and Bontis 2002a, Easter-Smith and Lyles 2003b; Stankosky, 2005a). The last section in Chapter 3 showed how the field is moving towards an integration of these different disciplines.

It is the intention of this chapter to present a holistic model for knowledge management specifically directed towards the study of knowledge-intensive SMEs, putting a major emphasis on the lifelong learning implications of the model. The model is specifically adapted for the study of SMEs in education and consultancy in Sweden. However, a certain degree of generalization is presumed and it is argued that the model could be adapted easily to meet the demands of bigger organizations.

The model consists of specific characteristics that knowledge-intensive SMEs hypothetically possess. The intention of the dissertation is to explore to what extent these characteristics appear in SMEs and in this way explore the knowledge management approach of each company in relation to the proposed model. Assumptions and findings from the fields of human capital theory, intellectual capital, organizational learning, the knowledge-creating company and human resource development are brought together to create a holistic model for knowledge management. The model assumes that knowledge management implies much more than the use of information technologies (IT) for internal business processes. In the model knowledge management takes into account the tacit nature of knowledge as well as its transformation into information. The model's main foci are on human capital (or individual competences) and organizational capital (or internal structure) (see Chapter 3). The framework pays special attention to the processes directed toward the creation of knowledge, both formally and informally. It is important to note that the model constitutes a tentative hypothesis on how the companies under study are knowledge intensive firms.

The theoretical framework for knowledge management in SME's is presented in Figure 4.1. It is composed of three main areas, discussed below, that include the four focal processes traditionally defined within knowledge management: knowledge creation; distribution; storage; and, use (see e.g. Wiig, 1997; Coleman, 1999; Hellström *et al.*, 2000; Leech and Sutton, 2002). It is important to mention that although the literature on knowledge management uses the expression "distribution or storage" of knowledge, it is information that is distributed or stored not knowledge. Knowledge is only kept in people's minds. Knowledge-creation processes refer to the activities intentionally directed towards learning at any level of the organization. Distribution processes refer to the exchange of information and the transfer of tacit knowledge. This can occur in any kind of gathering among employees as well as through exchange of ideas through email or other means. Storage processes refer to the codification, organization, and storage into databases of explicit knowledge. It also includes the internalization among employees of working routines. Knowledge use processes refer to the application of the knowledge created into products or other visible outputs that create revenues directly or indirectly for the company.

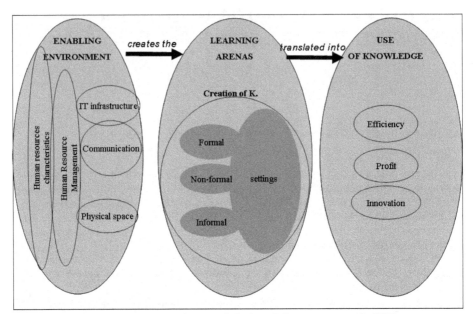

Figure 4.1: Theoretical framework for knowledge management in SMEs

It is hypothesized that knowledge intensive organizations foster knowledge creation, distribution, storage and use processes through strategic actions directed towards the management of knowledge. These actions, which constitute the knowledge management approach of each company, have been grouped into three main areas: the knowledge-enabling environment, learning arenas and knowledge use. These three areas (see Figure 4.1) are somewhat artificial since the separation of the different aspects of an organization is not uniform.

The knowledge-enabling environment refers to the organization of a company, the ways of working and the facilities that employees have in order to deliver services and constantly upgrade their knowledge. Such an environment constitutes a knowledge-intensive organization (where knowledge is produced and sold). As it is used here, the concept of knowledge-enabling environment encompasses more features that the ones described in Chapter 3 (see von Krogh *et al.*, 2000, Ichiyo, 2004). In this thesis, the knowledge-enabling environment is divided into four main areas: human resources and its management; communication activities;, information technology infrastructure; and, physical space arrangement. The four areas include different ideas presented in the previous chapters related to the management of knowledge. The next section of this chapter presents a discussion of each of these areas and how they are viewed in the model. Chapter 7 presents the results of the exploration of this environment.

Learning arenas refer mainly to activities directed specifically towards the creation of knowledge, such as training events. Learning activities can be placed within the life-wide dimension, from informal learning to formal learning. Informal unintentional learning (as defined by Livingstone, 2000a, 2001) occurs almost constantly in our daily activities. It is, thus, almost impossible to account for it. However, the assumption is that a knowledge-enabling environment will promote unintentional learning. In addition, a knowledge-enabling environment should also foster the creation of knowledge intentionally, through planning of events, time and investments in learning activities. In this study, the demand for training is used as an indication of the knowledge creating effort of the company. As such learning arenas, knowledge creation and demand for training are sometimes used interchangeably. Chapter 8 presents the exploration of this area.

The distinction between learning arenas and the knowledge-enabling environment is to some degree artificial. For example, informational meetings that have an information-sharing objective are considered within the enabling environment. However, it is very likely that this sharing constitutes new knowledge for many of the participants. However, for analytical purposes, only activities directed exclusively to the improvement of the human capital are considered within the learning arenas. In other words, learning arenas are made up of activities exclusively directed towards learning new knowledge or skills. Other activities such as meetings, that might promote learning but are not primarily directed toward these objectives, are considered part of the enabling environment.

Finally, the use of knowledge refers to the outcomes of the knowledge-enabling environment and learning activities. Any service or product is the result of a knowledge production process, especially in knowledge-intensive companies. The services that companies provide are knowledge-products; specifically, they are professional's knowledge translated into a service for a client. The ultimate objective of knowledge management in an organization is to improve company profitability, efficiency or effectiveness, as well as to assure quality in the service delivered.

Especially interesting is how this knowledge-enabling environment facilitates product or service innovation. In addition, the output of a knowledge-enabling environment should be that employees are willing to share their knowledge, improving the overall collaborative climate of the company.

4.2 The knowledge enabling environment

4.2.1 Human resources and its management

Human resource characteristics

The knowledge-enabling environment is divided in different sections in order to be able to more easily study its characteristics. The first feature is the human resource characteristics or the employees. It is the employees who play a central role in creating the knowledge-enabling environment. Since knowledge belongs to individuals it is necessary to start by understanding the characteristics of the people that work at the company as the point of departure for any knowledge management strategy. Company's employees are usually referred to as the human capital or human resource of the firm. Barney's (1991) resource-based theory of the firm maintains that a company's survival depends on having rare, non-imitable resources that can create a competitive advantage in the market. Ferris et al. (1999) argue that in the last 15 years a certain degree of agreement has coalesced around the idea that the most rare, non-imitable resource which can provide a competitive advantage is the knowledge embodied in employees. In the resource conversion theory (Coleman 1971, 1990), companies transform human capital into financial capital. That is, a company will rent the human capital of a person in order to create a product or service that will bring revenue. Understood either as a resource or as a type of capital, employees, more specifically their knowledge, are the main sources of profit in a knowledge-intensive company.

Traditionally human capital has been measured in terms of years of schooling or educational attainment. As a factor of the production process, human capital has also been measured as experience; assuming that more experience increases the human capital that one possesses. Similarly, age has also been used as a measure. In the present model, these meaures are not used to gauge the level of human capital that the company has, but rather to evaluate the "readiness to learn" of a company's workforce (Desjardins, 2004). From a lifelong learning perspective, studies within human capital theory have shown that educational attainment is an important predictor for participation in adult training (Mincer, 1989, Boudard, 2001). In other words, it seems that people with higher levels of educational attainment are more likely to demand and participate in knowledge creating activities. On the other hand, age is traditionally associated with lower levels of participation in training (Livingstone, 2000b, 2004). It is important thus, to take into account these variables in order to understand the knowledge-enabling environment and the demand for training.

Intellectual capital accounting has also used education, age and experience on the job to measure human capital or individual competences within a firm (see e.g. Sveiby, 1997; Harrison and Sullivan, 2000; Lundquist, 2000; Ordoñez de Pablos, 2002). Sveiby (1997) also differentiates between professional know-how and managerial know-how (see Chapter 3). For him, knowledge-intensive companies should be comprised mainly of personnel with a high level of professional know-how (see also Sveiby and Lloyd, 1987). Nonaka and Takeuchi (1995) and von Krogh *et al.* (2000) identify the importance of mobilizing "knowledge activists". They present two archetypical actors with professional know-how (the knowledge specialist and the knowledge operator) and one archetypical actor having both high managerial and professional know-how (the knowledge engineer), usually referred to as the middle manager (see Chapter 3).

Another important characteristic of a work force is variety. Nonaka (1988, 1991) argues that the greater the varieties of knowledge perspectives the more knowledge creation possibilities exist. The greater the variety in the labor force of a firm the greater the number of meanings of expressions that have to be constantly negotiated in order to agree on what is meant by an expression. This then encourages more communication among employees which in turn improves the possibilities for innovation and knowledge creation.

Human resource management

Human resource management (HRM) refers to certain actions directed towards maximizing the use of human resources. Roos *et al.* (2004) have noticed that in recent years, HRM has shifted from being a marginal executive management function to that of having an important strategic role in an organization (see also, Ferris *et al.* 1999). Accordingly, human resource practitioners have highlighted their importance within knowledge management initiatives (Filius *et al.*, 2000; Stovel and Bontis, 2002; Yakya and Goh, 2002; Gloet and Berrel, 2003; Hislop, 2003; Rodriguez *et al.* 2003; Oltra, 2005). Hislop (2003), for example, maintains that HRM plays an important role in providing the necessary incentives and conditions for employees to share their knowledge in knowledge management initiatives. Gloet and Berrel (2003) claim that, since human capital and intellectual capital are the core focus of HRM, human resource practitioners play a key role in the understanding of necessary approaches for knowledge management.

According to Fombrum *et al.* (1984), HRM encompasses four "generic" functions: (1) selection; (2) appraisal; (3) rewards; and, (4) development (see also Storey, 1992). In the present model, HRM includes only selection and reward functions. Appraisal functions are considered together with the rewards system and development is studied separately within the learning arenas.

Recruitment and selection procedures and new employees

The type of employees that a company has depends largely upon the selection and recruitment processes it uses. The selection process involves the manner in which companies choose suitable employees and the criteria used for selection. Recruitment refers to the pro-active process of soliciting specific persons for employment. In addition to determining the type of individuals a company hires, selection and recruitment processes provide information as to a company's approach to human capital. For example, some companies might be more interested in the personality of a prospective employee, while others might focus on skills. Quinn *et al.* (1998) maintain that the first step in strategic management of intellectual capital is recruiting candidates that best suit the company. Sveiby (2001, p. 350) also refers to recruitment as a strategy to improve the collaborative professional climate by recruiting people who are willing to share their knowledge.

Within HRM, attention needs to be given to company procedures dealing with new employees. Quinn et al. (1998) refer to having a mentor as a way of helping new employees more readily integrate into the company. A mentor system is also a way of reinforcing tacit to tacit knowledge conversion (Nonaka and Takeuchi, 1995; Diakoulakis et al., 2004). Svensson (2005, p. 289) refers to mentors as a way of improving the learning opportunities of employees. Employee handbooks or manuals also provide a means for integrating new recruits to a company's culture. A handbook that shows company rules and procedures is an attempt to externalize the firms working routines and values.

A final aspect related to selection worth considering is employee turnover. On the one hand a high rate of employee turnover can create instability in a company. Jasimuddin et al. (2005) have pointed out that losing employees implies a loss of the tacit knowledge they possess (see also Boiral 2002, p. 296). This loss in human capital might be difficult to replace. Tacit knowledge builds up over the years through interactions with other company members and thus it takes time for a new comer to get to the same level of understanding of company routines and ways of working. Further, if key employees transfer to a competitor, they might take with them experience and knowledge that could endanger the competitive advantage of their old firm (Stovel and Bontis, 2002). On the other hand, Takeuchi and Nonaka (2004a) note that employee turnover can play an important role in knowledge creation. High employee turnover and new recruitment can bring new insights and visions to a company by creating more heterogeneity within the firm and increasing possibilities for innovation and organizational learning (see also Argyris, 1993; Nonaka and Takeuchi, 1995). Further, former employees working in other companies can become clients or valuable partners (Keseels and Keursten, 2002).

In this way, Takeuchi and Nonaka (2004a) talk about creating a third way through synthesizing these two apparently opposing options: high employee turnover and stability of the workforce. In relation to workforce stability, companies might decide to have a higher proportion of temporary workers in order to have a workforce that is more adaptable to the constantly changing necessities of the marketplace. In other cases, companies might prefer to have permanent employees in order to build up human capital associated with the company.

Reward system

A second function usually associated with HRM is the reward system. Hurwitz et al. (2002, p. 58) present a total rewards framework. They divide it into four areas: (1) pay; (2) benefits; (3) learning and development; and, (4) work environment. Only the first will be considered in this thesis within the reward category. This is because benefits are usually compulsory within the Swedish context and learning and development and work environment are included within other parts of the model. Therefore, in this model the reward system refers to the salaries that employees receive as payment for the rent of their human capital. Hurwitz et al. (2002, p. 58) include within the "pay" area bonus systems, such as target bonuses, actual bonuses and long-term compensations (stock and others). Bonuses refer to extra payments or any other reward given after an objective is accomplished.

Yakya and Goh (2002) studied HRM functions in relation to knowledge management strategies in 300 Malaysian companies. They conclude that reward systems can be used to change employee's behavior in relation to knowledge. Foss and Mahnke (2003) maintains that economic rewards can be used to increase employee participation within a company. Hislop (2003) has pointed out that rewards can be used to enhance employee's interest in sharing information. Davenport and Prusak (1998) maintain that a reward system should be linked to participation by the employee in knowledge repositories or other types of knowledge management activities within the company. Knowledge repositories or even knowledge management activities are not likely to appear in SMEs. Therefore, for the model presented here, it is almost impossible to find reward systems directly linked to the employee's contribution to the knowledge capacity of the company. However, it is possible to inquire how salaries are determined. The different criteria used to determine the salary of an employee can show if the company is explicitly linking employee's knowledge to remuneration.

Organization of work

The organization of work can be considered part of HRM. It refers to ways of making human resources more effective through the way their work is structured. The present study enquires as to whether or not companies work in teams. In the case of education, "teams" refers to groups of teachers in the same subject working together with a similar group. In the case of consultancy, "teams" refers to group of consultants with the same type of expertise working together. "Cross-functional teams" refer to companies that are organized in groups of people with different expertise and competencies. In the case of education, it refers to groups of teachers from different subjects working together with the same kids at the same time at the classroom.

Working in teams is usually viewed as one feature of knowledge-intensive organizations (Taylor, 1998, p. 97). Grandberg and Ohlsson (2005, p. 292) maintain: "Teams support and facilitate learning and competence enhancement". Specifically, cross-functional teams and multidisciplinary teams are crucial in a knowledge-intensive company (Taylor, 1998; Sole and Edmondson, 2002; Johnsson, 2003). Nonaka and Takeuchi (1995) maintain that cross-functional teams are better at working with the archetype created through the spiral of knowledge. Cross-functional teams, in addition, will likely create a higher level of communication among employees, since different perspectives have to be integrated (see Harrison, 2000). Fong (2003) maintains that cross-functional teams allow for different perspectives in problem solving and can better integrate different client needs into product development. The APQC (2000) published a report showing that knowledge management initiatives were more likely to succeed if cross-disciplinary teams were involved in the initiative.

In addition to having cross-functional teams, the structure of a knowledge-intensive business has been characterized as a "flat" organization (Drucker, 1988; Halal, 1998). In a similar vein, Sveiby (1997) maintains that knowledge professionals are unwilling to work under strong hierarchies with a high degree of control over their work. Nonaka and Takeuchi (1995) maintain that companies should have middle managers who serve a bridge between the management structure and the production line (see also, Nonaka et al., 2000). Thus, it appears that a knowledge-enabling environment in a knowledge-intensive SME will be characterized by a flat structure with no hierarchy and a high percentage of professional workers.

Table 4.1 summarizes the different aspects within human resources and its management that this thesis explores.

4.2.2 Communication activities

Communication refers to the exchange of information between people. Information comes from the knowledge that one person holds. As stated in Chapter 2, our tacit knowledge is partially made explicit by producing information which is shared with others. It is through communication that the process of teaching and learning takes place. Von Krogh et al. (2000) consider "manage conversation" one of the enablers of the knowledge creating process. They maintain that through conversation meanings are both discussed and justified. This creates a concept that is shared within an organization at different levels and which then becomes an archetype used later for product development (see also, Nonaka and Takeuchi, 1995, von Krogh and Roos, 1996; Ichiyo, 2004). Webber (1993, p. 28) puts it this way: "Conversations are the way knowledge workers discover what they know, share it with their colleagues, and in the process create new knowledge for the organization". Communication is, therefore, a central characteristic to look at in a knowledge-enabling environment.

Table 4.1: Summary of the aspects within human resources and its management

General
• Total Number of Employees
Human Resource Characteristics
• Educational attainment
• Age
• Number of years working in a similar area
• Number of foreigners in the workforce
• Percentage of professionals in the workforce
• Percentage of women in the workforce
Human Resource Management
Recruitment and selection procedures
• Method of advertising available positions
• Method of selection procedures
• Different criteria used for recruiting
New recruits
• Having a mentor for new recruits
• Having a standard procedure for new recruits
• Having a handbook for the company
Stability of the workforce
• Employee turnover
• Number of years working in the company
• Number of employees with a permanent contract as a percentage of total number of employees
• Number of employees with permanent contracts as a percentage of total number of employees with temporary contracts
Rewards
• Salary level
• Criteria to determine salary level
• Bonuses
Organization of work
• Cross-functional teams
• Having middle managers
Other
• Manager is a professional
• Manager is owner
• Having a specific person for Human Resource Management

As already stated, the teaching and learning process occurs through communication. The listener or reader internalizes information created through the externalization process and in this way creates knowledge. The socialization process also pertains to the creation of knowledge and not only to its distribution. In the socialization process, internalization of common routines, for example, constitutes informal un-intentional learning (see Chapter 3).

These communication activities, and hence the different types of knowledge conversion, are the main tools for transforming human capital into organizational capital, and making individual knowledge available at a group level. In other words, through the process of communication different employees can have a similar understanding of the surrounding world.

In the present model, communication activities are understood as a tool for information distribution, and not for the creation of knowledge. It is important to note that the analysis in this thesis does not look at information and knowledge distribution processes, which would be virtually impossible, but rather looks at the communication activities promoted at the company level. Despite the considerable reductionism this measure implies, it is practical and deemed necessary in order to have a workable exploratory model.

The main activity undertaken by a company for the distribution of information is to hold meetings. Meetings clearly encompass externalization, combination and very likely internalization and socialization. It is, however, impossible to determine if the information shared has or has not been transformed into knowledge (internalized) by the employees who attend the meeting. However, meetings are indications of a company's effort to share information. Meetings specifically directed towards learning skills or acquiring competences are not considered within communication activities, but rather as knowledge creation initiatives. This study includes only meetings that are directed towards the distribution of information among company members.

Another interesting action that companies might use for information distribution is a newsletter. Newsletters can provide general information for employees and clients on interesting issues related to company activities. In addition, they can provide a perfect platform to express the vision and ideals of a company. In other words, newsletters are a tool which can be used to enhance the vision of the company, and in this way promote organizational intentions (Nonaka and Takeuchi, 1995) or knowledge vision (von Krogh *et al.* 2000).

IT plays a major role in the distribution of information since it is such a powerful information dissemination tool. Emailing, chat rooms, blogs, etc. are all IT tools for communication. But in the present model, IT-related variables are considered separately. They have traditionally played a major role in knowledge management literature and there are many publications and companies dedicated only to information technology solutions for knowledge management (see Rao, 2005b, for an overview of knowledge management technological solutions).

Table 4.2 summarized the different aspects within the communication activities explored in this dissertation.

Table 4.2: Summary of the aspects within the communication activities of the company

Meetings
- Frequency of informational meetings
- Scheduled meetings for professional workers
- Number of hours spent at formal regular meetings with other colleagues
- Number of hours spent at informal regular meetings with other colleagues
- Having a newsletter

Individual communication activities
- Number of emails from colleagues per day
- Number of emails from customers per day
- Number of telephone calls from colleagues per day
- Number of telephone calls from customers per day
- Number of materials WRITTEN last year
- Number of materials READ per week

4.2.3 Information technologies infrastructure

An important enabler of knowledge is IT. Traditionally knowledge management has been linked with the use of IT in companies. In many instances, knowledge management strategies have been used together with IT in the work place. The first generation of knowledge management was mainly driven by the use of IT (Tuomi, 2000; McElroy, 2000). As already mentioned, a holistic model for knowledge management necessarily encompasses more than the use of IT for company purposes. IT for knowledge management have to recognize the existence of tacit knowledge. In other words, IT can be used as a tool for knowledge management, but the most important thing in implementing knowledge management is gearing it toward the sources and final users of the knowledge: the employees. IT are therefore enablers of the process for managing knowledge but not drivers.

IT are referred to in economic theory as factors to increase productivity (see e.g. Mata *et al.*, December 1995; Kohli and Devaraj, 2003a). Higher investments in technology are associated with higher company performance (see Kohli and Devaraj, 2003b for a literature review). Tanriverdi (2005) has argued that knowledge management serves as a mediator between IT and performance. In other words, the impact of IT on performance depends on the actions directed toward the management of knowledge.

IT in relation to knowledge management are extremely useful for the distribution and transfer of information. The combination conversion (explicit-to-explicit) of knowledge is easily carried out through emailing or other digital forms of sharing information. The latest developments in technology also allow for certain socialization (tacit-to-tacit) conversion of knowledge. BP, for example, as reported in Ahmed *et al.* (2002, p. 156-165), has successfully added video-conferencing systems to allow for the transfer of tacit knowledge without the requirement of physical presence.

In addition to using information technology for distribution of information, or as a factor to enhance productivity, they are widely employed as storage tools. Databases and other forms of storing information are common among companies in order to keep important information available to be re-used. Intranet systems can also provide access to a variety of important company data. In fact, nowadays, the Internet can be considered an endless database, where all sorts of information can be found. There is, thus, a vast amount of information available that has to be channeled and organized in a way that makes sense to company employees. Programming languages such as XML or search engines such as "Google ^{TM}" are examples of information technology developments that can handle various information sorting requirements. Recent developments in the use of IT for knowledge management have also included ways of promoting discussion. Forums, communities of practices, bloggs and other types of web-based solutions are not only means of sharing information but also ways of initiating discussions that can create new insights and developments (see e.g. Plaskoff, 2003).

In sum, IT provide a new way of working that also result in challenges in the everyday life of an organization. They provide a tool for the distribution and storage of information as well as a tool for connecting people who are physically distant. It is therefore important to look at how companies are investing in IT, what kind of information technology systems they have and how they relate to the overall structure of the knowledge management processes. In SMEs it is very unlikely that companies will be using sophisticated software catalogued as knowledge management platforms. It is important, therefore, to consider IT only as a possible feature and not as a necessary tool for a knowledge-enabling environment. Table 4.3 presents a summary of the aspects explored within the IT infrastructure.

Table 4.3: Summary of the aspects within the Information Technology infrastructure

Facilities
  • Number of computers per employee
  • Having access to the Internet
Databases
  • Having databases
  • Content of the databases
  • Accessibility of the databases
Investment
  • Investment in IT years

4.2.4 Physical space

Finally, the physical space where work takes place can play a role in the creation of a knowledge-enabling environment. In the field of architecture, Hillier (1996, p. 248) indicated that all human spatial organization does not only reflect some sort of knowledge, but "can also be generative" of knowledge. Building on the work of Allen (1977) on R&D groups,

Hillier (1996, p. 257) concludes: "Because all spatial structure has the capability to generate patterns of co-presence through movement, it also has the potential to generate ties". These ties refer to the communication between employees. Or said in another way, space can generate a higher level of exchange of ideas (see also Johnsson, 2003, p. 180). Drucker and Prusak (1998, p. 90) have referred to the "water coolers" as meeting places where the informal exchange of ideas can be of enormous value for the company.

Sveiby (1997) maintains that knowledge intensive companies should have open spaces with no walls. This can provide an easier and faster way for the exchange of ideas. Takeuchi and Nonaka (2004a) have pointed out the importance of designing spaces that reflect the vision of the company. They also encourage organizations to provide symbols that embody the culture of the organization.

In sum, it seems that the physical configuration of the working space is another aspect to look at within a knowledge intensive organization in order to see if it is or is not in line with the theoretical approaches on innovation. Unfortunately, the present study could not look systematically into the configuration of space in the companies.

4.3 The learning arenas

4.3.1 Introduction: creation of knowledge

In this thesis, the model for knowledge management in SMEs is especially interested in the creation of knowledge or what Hedlund and Nonaka (1991) refer to as generation of knowledge. Junnarkar (1997) using the SECI model maintains that knowledge creation in individuals is the tacit- to- explicit-to-tacit conversion of knowledge. Socialization-to-internalization refers to how individuals collectively create insights. As presented in Chapter 2, the transfer tacit-to-explicit-to-tacit is the process of teaching and learning and it occurs at the individual level. When knowledge is internalized into organizational routines or when the employees' mental models change, one could say that the organization has learned. Thus for this study, knowledge creation refers to the process of learning both at the individual level as well as at the organizational level.

The explanation of the life-wide dimension of learning in Chapter 3 showed that the process of learning can take place in many different situations and in many different forms. As stated above, activities primarily directed toward information distribution might result in informal learning (there is no structure, no institutionalization of the process, no "teacher", no "student") or un-intentional informal learning. The outcome of these distribution activities is difficult to predict or determine. Thus, these activities are considered within the knowledge-enabling environment and not specifically as knowledge-creating activities. Only intentional learning activities directed explicitly toward the acquisition of new knowledge or skills are considered within the learning arenas.

Another process usually referred to as a way of bringing new knowledge into a company is the recruitment of new personnel (see e.g. Sveiby, 1997). A new employee can be hired in order to bring certain expertise into the company. It is not automatic, however, that adding a new individual to the company will increase the human capital, and it is even less clear that new human capital will be transferred into organizational capital. For this reason, hiring new personnel is only considered as an enabling factor of knowledge creation and not as a specific action for knowledge creation.

Accordingly, an activity directed specifically towards learning will not automatically increase human capital or the knowledge of any employee. However, at the organizational level this action unequivocally promotes the creation of knowledge. In the model, therefore, formal and non-formal training activities are seen as main actions for the creation of knowledge. They constitute human capital formation activities since the activity is directed towards increasing one person's knowledge or competencies. In a similar way, intentional informal learning activities, or what Livingstone (2001, 2004, 2005) refers to as self-directed learning, are also considered a form of human capital formation. It is important to keep in mind, in any case, that it cannot be automatically assumed that the whole company has gained knowledge. The individual acquires the knowledge and through the enabling environment this knowledge can be incorporated into the organization, contributing in this way to the organizational capital of the firm.

4.3.2 Formal and non-formal training activities

The model considers training activities as the main method for the creation of knowledge. All training activities can be placed within the life-wide dimension (see Chapter 3): training can take place in formal, non-formal or informal ways. Training activities are considered formal or non-formal because their learning is intentional, organized and structured (EUROSTAT, 2001, p. 11). First, they are intentional because employees consciously decide to participate and to learn something. Second, training activities have a certain degree of organization. They have a predetermined time and place and they have associated costs. Thirdly, they are structured in the sense that there is a content plan for what to present and how to present it. Formal learning is considered here as training that takes place in a formal institution such as a university or college. Non-formal learning can take place internally through seminars conducted at the company's site or externally at non-formal types of institutions.

Traditionally training has been studied using three main parameters: training incidence, participation and cost. Training incidence can be looked at both as time spent on training and as number of training events employees attend. In terms of participation, percentage of employees participating in training is traditionally considered as an indicator for the demand for training. For this thesis, the demand for training cannot be considered in the traditional sense, since companies plan the training for all employees (see Chapter 5 and 9). In this way, the demand for training is studied in an ideal situation where firms plan training for all their employees.

Finally, the training cost also provides an indication of a company's training efforts. The study of educational costs includes indirect as well as direct expenses. Direct cost refers to the actual price of the course (the hiring of the teacher, the renting of the installations, etc.) Indirect expenses, also denominated as labor cost, refer to the cost associated with the time the employee is not producing while s/he is training.

4.3.3 Informal learning

While the identification of formal and non-formal activities is relatively easy, informal learning is more difficult to pinpoint. Informal learning is qualitatively different from non-formal and formal learning (Tuijnman and Boström, 2002). In order to be able to study informal learning it is necessary to imply certain delimitations. Following the recommendations from the European Task Force for the measurement of lifelong learning, the model here considers only informal intentional learning (EUROSTAT, 2001, European Commission, 2005b). Thus, socialization activities, such as the ones defended in the SECI model, are not considered within informal learning but rather as part of the enabling environment.

Accordingly, informal learning activities refer to self-directed activities that the employee engages in. They do not necessarily have to be directed to learning or improving job-skills. In fact, they can be directed towards learning virtually anything. It is debatable, therefore, to what extend they produce human capital, since it is not clear how useful this knowledge might be for the company. However, it is assumed that informal learning activities somehow enrich a person's mental model. It is important to explore how this informal learning relates to formalized demand for training and how is it related to a person's position within the enabling environment.

Table 4.4 summarizes the different aspects within the learning arenas that are explored in the present dissertation.

Table 4.4: Summary of the aspects of the learning arenas

Formal and non-formal training activities
Training events and time
• Number of training events per company
• Number of hours of training per company
• Number of hours of training per employee
• Number of courses demanded per employee
Participation
• Number of participants per course
• Number of employees in a course as a percentage of the total number of employees
Training costs
• Direct costs
• Indirect costs
• Other costs
Purpose of the training
• Professional vs. Support training
• Subject area of the training events
Informal learning activities
• Frequency of reading manuals
• Frequency of going on guided tours
• Frequency of using media-assisted products to learn
• Frequency of asking colleagues for help
• Frequency of watching, getting help or advice from others
• Frequency of learning by watching or trial and error
• Frequency of learning using the Internet

4.4 The use of knowledge

The products and services that knowledge-intensive companies offer, more specifically consultancy and educational services, are indeed knowledge products. The central element in the service provided to the client is the professional's knowledge (Carmel, 2005). The knowledge held by employees and the constant updating of this knowledge is crucial to being able to provide state-of-the art service.

The knowledge-enabling environment is supposed to create a working place for knowledge creation. This creation of knowledge has the objective of creating better and more innovative products that will provide a sustainable competitive advantage for the company. Knowledge management is meant to direct the employee's competencies to improve the services which can be delivered to clients. In other words, the knowledge that employees gain through training or through working in a knowledge-enabling environment has to be used. Said another way, the knowledge has to be put into practice. The ultimate purpose of knowledge management is that the knowledge that the company has (within its human capital, or in its structural capital) be used to create profits for the company (see e.g. Demarest, 1997). The objective is, therefore, the exploitation of knowledge.

Although not a crucial part of this model, which explores knowledge management but not its results, the relationship between the enabling environment and product innovation as well as other business performance measures are also important. Innovation is defined by the European Commission (2004, p. 11) as: "new or significantly improved products (goods or services) introduced to the market. It also covers - as process innovation - new and significantly improved production technology, and methods of supplying services and of delivering products."

The topic of innovation is a complex one especially with respect to the two sectors, education and consultancy, selected for this study. In both these sectors, innovations are frequent since each service provided (giving a class or providing some consultancy) involves creativity and thus, likely requires ongoing innovation. In this study innovation has been delimited to "product only innovation" (European Commission, 2004). In consultancy, a new product refers to a service that was not being provided previously. Similarly, in education it denotes new courses or activities that did not formerly exist.

In addition, a knowledge-enabling environment is meant to increase not only the innovation and profitability of a company, but also the overall collaborative climate within a company. Sveiby and Simon (2002, p. 421) define collaborative climate as a specific aspect of the organization's culture. For them, it refers to the "values, beliefs and assumptions that influence the behaviors and the willingness to share knowledge". They developed a tool, the Collaborative Climate Index, that this dissertation uses as an indicator of effectiveness of the knowledge enabling environment.

Table 4.5 summarizes the different aspects explored within the use of knowledge in the knowledge intensive companies under study.

Table 4.5: Summary of the aspects of the use of knowledge

Collaborative Climate Index (CCI)
Innovation
•   Having a new product or service in the last year
•   Number of new products as a percentage of all products
•   Number of new customers
Profit
•   Monetary profit as a percentage of the total turnover

This chapter has presented the theoretical model that will be used in the present dissertation to explore the management of knowledge in the selected companies. The next chapter presents the context within which companies under study operate. Chapter 5 explains the program the companies participated in and from which they have received financial aid for training and development. In addition it provides an overview of the Swedish position in specific indicators on research and development, innovation and training. This provides an indication on the Swedish efforts in developing knowledge intensiveness in companies.

PART III CONTEXT AND BACKGROUND

CHAPTER 5: THE EUROPEAN SOCIAL FUND AND THE SWEDISH POSITION IN RESEARCH AND DEVELOPMEN, INNOVATION AND TRAINING

5.1 Introduction

This dissertation features 18 case studies of companies which are a self-selected sample of a very particular kind. In addition to belonging to knowledge-intensive sectors and having knowledge as a main product, they all participated in a special program financed by the European Social Fund (ESF). This indicates that these companies are eager to promote employees' learning and competence development. These measures have specific objectives and procedures that shape the nature of the data described later in Chapters 7 and 8. Thus in order to fully understand where the data comes from and how and why it was generated it is important to understand the ESF in general, these measures in particular and the context of the ESF in Sweden.

This chapter presents a brief historical review of the European Structural Funds and more specifically one of these funds: the ESF. After this review, the chapter focuses on the Swedish approach to the ESF and the different measures undertaken during the programming period 1999-2006.

5.2 The European Social Fund

5.2.1 The European Social Fund within the context of the European Structural Funds

The Structural Funds of the European Union are the "main financial instrument used to reduce the gap in living standards between regions and between people and to promote economic and social cohesion across Europe" (see European Commission, 2000a). There are four structural funds: The European Regional Development Fund (ERDF); the European Social Fund (ESF); the Financial Instrument for Fisheries Guidance (FIFG); and, the European Agricultural Guidance and Guarantee Fund (EAGGF). Each of these has different objectives and provides money to particular European regions.

The ESF is the oldest of the Structural Funds. It was set up by the Treaty of Rome in 1957 (Article 123) to improve job opportunities in the Community. For more than 40 years it has invested, in partnership with Member States, in programs to develop people's skills and their potential for work (European Commission, 1998). It has undergone major changes through the years to adapt to the changing demands of the European Union.

In the first phase, 1957 to 1971, "the objective was to assist workers moving from one region to another in search of work and those needing to acquire new skills in sectors undergoing modernization or conversion of production methods" (European Commission, 1998). The fund reimbursed public authorities in the Member States with half the cost of vocational training and resettlement allowances and grants to workers suffering a temporary drop in wages during restructuring operations in their enterprises. Specifically excluded for reimbursement was training for the public sector and the self-employed. The fund's rationale was "redistributive" in that countries such as Italy that contributed less to the fund were meant to be its main beneficiaries. From 1960 to 1971, the ESF provided grants for the retraining of almost a million workers and the resettlement of 700,000. Italy was the main beneficiary at the beginning of this period. However, from 1967 onwards, Germany, the most prosperous Member State at that time, became the main beneficiary. This was clearly contrary to the idea of redistribution.

With this in mind and structural unemployment increasing across Europe (European Commission, 1998) the Fund was reformed in 1971. In its first two years the new fund exceeded the total budget of the previous 12 years. Instead of the retroactive funding system used in the first phase, Members States now had to submit an application prior to the beginning of operations. In this period there were two types of interventions included in the text of Article 4 and Article 5. Article 4 was directed toward improving the balance between supply of and demand for labor within the community. Article 5 sought to provide support for actions aimed at promoting employment in less developed regions as carried out within the framework of national policies. The activities supported included training and re-settlement as well as allowances for training of instructors and trainees. During this period ESF aid was opened to the private sector. It also provided support for pilot activities to promote innovative training.

In 1977 the Fund expanded the beneficiaries of Article 4 to include: migrant workers and their families (Council of the European Union, 1977a); women over 25 who were unemployed and wanted to work (Council of the European Union, 1977b); and, unemployed young people under 25 (Council of the European Union, 1977c). In addition, following the establishment of the European Regional Development Fund (ERDF) in 1975, increasing attention was given to specific regions with major unemployment or industrial re-structuring problems. In 1978 the ESF was empowered to provide additional help to create employment through financing young job-seekers under 25 in jobs which were likely to provide them with experience to obtain permanent positions(Council of the European Union, 1978).

In 1983 the ESF was judged to be too rigid to cope with the constantly changing needs of the Community (European Commission, 1998). As a result of this revision, ESF actions were mainly directed toward combating youth unemployment and matching graduate level qualifications with labor market demand. In addition, this reform accentuated the regional focus of the ESF by allocating 40 percent of the budget to the most disadvantaged regions. These regions were determined based on unemployment statistics and GDP. Many of these regions coincided with regions eligible for the ERDF. Another interesting change was the inclusion of grants for training and modernization of small and medium enterprises (SMEs). However, this new ESF system was difficult to manage. For one thing, the sheer number of applications from Member States was too large for Brussels to handle effectively. This raised concerns with the project promoters and eventually led to the development of a new approach to the Structural Funds in 1988.

The adoption of the Single European Act, which entered into force on 1 July 1987 (European Commission, 1987), had a strong impact on the reform of the Structural Funds and specifically on the ESF (European Commission, 1998). The Single European Act worked towards the completion of a single European market and incorporated a new commitment to economic and social cohesion. Article 130a obliged the community to ensure the reduction of disparities between regions and to improve the position of the least-develop regions. The Structural Funds were given a major role toward this end. Article 130d called for the different Structural Funds to coordinate their activities, work together, and improve their efficiency. This new approach was built on four basic principals: concentration, partnership, programming, and "additionality".

Concentration referred to the "targeting of regional aid on specific development objectives" (Bradley, 2000, p. 9). Five objectives were set out for the period 1989 – 1993 (see Table 5.1). The different funds were meant to work together in a coordinative manner. In addition, concentration referred to the focus of resources on the least developed regions. *Partnership* and *programming* dealt with fund implementation. A Community Support

Framework (CSFs) was developed for each Member State in partnership between the national, regional and local authorities and together with the Commission. These CSF's set out the priorities and the allocation for each of the funds for the entire programming period 1989-1993. Member States were also to submit an Operational Program (OP) that provided more detail on how and where the funds were to be spent, monitored and evaluated. Finally, the "*additionality*" principal required that the funds were not to replace but rather to complement national funds.

Between 1989 and 1993 about 85 percent of the budget was allocated to activities under the CSFs. The remaining 15 percent was used to finance Community initiatives and innovative actions and studies related to new approaches in vocational training and employment policies. Here Community initiatives referred mainly to transnational projects that included a European Community dimension.

In 1993 the white paper on Growth, Competitiveness and Employment (European Commission, 1993) proposed solutions to combat rising unemployment through increasing the competitiveness of the European Union. The white paper identified four inter-dependent targets (European Commission, 1998):

> (1) Adapt working time and incidence of taxation to encourage job creation and labor market flexibility;
> (2) Improve the employment situation in the least-developed regions and for socially disadvantaged groups; tackle youth and long-term unemployment and social exclusion; and promote equal opportunities. Employment services to become more productive;
> (3) Increase the stock of human capital through life-long learning and upgrading of skills; including basic training for new technologies; and,
> (4) Develop new, labor intensive opportunities in environment, health and care sectors and boost employment in the audio-visual sector, arts, culture and tourism. Emphasize SMEs.

The white paper called for development of new economic activities in viable sectors. It expressed concern about youth and adult long-term unemployment. It included additional considerations on the importance of equal treatment between men and women and participation of groups at risk of social exclusion. It acknowledged the importance of preventive measures such as providing incentives in anticipation of changes in the types industrial job skills needed. All these had significant implications for the Structural Funds. The tasks of the Structural Funds were redefined (Council of the European Union, 1993a) as to how they should coordinate with the European Investment Bank (EIB). Council regulation No. 2082/93 (Council of the European Union, 1993b) contained further provisions which affected all Structural Funds. Finally, the Council regulation No. 2084/93 also contained regulations for the ESF (Council of the European Union, 1993c).

As illustrated in Table 5.1 the fund objectives for this period changed. A new Objective 3 combined the previous Objective 3 and 4. A new Objective 4 was created with no regional limitations on the provision of training and guidance for workers facing changes in industrial or production systems. A new Objective 6 was created on January 1995 to deal with problems associated with the new Member States, Sweden and Finland, since areas with extremely low population density posed problems not previously covered. However, concentration, programming, partnership and additionally remained as guiding principles. The regional eligibility criteria for the Objectives 2 and 5(b) were widened and relaxed. In order to reduce programming procedures, an option was provided to replace the previous CSF with a Single Programming Document (SPD). The partnership requirement now included economic and social partners. This is especially important for the ESF under Objectives 3 and 4 where a bottom-up approach is necessary and where many of the problems related to social exclusion and industrial change are outside the public sector (European Commission, 1998).

The ESF-Committee played a major role during this period. It was set-up by the Treaty of Rome and included representatives from governments, trade-unions, and employers. Its mission was to advise the Commission on proposals relating to the ESF and provide a forum for discussion on implementation of ESF. The additionality requirement was reinforced by making Member States maintain the public expenditures at level at least comparable to the previous programming period. In addition, Members States were required to implement measures to advertise and attract potential beneficiaries of the Structural Funds.

In the period 1994-1999 the budgets for the various structural funds were almost doubled from the previous period (European Commission, 1998). In addition, a new Structural Fund was instituted to assist in restructuring the fisheries sector, the Financial Instrument of Fisheries Guidance (FIFG).

In March 1999 the European Council reached political agreement in Berlin on the "Agenda 2000" financial package for the period 2000 –2006 and drafted regulations for the Structural Social funds (European Commission, 1999a, p 3). For the six year period, new general and specific regulations were adopted, and the number of priority objectives was reduced from six to three (see Table 5.1):

- Objective 1: promoting the development and structural adjustment of regions whose development is lagging behind.
- Objective 2: supporting the economic and social conversion of areas facing structural difficulties.
- Objective 3: supporting the adaptation and modernization of education, training and employment policies and systems.

Objective 3 brings together the previous Objective 3 (combating long-term unemployment and integration of young people and of those excluded from the labor market) and Objective 4 (facilitating adaptation of workers to industrial changes and changes in production systems). This new Objective 3 "constitutes a reference framework for the development of human resources throughout the Member States, notwithstanding regional specificities" (European Commission, 1999a, p. 5).

For this current period, Member States are recommended to do their programming through SPD, especially when dealing with Objective 2 and 3. Within these SPDs there is no requirement for detail on the type of measures to be funded, which differs from the previous period. In addition, the new regulations stipulate that after adoption of the SPDs or the OPs the Member States, or the responsible regions, have to create new, complementary programming documents for each programme, which primarily indicate the beneficiaries and the financial allocations for the measures proposed.

The partnership principle remains both at the planning and creation phase of the SPDs as well as at the monitoring phase. Member States are required to designate a single managing authority responsible for supervising the implementation, on going management and effectiveness of the program. This authority is in charge of drawing up and submitting annual and final program reports to the Commission as well as organizing mid-term evaluations. The Commission reviews the yearly reports and can transmit comments or suggestions for improving program implementation. Monitoring committees are given an expanded role and their agreement must be obtained for supplements or adjustments to the program.

Community Initiatives are narrowed down to four: (1) INTERREG: Transnational, cross-border and inter-regional and designed to stimulate the balanced and harmonious spatial planning of the European territory; (2) URBAN: Economic and social conversion of towns, cities and urban areas in crisis in order to promote sustainable urban development; (3) LEADER: Rural development initiatives developed by local action groups; and, (4) EQUAL: Transnational cooperation designed to promote new means of fighting all types of discrimination and inequality in the labor market.

During the period 1993-1999, monitoring "additionality" was a complex process. In order to simplify this process, the geographical level of verification was simplified and verification was restricted to three parts in time: following the adoption of the CSF or the SPD; mid-way but before 31st December 2003; and, towards the end of the period but before 31st December 2005.

Table 5.1: Evolution of the Objectives of the Structural Funds (1989 - 2006).

	Period 1989-1993			Period 1993-1999			Period 2000-2006		
	Objective	Funds involved	% of budget	Objectives	Funds involved	% of budget	Objectives	Funds involved	% of budget
	1. Development of least prosperous regions	ESF, ERDF, EAGGF	54.8	1. Development of least prosperous regions	ESF, ERDF, EAGGF, FIFG	47.6	1. Promoting the development and structural adjustment of regions whose development is lagging behind.	ERDF, ESF, EAGGF, FIFG	67.7
	2. Regions hit by industrial decline	ESF, ERDF	7.1	2. Regions hit by industrial decline	ESF, ERDF	7.8	2. Supporting the economic and social conversion of areas facing structural difficulties.	ERDG, ESF	11.5
	3. Combating long-term unemployment	ESF	32.3	3. Combating long-term unemployment and integration of young people and of those excluded from the labor market	ESF	27.4	3. Supporting the adaptation and modernization of education, training and employment policies and systems.	ESF	12.3
	4. Employment pathways for young people	ESF		4. Facilitating adaptation of the workforce to changes in production	ESF	4.9			
	5. (a) Adaptation of agricultural structures	EAGGF	1.5	5. (a) Speeding up the restructuring of agriculture and fisheries	EAGGF, FIFG	2			
	5. (b) Development of rural areas	ESF, ERDF, EAGGF		5. (b) Furthering development of rural areas	ESF, ERDF, EAGGF		Integrated in Objective 2		
				6. Assisting development of sparsely populated areas	ESF, ERDF, EAGGF, FIFG	0.4	Integrated in Objective 1		
	Community Initiatives					9			

In this current period Objective 3 is financed entirely by the European Social Fund (ESF). In this way, the ESF constitutes the main financial tool through which the European Union implements its European Employment Strategy (Council of the European Union, 1999). This strategy has four key areas (European Commission, 2002c):

(1) Employability: helping both employed and unemployed and workers develop appropriate skills;
(2) Entrepreneurship: making it easier to start and run a business and to hire employees;
(3) Adaptability: modernizing skills and ways of working in a rapidly changing world; and,
(4) Equal Opportunities: equal access to jobs for men and women, and assistance in balancing work and family life.

Sweden places major emphasis on adaptability. Since this study is based in Sweden, it is also important to present the Swedish approach to implementation of the fund. Of particular interest for this dissertation is Objective 3 of the European Structural Funds: "supporting the adaptation and modernization of education, training and employment policies and systems".

5.2.2 The Swedish Objective 3 and SPD

In Sweden, the ESF serves as a complement to the Swedish government economic policy aimed at promoting growth and increased employment (Swedish Ministry of Finance and Ministry of Industry, Employment and Communications, 1999, 2004). The ESF cumulative grant is about equal to three percent of the resources allocated to the national labor market policy. However, the measures associated with the ESF are development-oriented and in many cases experimental which "can be regarded as a considerable contribution to the implementation of the employment strategy" (Swedish Ministry of Finance and Ministry of Industry, Employment and Communications, 1999, p. 29).

The Swedish Objective 3 is built on: (1) continuous development of the conditions in working life; (2) lifelong learning for individuals; (3) a "close to down to earth kind" of definition of the concept learning/skills development; (4) flexibility in the educational system; (5) innovative addition to the development of national policy; (6) decentralized implementation with regional/local perspective; and, (7) active partnership (Swedish ESF Council, 2000).

The Swedish plan places more emphasis than any other Member State on skills development of employees in enterprises. This is reflected in the proportion of funds allocated to this activity which constitutes about half of the total (European Commission, 2005c). The total budget for the whole six-year period is 747 billion Euros. The plan facilitates the participation of small SMEs (less than 50 employees). Work organization and the competencies of the labor force are also a focus (Swedish ESF Council, 2001).

The Swedish SPD defines five priorities for the programming period. Priority 1 is centered on competence development for employees. Since it is the main focus of the study presented in this dissertation, it will be treated in detail below. Priority 2 deals with increasing employability and entrepreneurship. It is directed towards employed and unemployed people in job-rotation (Measure 2.1) and to people totally outside of the labor market (Measure 2.2). Priority 3, entitled "integration, multiplicity and equal opportunity" has two measures. Measure 3.1 is directed toward integrating foreign born-persons into the labor market and helping people with disabilities participate in the labor market. Measure 3.2 is directed toward increasing women's employment rate and possibilities for women to start their own businesses. While interest in gender is integrated into the other priorities it is also given special emphasis through its own measure. Priority 4 deals with local development and is directed toward supporting well justified local projects that are too small to be treated under other priorities. Finally, priority 5 encompasses all technical assistance activities.

Going back to Priority 1, "Competence development for the employees", this is "the main trust" of the program. It was allocated 38.7 percent of the budget for the whole period, 42 percent during the first three years and 36 percent during the rest of the period. It consists of two measures:

> Measure 1.1 "support for the analysis of the competence development and support for the competence development"; and,
> Measure 1.2 "general stimulus for skill development" (Swedish ESF Council, 2001).

Priority 1 follows the successful two-step model from the former Objective 4. Measure 1.1 is a prerequisite for participation in Measure 1.2; that is to say, companies are required to prepare a competence analysis plan as part of improving work organization (Verksamhets- och kompetensanalys), thereby formulating related skills development needs (kompetensutveckling) (Measure 1.1). This in turn is a prerequisite for participating in the general stimulus measure (Measure 1.2). General stimulus consists of the actual training of employees, co-financed by the ESF (European Commission, 2002d). The companies provide one third of the costs associated with the employee training. One third is provided by the ESF and the last third is provided by national public authorities.

In the six year programming period (2000 – 2006), Measure 1 has had more than one million participants (Ramboll management, 2005) and 55 percent of these have been women. Of the 37000 organizations that have participated in the measure, 88% of then had less than 50 employees.

According to the final evaluation which included data up to June 2005 (Ramboll Management, 2005), Measure 1.1 had more than 500000 participants in more than 18000 projects. Private companies represented around 70 percent of this total. The average cost per project was around 68000 SEK, which equals about 3000 SEK per participant. Measure 1.2 had a little more than 400000 participants of which 55 percent were women. Forty one percent of the projects were granted to companies with less than 10 employees, and 47 percent to companies with 10 to 49 employees. Almost all, 96 percent, of the companies participating in this measure were private.

Objective 3 and specifically its Measure 1 can be regarded as having a positive impact on the participating company in relation to creating awareness as to the importance of competence and skills development (Ramboll management, 2005). Of the companies participating, 61 percent maintain that the project resulted in a sustainable plan for competence development. It is also interesting to note that Measure 1 can be regarded as the initial step in the identification of a company's intangible assets. Through the analysis of their business activities companies have had to evaluate what defines them as business and in what direction they want to evolve.

This indicates that the 18 companies under study, all of which participated in Objective 3 activities, are of a particular breed. They are especially interested in their employee's skills and knowledge. They are proactive in looking for funding to provide competence development and they completed a major review of their business activities before the study was conducted. To a certain degree, thus, it is likely that these companies are more interested in learning and knowledge development than their Swedish counterparts. The next section in this chapter looks more closely at Sweden and indicates how this country can be regarded as a leader in the promotion of innovation and skill development in companies.

5.3 Swedish position in research and development, innovation and training

5.3.1 Swedish position in research and development, and innovation

This section presents secondary data that may be seen as supporting the concept that Sweden provides a positive environment for knowledge management. First it looks as Sweden in relation to other countries in terms of research and development (R&D), and innovation. Then it presents some comparative analyses related to education and training provided by companies.

The indicators in R&D discussed below, attempt to measure country efforts in promoting the creation of knowledge. In addition, other indicators of factors influencing innovation such as Internet use or investment in telecommunication technologies are presented. The intention here is to address to what extent companies and governments in different countries support innovation. The indicators can be roughly divided into input and output indicators (European Commission, 2004). Input indicators are, for example, expenditure in R&D, Internet use and personnel working in R&D. Output indicators refer mainly to patent production and innovation resulting in the creation of new products. The data presented here come from the European Statistical Office (EUROSTAT). Some of the data is obtained directly from the Internet (http://epp.eurostat.cec.eu.int/), while some has been adapted from various European Commission publications (European Commission, 2002b, 2003, 2004). Figures for the years 2002 or 2003 are presented. This focus is justified because the companies under study provided 2002 data. Thus, the figures provide an overview of the Swedish operating environment during the time the Swedish companies were under study.

Andriessen and Stam (2004) use some of the indicators presented in this chapter as a way of measuring the intellectual capital of a nation. Using 38 indicators they develop an Intellectual Capital Monitor. They divide the intellectual capital measurements into human capital, structural capital and relational capital (see Chapter 3 for an overview of the concepts). Each of these three classes of intellectual capital has "three different perspectives in order to stress the differences between the past, present and future" (Andriessen and Stam, 2004, p. 11). These perspectives are referred to as (1) assets (present), (2) investment (future), and (3) effects (past). In line with the conclusion of this chapter, Andriessen and Stam's (2004) analysis places Sweden, Denmark and Finland among the countries in Europe with the highest level of intellectual capital assets and investment. According to their report, Sweden is second only to Denmark in terms of the level of Intellectual Capital investment and is the highest of all the 15 EU countries (countries in the EU prior to May 1, 2004) in intellectual capital assets. Thus Sweden can be seems particularly keen on investment in structural capital.

Figure 5.1 shows expenditure in R&D as a percentage of the GDP in EU countries, the US and Japan. Sweden is the country that invests the most in R&D measures, spending four percent or over two percent higher than the mean of the 15 European Union countries. The

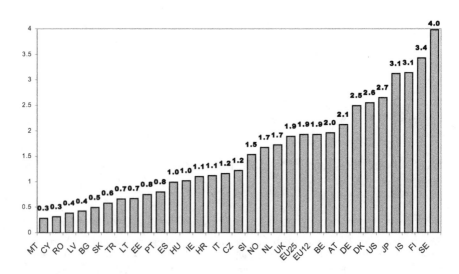

Figure 5.1: R&D expenditure as a percentage of GDP, 2002. Source: EUROSTAT

countries nearest in expenditure in R&D such as Finland, Iceland and Japan and the US, spend from two and a half to three and a half percent. In Sweden almost 72 percent of the financial resources for R&D come from industry, while government accounts for 21 percent of the total R&D expenditure (see Figure 5.2).

In Sweden the R&D expenditure in the business enterprise sector (BES) as a percentage of the GDP is three point three percent, indicating that Swedish companies invest

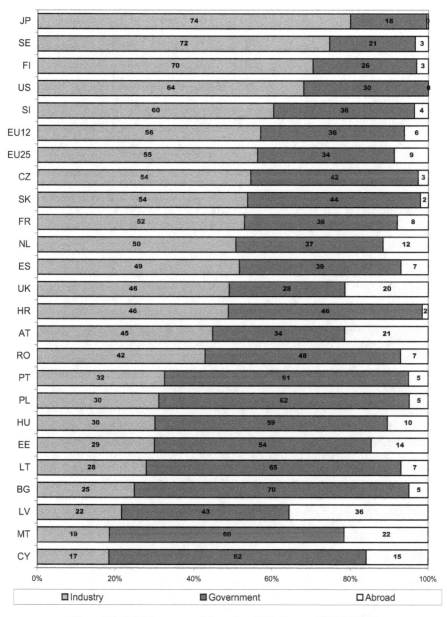

Figure 5.2: R&D by source of financing, 2002. Source: EUROSTAT

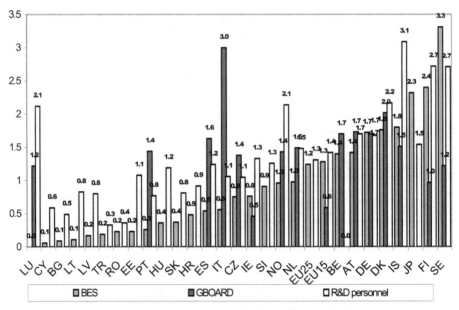

Figure 5.3: R&D investment in the Business Enterprise Sector (BES), Government budget appropriations or outlays on R&D (GBOARD), percentage of labor force in R&D (R&D personnel) 2002. Source: European Commission, 2004.

comparatively more in research than their counterparts in, for example, Finland, the United States or Japan (see Figure 5.3). However, the Swedish Government allocates comparatively less resources of its budget to R&D. Figure 5.3 also shows the government budget appropriations or outlays on R&D (GBAORD). It refers to the money allocated to R&D in central or federal government budgets. Sweden allocates little more than one point two percent of its total expenditures, lower than many European countries such as Iceland, France or Spain. In terms of R&D personnel, Sweden is among the countries with highest proportion of its labor force involved in R&D activities with two point seven percent (see Figure 5.3).

Other indicators usually assumed to be inputs for R&D are related to the use of information and telecommunication technologies. They point to the effort of enterprises to use these technologies, which are considered among the main sources of innovation in our time (European Commission, 2001d). Figure 5.4 shows the percent of enterprises with more than nine employees having access to the Internet. Sweden is among the three countries having the highest access, right behind Finland and Denmark. Virtually all Swedish companies have access to the Internet. In addition, Figure 5.5 shows that Sweden is first in Europe with regard to expenditures on IT as a percentage of GDP. This figure refers to annual data on expenditures for IT hardware, equipment, software and other services as a percentage of GDP.

The figures 5.1 to 5.5 show all the main input indicators for R&D and Sweden ranks the highest or among the highest in all of them. This shows that Swedish companies seem to invest in and promote R&D more than their European counterparts. Figure 5.6 and 5.7 presents output indicators of R&D. Figure 5.6 shows the number of patent applications received at the European Patent Office (EPO), per million inhabitants and patents per million inhabitants granted by the United States Patent and Trademark office (USPTO). Sweden has the highest number of applications per million inhabitants to the EPO. In the case of USPTO, Sweden is the European Community country granted the most patents, behind the United Sta-

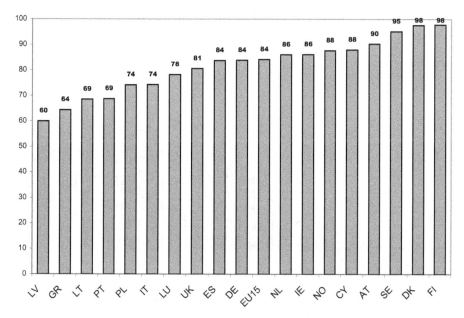

Figure 5.4: Percentage of enterprises having access to the Internet, 2003. Source: EUROSTAT.

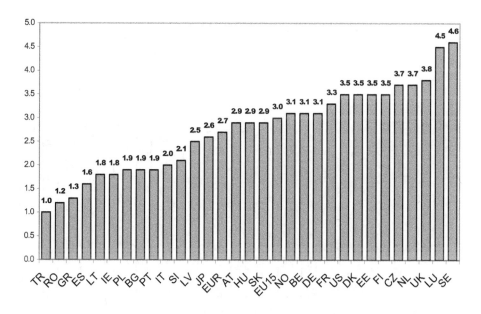

Figure 5.5: Expenditure in telecommunication technologies as a percentage of GDP, 2002. Source: EUROSTAT.

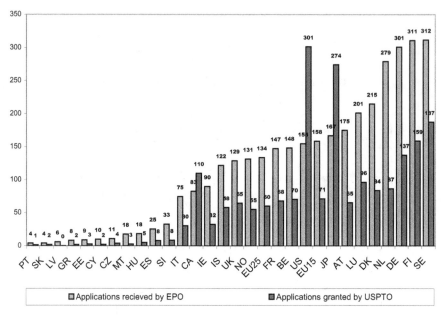

Figure 5.6: Applications received by the European Patent Office (EPO) and patent granted by the United States Patent and Trademark office (USPTO), 2001. Source: EUROSTAT.

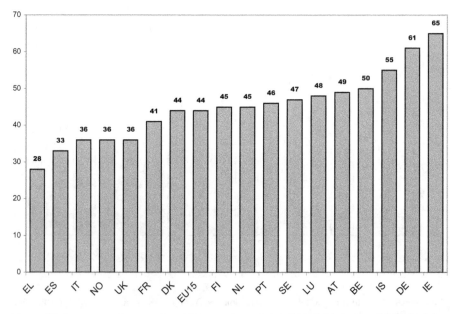

Figure 5.7: Percentage of companies with innovation activity, 1998- 2000. Source: EUROSTAT.

tes, Japan and Switzerland. Therefore, one can conclude that Sweden not only invests in R&D but is also an innovator.

In addition to patents it is possible to inquire into innovations produced by companies. The European Union's Community Innovation Survey (CIS3) contains data on various aspects of innovation between 1998 and 2000. The EU states that "(a)n innovation covers new or significantly improved products (goods or services) introduced to the market. It also covers - as process innovation - new and significantly improved production technology, and methods of supplying services and of delivering products." (European Union, 2004, p.11). Figure 5.7 shows the percentage of innovative companies, that is to say, companies that have released a new product in the last two years. Sweden comes in at 47 percent and in seventh place among the 15 European countries that participated in the survey. From this information, it seems Swedish companies are more successful in producing patents than new products.

The information presented above provides a context for the study presented in this dissertation. What is clear is that Swedish companies are in an environment where knowledge creation (if we consider innovation and R&D indicators of this) is both promoted and relatively successful.

5.3.2 Swedish training and education

Another very important aspect of the study is the training that companies provide. The European Community released data on training within companies in the Second Continuing Vocational Training Survey (CVTS2). Sweden did not participate in the first CVTS so the data presented here is from the last CVTS, containing figures from 1999. If indicators on R&D locate companies within the context of promotion of innovation, indicators on training activities place companies within the context of skills and knowledge promotion. Figures5.8 to 5.11 present various aspects of training activities and are compiled from data taken from CVTS2.

"Training enterprises" are defined as companies that provide continuing vocational training as opposed to those that do not. EUROSTATS defines continual vocational training as:

> ... training measures and activities, which the enterprises finance, partly or wholly, for their employees who have a working contract. Continuing vocational training measures and activities include continuing vocational training courses (CVT courses) and other forms of continuing vocational training... The primary objective must be the acquisition of new competencies or the development and improvement of existing competencies (European Commission, 2002b, p. 8).

Continuing vocational training courses consist of internal and external courses depending upon whether they are designed and managed, or not, by the organization. Other forms of continuing vocational training include planned periods of training, instruction or practical experience, job rotation, quality/learning circles, self-learning and instruction at conferences or workshops. The data excludes initial vocational training and, therefore, it does not include employees in internships or apprentice positions.

Figure 5.8 shows the percentage of companies from all the companies that provide some sort of continuing vocational training (CVT courses and other forms), and what here will be called training enterprises. Sweden has the second highest percentage in Europe in terms of training enterprises, with 91 percent of its companies providing training. Only Denmark enjoys a higher percentage, with 96 percent of its companies acting as training enterprises. The EU-15 average is 62 percent. Figure 5.8 also shows the percentage of companies that provide CVT courses. Sweden, again, is in second place following Denmark, with 83 percent of its companies providing courses. The percentage of companies providing other types of training is also illustrated in Figure 5.8. In this case, Sweden ranks third after Denmark and the United Kingdom. From this data it appears that Swedish companies supply a comparatively high level of training opportunities for their employees, both through courses and other less traditional forms.

Figure 5.9 indicates that 98 percent of employees in Sweden are employed by training enterprises, with only Denmark having a higher slightly percentage in the region. Figures 5.8 and 5.9 refer to the supply side of lifelong learning in enterprises. In other words, they give information on the providers of training opportunities (in this case the companies). Clearly, Sweden has a large supply of training opportunities within the business sector.

As for the demand side of lifelong learning in companies, Figure 5.10 shows that the percentage of employees who participate in CVT courses in Sweden is the highest in Europe, with 61 percent of all employees engaged in training. In addition, Sweden is also the country with the highest percentage of employees participating in courses in companies that provide CVT courses.

Training time per participant in Sweden, however, is lower than in many other European countries, as is shown in Figure 5.11. Employees participating in CVT courses engage in training courses an average of 31 hours per course, the same amount as the 15-member EU average. Sweden ranks eleventh position of all countries in the sample in terms of training time per participant.

Thus, with regards to training supply and demand, Sweden appears to occupy a leading position within the EU, exceeded in some cases only by Denmark. On the other hand, according to the evidence presented above, Swedish companies provide shorter training time per participant than many of their European counterparts.

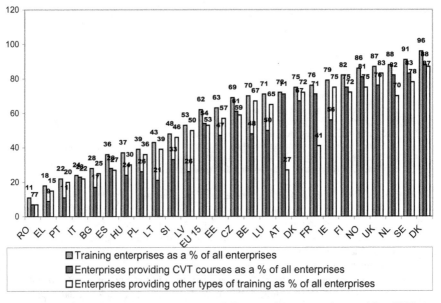

Figure 5.8: Training companies as a percentage of all enterprises, companies providing CVT as a percentage of all companies and, companies providing other type of training as a percentage of all enterprises, 1999. Source: European Commission, 2002b.

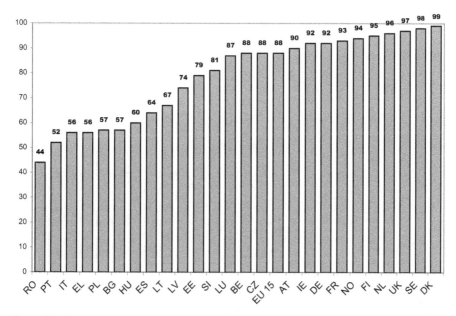

Figure 5.9: Employees in training enterprises as a percentage of all employees, 1999. Source: European Commission, 2002b.

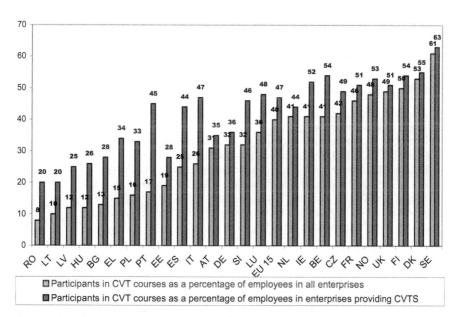

☐ Participants in CVT courses as a percentage of employees in all enterprises
■ Participants in CVT courses as a percentage of employees in enterprises providing CVTS

Figure 5.10: Participants in CVTs as a percentage of all employees and participants in CVTs as a percentage of employees in companies providing CVTs, 1999. Source: European Commission, 2002b.

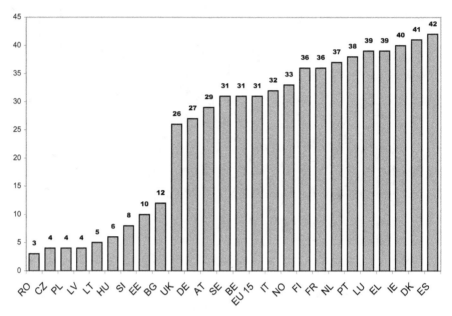

Figure 5.11: Training time per participant in CVTs (in hours), 1999. Source: European Commission, 2002b.

5.4 Knowledge intensive businesses services, the case of education and consultancy

5.4.1 Understanding knowledge intensive business

The indicators on training discussed above deal with Sweden at the national level, and the data refer to the entire spectrum of business activities in industry and services. This section looks into the specific business activities that the study is focused on, namely, consultancy and education. These two business activities will be referred as sectors.

The study is interested in looking into the management of knowledge in SMEs in the so-called Knowledge Intensive Business Services (KIBS). Studying innovation in services, Butler *et al.* (2000, p. 8; see also Bilderbeek *et al.*, 1998; Miles 2000) defined Knowledge Intensive Business Services as those which:

(1) rely heavily upon professional knowledge;
(2) supply products, which are themselves primarily sources of information and knowledge to their users;
(3) or use their knowledge to produce services which are intermediate inputs to their clients' own knowledge generating and information processing activities; and,
(4) have other business as their main clients.

OECD (2001b) has tried to define knowledge intensiveness through the study of investment in knowledge. OECD (2001b, p. 3) defines and calculates investment in knowledge as "the sum of expenditure on R&D, on total higher education from both public and private sources and software" with some transformation of the data to avoid overlaps of the components. OECD (2001b) acknowledges that a more complete picture would also include data on expenditures on the design of new goods, on job-related training and other components such as costs related to organizational change.

With the data available, OECD (see e.g. OECD, 2001b) divided manufacturing industries and services according to "technology and knowledge intensity". Services are classified according to their knowledge intensity. The measures are based on previous analyses of users of embodied technology (based on input-output tables), R&D intensities for the service sector and a preliminary evaluation of the composition of workforce skills by activity. There is not a clear gradient of knowledge intensity and only few sectors are selected as knowledge-intensive. Following, ISIC Rev. 3 (which is equivalent in this case to NACE Rev.1) OECD (2001b, p. 12) identifies these sectors as knowledge intensive:

Division 64:	Post and Telecommunications;
Divisions 65-67:	Finance and insurance;
Divisions 71-74:	Business activities (not including real estate); and,
Divisions 80 and 85:	Education and Health which are also seen as knowledge intensive sectors but are considered "not-market" services.

The European Union follows a similar classification of knowledge intensiveness, but they include some more additional services in their classification, namely: Division 62 "air transport" and Division 63 "supporting and auxiliary transport activities; activities of travel agencies" (see EUROSTAT, 1996; European Commission, 2001c). The European Commission (2001c, p. 58) agrees with OECD that further development has to be done in defining knowledge intensity:

> Using highly aggregated 2 digit level of the NACE (or ISIC) classification does not allow a fine distinction between those services that may be highly knowledge intensive and those which are not. Further improvements in the classification of these services will be necessary.

Thus, this study has chosen to use a 3-digit classification of these sectors, see Table 5.2. The study features companies from the Division 74: "other business activities" and from the Division 80: "Education". Within Division 74 only specific sectors that are called "consultancy" were considered. Consultancy companies refer to companies that have as their main activity the provision of counseling to their clients. They sell professional knowledge; they provide a service to the client through the knowledge of their professional workers, such as legal, accounting or management advice, etc. Thus for consultancy, sectors (under the classification NACE rev. 1) 741, 742, 743, 744 and 745 are included in this study.

Table 5.2: Companies activities selected for the study

Sectors selected (NACE Rev.1 codes, 3 digits)	
CONSULTANCY	
741	Legal activities
742	Architectural and engineering activities and related technical consultancy
743	Technical testing and analysis
744	Advertising
745	Labor recruitment and provision of personnel
EDUCATION	
801	Primary education
802	Secondary education
804	Adult and other education

In education the sectors used here (under the classification NACE rev. 1) are 801, 802 and 804. However the Education division (80) includes:

> ...public as well as private education at any level or for any profession, oral or written as well as by radio and television. It includes both education by the different institutions in the regular school system at its different levels as well as adult education, literacy programmes, etc... This division also includes other education such as driving schools, but excludes education primarily concerned with recreation such as bridge or golf (EUROSTAT, 1996c, p. 158).

In order for educational and consultancy services to be more comparable, only privately owned education companies are included in this study. This means, there are no public institutions in the sample.

Despite the difficulties in defining knowledge intensiveness, it seems possible to say that the two selected sectors both have employees with a relatively high degree of educational attainment and have as their main activity providing the client with certain specific knowledge. Understood in this way education and consultancy can be considered as knowledge intensive services. Being representative of knowledge intensive services these sectors are assumed to provide interesting material for research on competence development since they place high demands on their employees for continuous learning.

Consultancy services provide clients with knowledge and advice on specific areas of expertise. The work of these companies is based on professionals with specific expertise (accounting, legal, management, marketing expertise). They provide other businesses with support in such areas. In this context, they constitute an important resource for other business activities. Consultancy companies, therefore, continually need to adapt to client and market needs. Competence development and updating of employee's knowledge is essential in order to be able to provide quality services.

Educational companies (they will be called companies throughout this dissertation), provide students with knowledge at different levels. Thus, if students are considered clients, educational companies provide their clients with certain specific expertise, just as a consultancy company usually does. The role of the consultant and of the teacher is not as different as it might appear. In the last few years there has been an increasing debate on the role of the teacher in education. Teachers are seen as a key element in providing quality education (Council of the European Union, 2004, European Commission, 2005a). The "professionalization" of teachers including the necessity of constantly upgrading their knowledge is recognized as an strategy for further improving the quality of education (Council of the European Union, 2004, European Commission, 2005a). Comparing both sectors, it is possible to study similarities and differences between these two types of professionals in upgrading of their skills and knowledge.

5.4.2 Consultancy and Education in Europe and Sweden

This section provides specific information about the two sectors under study. The information is extracted from the annual Labor Force Survey from EUROSTAT, for 2002 and from the Statistical Office in Sweden (www.scb.se). Figures 5.12 through 5.15 show statistics on Division 74 and Division 80 of the NACE rev. 1: "other business activities" and "education" respectively. It is important to mention, that Division 74 includes some other sectors that are not part of the study and that cannot be considered consultancy, such as "investigation and security activities" or "industrial cleaning". Unfortunately, it was not possible to obtain data at the three digit level. For practical reasons, the Division 74 will be called "consultancy" despite the fact that it includes certain activities that would not otherwise belong to consultancy. Given these variations, the figures can only give a general overview of the status of the sectors under study, providing an approximation of their general characteristics.

Figure 5.12 shows the employees in each of the sectors as a percentage of the total employed population by country in the year 2002. Education provides more employment than consultancy in almost all countries, with the exception of Sweden and the Netherlands. In the case of Sweden the difference between the sectors is only three tenths of a percent. Sweden has the second highest proportion of consultancy employment in Europe.

One of the characteristics of knowledge intensive services is that their labor force is composed of more educated employees than in other services. Figure 5.13 shows the educational attainment by business activity, comparing the average proportion of all European Employment Area (EEA) countries and Sweden. Educational attainment is coded according to three levels. "Low" refers to at most lower secondary education (ISCED 0 to 2). "Medium" refers to upper secondary education (ISCED 3 to 4). "High" refers to tertiary education (ISCED 5 and 6). As expected, the two sectors under study have more qualified employees than the remaining sectors. Sweden has slightly more high-educated people (ISEDC 5 and 6) in education than the average EEA countries, but in consultancy the proportion is not as high as the average in EEA countries. In fact, Sweden, with 31 percent, has the second lowest proportion of employees with high educational attainment in the consultancy sector in the EEA countries. This proportion is far below countries such as Spain (74 percent), Iceland (60 percent) or Malta (67 percent) (see Villalba, 2004, p. 41). It is important to remember, however, that within the generic Division 74 there are other sectors such as "industrial cleaning" or "investigation and security activities" that might lower the rate, but this is equal for all the countries in Europe.

Figure 5.14 shows, by sector, the proportion of employees that report having attended training in the four weeks prior to responding to the survey with Sweden being compared to the average of all the EEA countries. Sweden has, in general, a higher proportion of employees attending training courses, as CVTS2 has already shown. In Sweden, consultancy companies have fewer people participating in training than the remaining sectors, while the opposite holds true for education. In relation to the rest of the European countries, Sweden has higher rates in the two sectors under study, particularly in education, where it is four percent higher than the European average.

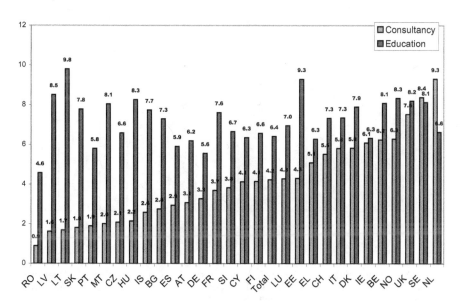

Figure 5.12: Employees in consultancy and education as a percentage of the labor force, 2002.
Source: LFS, 2002.

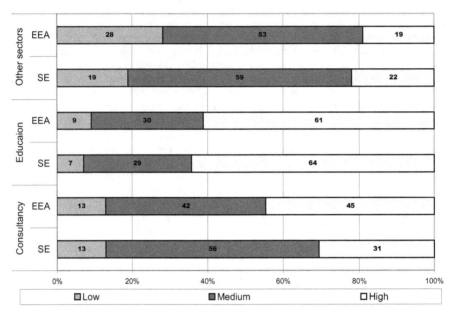

Figure 5.13: Employee's educational attainment in consultancy, education in Sweden and European Employment Area, 2002. Source: LFS.

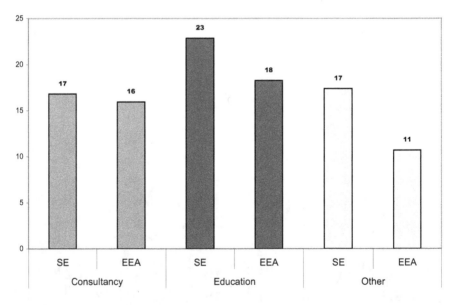

Figure 5.14: Employees that attended training in the last 4 weeks as a percentage of all employees in consultancy, education and other sectors in Sweden and in the European Employment Area, 2002. Source: LFS.

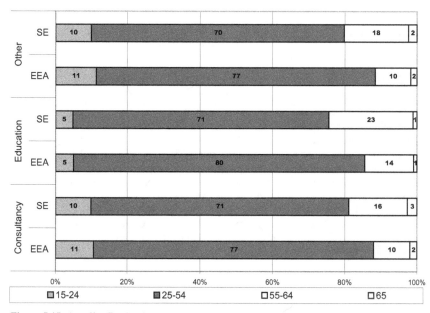

Figure 5.15: Age distribution in consultancy, education and other sectors in Sweden, and the European Employment Area, 2002. Source: LFS.

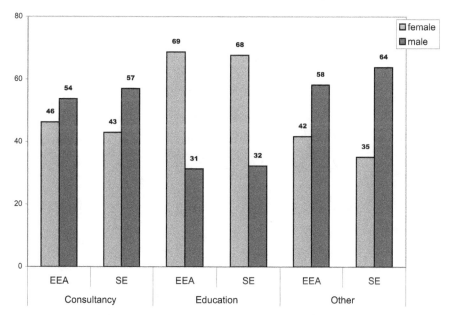

Figure 5.16: Gender distribution in consultancy, education and other sectors in Sweden, and the European Employment Area, 2002. Source: LFS.

Figure 5.15 shows the percentage of employees in Sweden and the EEA average by age cohort. According to the figure, educational companies generally employ more people over 54 than in consultancy or other sectors. The percentages of older employees are higher in Sweden than the EEA average in all sectors.

Figure 5.16 shows the proportion of male and female employees by sector in Sweden and the average for the EEA in 2002. In Sweden, educational services employ more than 65 percent women, while in consultancy more than 55 percent are male employees. In relation to the EEA, Sweden has a similar proportion of men and women in education but is slightly less male-oriented in consultancy than the EEA.

This chapter has presented specific indicators on R&D, innovation and training in Sweden in comparison to other countries. It has also compared Sweden with other European countries in terms of some basic indicators in the consultancy and education sectors, thus providing an overview of how these services are structured. Clearly, Sweden can be regarded as a leading country in the promotion of R&D and training in the business sector. That is, the companies under study function in an environment that seems more positive than other European countries towards the development of intellectual capital in organizations. The next chapter looks at the methodology and research procedures used to investigate the knowledge management approaches of these companies.

CHAPTER 6: METHODOLOGY AND RESEARCH PROCEDURE

6.1 Methodology

6.1.1 Hypothetical deductive rationale

This chapter presents the methodological rationale behind the study as well as the procedure used for data collection and analysis. Louis (1982, p. 9) points out that in order to understand the methodology of any study it is important to "examine the nature of the design and practice at three points in the study: during data collection, during database formulation and during actual data analysis". This chapter first discusses the theory of the methods used and then presents the procedure using the three points in the study.

The study is empirical in nature. As Blumer (1969, p.21) points out: "an empirical science presupposes the existence of an empirical world". The existence of an empirical world does not necessarily imply that there is a unique "Truth" (with capital T), but a variety of truths from different points of view (Phillips and Burbules, 2000). However, this study rejects the post-modern idea that all knowledge is equally valuable in science. A scientific work is meant to follow certain standards and procedures to maximize the reliability of the findings. As Kuhn (1970) indicates, these procedures might have to comply with the rules stated by the scientific community and specifically the predominant paradigm in the area of expertise. This study follows a hypothetical deductive rationale (see e.g. Popper, 1976). This means the creation of a hypothetical model that is later tested in empirical reality. This study does not, rigorously speaking, test the theoretical model, but carries out an exploration of empirical reality guided by the model. A rigorous testing of the model would imply a quasi-experimental methodology which was not possible to undertake. The study is mainly explorative and strives to understand rather than predict the management of knowledge in small knowledge intensive services.

To this end, this particular work will use what can be defined as a multi-site case study (see e.g. Stenhouse, 1982) or, as Stake (2000, p. 437) refers to it, a "collective case study". More specifically following Yin's (1993) typology of case studies, this research uses multiple and descriptive case studies. Descriptive case studies refer to studies that "present a complete description of a phenomenon within its context" (Yin, 1993, p. 5). "Multiple" refers to the several units of analysis that comprises the study. Case study, rather than as a specific method or technique, is usually seen as an "approach" to research which includes different ways of studying "a case" (Stark and Torrance, 2004). For Stake (2000) case study is not even a methodological choice "but a choice of what is to be studied, [...] the case". Methodologists, thus, seem to agree that case study methodology involves an in-depth study of a specific reality that seeks to understand the specific case and its conditions.

The unit of analysis (or the case) in this dissertation is the management of knowledge in organizations, specifically knowledge-intensive organizations. There are 18 cases in this specific study. The study tries to gain as much information as possible from each of the cases creating a "picture" of each company that can tell us something about how knowledge is managed in knowledge-intensive SMEs. The 18 companies are illustrative, not representative, of knowledge intensive SMEs in Sweden. The rich amount of varied information provides interesting insights as to how knowledge intensive SMEs manage their knowledge. Through the study of different regular business processes such as communication, investment in information technologies and training it is possible to obtain insights into the knowledge management activity of the firm.

An anthropologist would probably not classify this research as a case study, since it does not follow the traditional ethnography approach with extensive fieldwork on the case (Chapman, 2001). Thus, in order to get a "rich description" (Geertz, 1973) of each case, the study draws from different sources: documents, interviews and questionnaires. It does this at two different levels in each organization: individual and organizational. This allows for data triangulation in order to seek further validity of the findings. This 'picture' for each case is based on the theoretical framework that was presented in Chapter 4. This model is hypothetical since it is a proposal that is made in order to try to understand the case.

It is important to note that the study of organizations, especially private ones, have inherent problems such as accessibility and data reliability (Bryman, 1988; Lorens *et al.* 2004, p. 4). In this specific case, a certain degree of access was granted because the companies were receiving funding from the ESF-Council in Sweden. The companies however are self-selected (they were not obligated to participate in the study) and on many occasions it was difficult to arrange some meetings or gain access to certain documents. This caused difficulties and thus in some cases the data becomes fragmented. While the number of companies that decided to participate in the study was smaller than expected, this was not atypical for this type of study. However, this did result in a change in some of the original strategies for the analysis since it was not possible to create a statistical linear model with such a small number of cases. Also important to note is that this study can only provide a picture of a company at a specific moment in time. Data triangulation was used to ameliorate these problems.

6.1.2 Data and methodological triangulation

Introduction

This study uses what Denzin (1978) calls data triangulation and methodological triangulation, which is a combination of data and methodologies to study the same phenomena (Frankfort-Nachmias and Nachmias, 1996, p. 206). Data and methodological triangulation in this study is used to present a richer picture of each company. In order to use data triangulation it is necessary to have different types of data. In this dissertation the methods used to collect information are primary and secondary (see Bulmer, 2004, p. xiii). The data obtained is both quantitative and qualitative. Quantitative data implies that the empirical object of study can be measured in a certain scale, and the unit of analysis can be ordered according to its score in that specific scale. Qualitative data, on the other hand, refers to qualities of the studied entity.

As in the case of data, methods also can be separated into quantitative or qualitative. There is a continuing controversy among social scientists as to the degree of scientific validity of each method. Neuman (2000) points out four similarities between the two methods. First, they both involve inferences. Second, they both involve a public method; researchers systematically record data, making what they have done accessible to others. Third, both use comparison as a central process of the data analysis. Finally, they both try to avoid errors, false conclusions and misleading inferences. However, he also points out four differences: qualitative methods are less standardized; qualitative analysis usually starts early in the process of the research, while the data is still being collected; qualitative analysis may illustrate the theory but does not usually test hypothesis with empirical facts; and, they have different levels of abstractions with, qualitative analysis being less abstract since it is closer to raw data. For Neuman (2000, p. 419): "In qualitative analysis the researcher's goal is to organize a large quantity of specific details into a coherent picture, model, or set of interlocked concepts". The goal of this research is also to organize a large quantity of specific details into a coherent picture. While the study can be considered more quantitative oriented than qualitative, it does use some qualitative data and qualitative data analysis procedures. In general terms, the analysis tries to determine to what extent companies are knowledge oriented.

The data was collected using three different methods: document analysis, semi-structured interviews and questionnaires. Data triangulation provides a richer picture of the reality under study since information on the same entity come from different sources. This strengthens the findings and is especially useful when looking at organizations where there are many intervening factors.

Document analysis

The definition of what constitutes a document differs. Some authors consider written materials as well as verbal communication as documents (e.g. Fontana and Frey, 2000). In this study, only written materials are considered as documents. The materials used here were written in the name of the individual corporations under study. Two types of documents were analyzed: (1) documents that companies provided (copies of what was submitted to the ESF as the result of the activity analysis) and (2) company web pages if available.

Document analysis is part of non-reactive research measures (Neuman, 2000). Neuman (2000, p. 293) calls document analysis "content analysis". For him, content analysis "lets a researcher reveal the content (i.e. messages, meanings, symbols, etc.) in a source of communication (book, article, movie, etc.)." Atkinson and Coffey (1997, p. 61) have pointed out that documents are not accurate portrayals reality, but rather, documents construct their own kind of reality. For them, therefore, it is more important to study the form and the function of the texts than their content. In the present study, however, the form is comparatively irrelevant and the function is clear since the documents are written to apply for training aid. It is therefore more interesting to conduct content analysis rather than any other type of document analysis while still keeping in mind the very specific function of the documents.

Content analysis can be carried out quantitatively or qualitatively. Quantitative document analysis counts the frequency of certain expressions, its direction, its intensity and the size of the text (Neuman, 2000, p. 294). Qualitative document analysis, used in this study, looks for the underlying constructs that give meaning to a document. Neuman (2000) postulates four steps for content analysis: (1) question formulation to determine the objectives of the analysis; (2) decision as to the unit of analysis (the amount of text that is assigned a code); (3) sampling of the text; and, (4) constructing variables and coding categories. He also contends that the content analysis must be replicable. In order to be able to replicate the analysis, it is important to have a clear coding system: a set of instructions or rules as to how to systematically observe and record text content (see Annex I). The coding system operationalizes the constructs that the theory has identified. Neuman maintains it is important to start with open or basic coding in order to check different themes. Open coding then has to be narrowed down to more specific codes later on. This thesis uses a latent coding system that Neuman (2000, p. 296) defines as a coding procedure that: "looks for the underlying, implicit meaning in the content of the text".

Semi-structured interviews

Silverman (1993) believes we live in an "interview society" because of the extensive use of interviews for obtaining information. An interview can be defined as "active interaction between two (or more) people leading to negotiated, contextually based results" (Fontana and Frei, 2000, p. 646). Although interviews provide important and interesting data, as Nisbet and Watt (1980, p. 13) have pointed out, interviews only reveal how people perceive what happened and not what actually happened.

Cohen and Manion (1994, p. 273) talk about four types of interviews: structured, unstructured, non-directive and focused. In a structured interview "the contents and procedures are organized in advance". Unstructured interviews are conducted in an open situation and there is more freedom for respondents' answers. Non-directive and focused interviews refer to interviews that look for more subjective insight. Alternatively, Patton

(1990) uses interview instrumentation to define four interview types: informal; interview guide approach; standardized open-ended and close-ended; and, fixed field response interview.

Fontana and Frey (2000, p. 653) refer to the structure feature of the interviews as a "question format". For them structured interviewing aims at:

> ...capturing precise data of a codable nature in order to explain behavior within pre-established categories, whereas the [unstructured interview] attempts to understand complex behavior of members of society without imposing any apriori categorization that might limit the field of inquiry.

In an earlier work, Frey and Fontana (1991, p. 184) identify four dimensions in their classification of interviews: (1) setting, from formal to informal (or spontaneous); (2) role of the interviewer, from directive to non-directive; (3) question format, from structured to unstructured; and, (4) purpose, exploratory or phenomelogical. Creswell (1998, p. 124) adds another dimension to interview classification: how it is conducted. He refers to telephone interviews, focus group interviews or one-on-one interviews.

The present study conducted formal, semi-structured, one-on-one interviews. This type of interview was adequate to collect rich contextual information in the relatively short period of time available. The content and sequence of the interview was relatively fixed. The questions vary in format, from open-ended to close-ended. The latter asked for very specific information such as number of employees. In the open-ended questions, following Lazarsfeld (1944) method, a check list with possible answers was used in order to allow for faster codification.

Questionnaires

The third method used for data collection was questionnaires. Bulmer (2004, p. xiv) defines a questionnaire as "any structured research instrument which is used to collect social research data in a face to face interview, self-completion survey, telephone interview or web survey". As such, Bulmer does not make a major distinction between questionnaires and interviews. In this study questionnaires refer to a self-completion instrument with a set of predefined questions to gather data from the respondents, in this case company employees. In the case of the interviews, the questions are directed to one specific person and have a less pre-defined format.

The design of the questionnaire was inspired by several different instruments used in other studies (see Section 6.2.4). Bulmer (2004), building on Khan and Cannel (1957), makes the analogy between the design of a questionnaire and public speaking. The questionnaire, like a public speaker, has to "pitch the message ...in such a way that the majority of the audience can understand it and respond to it" (Bulmer, 2004, p. xvii). To this end, a variety of formats for questioning are available. A questionnaire, like an interview, can feature close-ended questions, which provide only few options to the respondent, or open-ended questions, which allows the respondent to speak freely about the question. Converse (1984) reviews the 1940's controversy about open-ended verse close-ended formats for survey questionnaires. Those in favor of an open-ended format, such as the group directed by Rensis Likert in Chicago, argued that the close-ended format was artificial, incomplete and tended towards rigidity. For them, close-ended questions could not grasp the richness of the social reality. On the other side, advocates of close-ended questioning argued that the open-ended format was impractical, too complex and too expensive, and usually less reliable. Converse (1984) offers Lazarsfeld's (1944) article as a sort of solution to the problem. Lazarsfeld (1944) proposed that it was possible to have open-ended questions with a previously defined checklist that would reduce the cost and increase the reliability of a survey.

Another widely used questionnaire format is the so-called Likert-scale. It basically consists of providing a statement and asking the respondent to what degree, in a scale from 1 to 5 or 7, s/he agrees or disagrees with the statement. A Likert-scale represents nominal data. The respondent selects one of the numbers as s/he identifies her/himself in the category of "never", "always", etc. However, Likert-scales also have certain ordinal characteristics. To some degree, it is possible to rank the answers using the categories. However it is difficult to assume that the distance between the points in a Likert-scale are equidistant. And further, it is not clear that a "never" for one respondent is the same as that for another. Despite these problems, Likert-scales are widely used in social science and, in many instances, are interpreted as interval type variables. In this research, equidistance between the categories in a Likert scale will be assumed.

The questionnaire used in this research uses the variety of the formats described above depending upon the type of information. Through the use of different formats, it is possible to collect a more robust data set. For example, although an important part of the questionnaire uses Likert-scales, each section ended with a space for additional comments. These spaces, however, were not very commonly used.

6.1.3 Statistical methods

The three data collection methods provide different types of information that have to be analyzed accordingly. In this way, the study features a multi-method approach for the analysis. Different statistical procedures are used in order to reduce the data and explore the sampled companies. Statistics are mainly used for illustrative purposes although certain inferential statistical methods are also used. Descriptive univariate statistics, such as measures of central tendency or measures of variance, are used to present the sampled companies. Bivariate statistics such as Pearson correlations are used in order to relate the different constructs identified in the theoretical framework. Inferential statistical methods are only used in an illustrative way, since the sample size does not usually allow for inferential analysis. When possible, however, certain inferential statistics were used.

Frequencies and cross-tabulation tables were used in order to explore the sample. Most of the tables are presented in Annex III and IV, since inclusion in the main text of the dissertation would have made it too dense and difficult to read. Only the main conclusions drawn from the analysis of such tables are presented in the body of the text.

Arithmetical averages are used to summarize both company parameters and sample parameters. The arithmetical average provides the "equilibrium point" of all the observations (Hays, 1988). The arithmetical average provides a parameter that unifies and reduces information from different cases for each variable. However, it is important to note that with the arithmetical averages it is not possible to detect extreme values. In this way, it is important to look into measures of variance. These are used to provide insight into how different the cases are within a specific group. This became very important since there are big differences among cases in this study. Thus the standard deviation is very high for certain parameters. The small number of cases also made the standard deviation relatively high. Ranges were used to illustrate how, for a specific variable, the highest score differs from the lowest.

The median split method

Another measure of central tendency is the median which is also used in this study. With the median it is possible to divide the sample in two subgroups, observations above and observations under the median. This can be interpreted as "high achievers" and "low achievers" with regard to a specific variable in relation to the other companies studied. This method will be referred as the median split method. This method of splitting the sample provides a division of the cases based on the data collected and not on external criteria. Also interesting to note is that through this method, the study divides the sample in two groups that will normally have the same number of cases each. Further, through the median split method, it is possible to relate all the different variables that have different measurement scales, and thus the outsiders disappear. Despite "losing" certain information, this makes it possible to use correlation measures in order to explore a wide variety of aspects of the organization which would have been difficult to interpret with different scales for each variable. The information "lost" is presented in the tables and, to certain degree, in the unvaried statistics.

The division of the companies in two groups for each variable referring to a specific characteristic can be interpreted as "companies that have" and "companies that do not have" that specific characteristic. In other words, each variable can be converted into a binary variable. This permits use of entropy analysis. Entropy analysis is a statistical technique that is based on conditional probability. The entropy analysis technique is similar to factor analysis but it is not based on the variability of the sample, but on the conditional probability that in having one aspect of the company another aspect is also given or assumed (see Frank, 2000). In a sequence of ones and zeros, the entropy analysis determines to what extend having one characteristic is associated with having another.

The main exploratory tool used in the study is the Pearson correlation. Measures of association indicate "in quantitative terms the extent to which a change in the value of one variable is related to a change in the value of another variable (Argyrous, 1997, p. 313). In this thesis, Pearson correlations are used to quantify the association between the different indicators recoded with the median split method. Ordinal type variables usually can be associated with Spearman correlation measures. For this case, however, both Pearson and Spearman coefficients are equal since there are only two levels in each of the variables.

In any associative measure it is important to look at the direction of the association. That is to say, the association can be negative or positive. Secondly, it is important to look at the strength of the association. In this study, associations from 0 to 0.3 are referred to as weak; associations between 0.4 and 0.6 are referred to as medium and associations between 0.7 and 1 are referred to as strong. Inferential statistics are not used in most of the cases, since they will not provide useful information due to the small sample size. In any case, in the study of the sample, these measures of association provide interesting insights into the relationships between the different constructs and indicators.

Analyses of variance (ANOVA) were conducted when possible to find if the differences between averages in the two services, consultancy and education, were statistically significant.

6.2 Research procedure

6.2.1 Sampling procedure

Each stage of the sampling procedure is based on a different rationale. From a pool of more than twenty thousand companies only 3376 could be considered as belonging to SMEs in education and consultancy services. Both sectors were selected because they are assumed to provide interesting material for research on competence development, since they both represent knowledge intensive services and place high demands on their employees for continuous learning (see Chapter 5). Smaller SMEs, what the European Union calls micro-companies, are particularly useful for the present study due to the fact that these organizations face the most serious challenges in providing training opportunities (see Chapter 3). In order to allow for the study of communication patterns and exchange of information, companies having less than 10 employees were excluded from the sample. In addition, only companies with less than 100 employees were included. Thus the sample was further reduced in size. Interestingly, none of the companies featured in the final sample have more than 70 employees.

Private companies were selected for two reasons: they have more market pressure to remain competitive and the sample can be homogenized in terms of environmental market characteristics thus reducing the number of intervening variables. The above criteria reduced the sample size to 512 companies. Finally, only the 119 companies that were already participating in Measure 1.2 of Priority 1 in Objective 3 of the ESF (see Chapter 5 for explanation) were chosen for the study since they had also planned for and were in the process of providing training for their employees. In order to gain the cooperation of these companies, two letters were sent to each company: one signed by the ESF-Council in Sweden and the other from the Institute of International Education which was conducting the study. Up to three reminders were sent via email and telephone contact between September and November 2002.

Fifty-two responses were received, constituting a 44 percent positive response rate from the 119 companies. In consultancy services the positive response rate was 43 percent while in education it was 46 percent. The 52 companies that agreed to participate in the study were then contacted for interviews with the person responsible for the ESF program or, if that was not possible, with somebody that had a good overview of the company. A total of 33 interviews were conducted. Since the study seeks to explore the knowledge-intensive environment it was important to have as much information as possible from each company. Finally, 18 of these 33 were selected because they provided richer amounts of information in terms of documents, interviews and completed employee questionnaires. Therefore this constitutes a self-selected convenient sample that meets certain predefined criteria. The sample cannot be considered representative of Swedish companies, but it is believed to be illustrative of how knowledge-intensive SMEs manage their knowledge.

6.2.2 Codification of documents and other written material

The documents analyzed are copies of documents the companies sent to the ESF-Council in order to gain monetary aid for employees training. As part of the Measure 1.1 (see Chapter 5), companies carried out an analysis of their business environment and an assessment of their competency needs. The documents collected totaled 302 pages, with an average length of 17 pages per company. The documents received differed in length from 6 page to 52 pages. They also varied greatly in terms of structure and content, making the analysis all the more complicated. The documents were translated into English, coded and analyzed using qualitative content analysis. Different strategies were followed depending on the type of information the document provided. Based on the framework presented in Chapter 4 a coding system was created. The coding system included the ability to identify both the source and the company thus allowing for later data triangulation.

For major parts of the documents an open coding strategy (basic coding) was used to bring major themes to the surface. The analysis was mainly semantic, not taking into account the exact words but rather the meaning of the text. This decision was based on the fact that the documents were translations of Swedish text. The different themes identified created the structure for a database where information from documents, web pages and interviews could be combined. The different units of text associated with each theme were later translated into variables. These variables were created together with the information from interviews. Different categories emerged from the data related to each variable. In addition, in some cases, specific information such as income level or employee age was inferred from the documents. Also information on company training activities was organized and codified from the documents. In these cases the information was recorded directly into different variables.

6.2.3 Visiting companies

With the insights gained through the document analysis, a script for a semi-structured interview was prepared. An interview guide was sent to the company prior to visiting it (see Annex II). The interview was divided into three major areas of interest: (1) the knowledge-enabling environment; (2) training activities; and, (3) knowledge products and innovation. Interviews attempted to ascertain more specific information about issues previously identified from the documents and from the theoretical framework on the company profile, not on the ESF program. Interviews collected both quantitative as well as qualitative information. All interviews were recorded and codified and later introduced into the database, thus combining the interview data with the documentary data. In this way, data triangulation was possible.

Visits to the companies were conducted between March and June 2003. One-on-one semi-structured interviews were conducted with the company's contact person in charge of the ESF program (Objective 3). In most cases, the contact person for the ESF program was the CEO or equivalent, but a number of interviews were held with someone in charge of Human Resources or a secretary. All the interviews, except for one, were conducted on company premises.

In many cases, together with the interview, it was possible to have a guided tour of the company site, thus seeing how the space and work were organized. Observations during these visits were not exhaustive or systematic, so no major conclusions can be taken from them. However, they provided rich qualitative information for a better understanding of the data collected from the documents and interviews.

6.2.4 Questionnaire analysis

Finally, questionnaires were created from various sources that touch upon aspects of the theoretical framework. The questionnaire has eight sections with several items in each section (see Annex I):

- Section A: personal information on the respondent;
- Section B: aspects of the knowledge-enabling environment in order to evaluate the learning climate ;
- Section C: information related to the immediate supervisor;
- Section D: informal learning activities;
- Section E: seminars and other group activities;
- Section F: aspects of information handling; and,
- Section G: the meeting habits of each employee, both formally and informally.

Sections B and C were taken from a questionnaire used with permission of Sveiby and Simon (2002) about collaborative climate in companies. Section D was inspired by the preliminary questionnaire for the Adult Literacy and Life Skills Survey (see Desjardins *et al.* 2005). Sections A and E were based on the first international Adult Literacy Survey questionnaire. Section F and G were originally created for this study, since no major pres-tested tools to measure these aspects could be found. The use of different sources to design the questionnaire allowed for the creation of a tool that did not need major revision and, with certain constraints, provided information that could be compared with other data.

Some questionnaires were given to the companies prior to the study visit while others were handed to the contact person responsible for Objective 3 during the visit. The contact person was asked to collect at least 10 questionnaires per company. In some cases only one questionnaire was received, while other companies supplied a questionnaire from virtually every employee. A total of 166 questionnaires were collected, codified and introduced into a master database. On average about 43 percent of the employees from each company answered the questionnaire. Due to the fact that most of the material from the questionnaires represents only a small fraction of the employees of each company, this data should be treated with caution. For instance, it is very possible that the employees who responded were people who had better relations with the person that gave them the questionnaire.

6.2.5 Data triangulation

Data combination

The three sources of information (documents, interviews and questionnaires) provide data referring to the same realities as well as aspects covered only in a single source. In order to organize the data four major databases were created. Each database had an identifier for each company and thus it was possible to combine different information from different datasets, allowing for data triangulation.

The first dataset was created mainly with information taken from the document analysis and the semi-structured interviews. The unit of analysis in this dataset is the company. This dataset is also the main source of information for the analysis, where summary information from the other datasets is retrieved and analyzed further. The major themes identified from the theoretical framework were used to develop an analytical tool for the data collected in the interviews as well as in the documents. Once all the data from the companies were reviewed, each theme was structured into different latent codes. These codes were later translated into variables that were further categorized if necessary.

The second dataset, mainly created from the document analysis, deals with the training activities planned by each company. The unit of analysis here is the training event. Summary information for each company can be obtained and introduced into the first dataset for further analysis. This second dataset posed significant challenges for the analysis since the identification of training needs differs substantially from company to company. First, they differ in time horizon: some companies plan their training for three years, while others plan for only one year. Second, some companies provide analysis centered on the individual, while others focus on the training events. Third, some companies provide a rich amount of information on cost, time and training participation, while others provide very little information. Finally, there is a significant amount of ambiguity in the data since some plans were not definitive.

The third dataset is derived from the codification of the questionnaires. The unit of analysis here is the individual. Many of the questionnaire items use continuous variables that can be obtained from company statistics. This information can be introduced and further analyzed in the first dataset. Likert-scale type variables can also be aggregated at the company level assuming that the distance between the points is equal and that each respondent perceives them in a similar way. This allows for the creation of a company level measure that can be related to other variables in other datasets.

The final dataset also refers to the individuals. The information is taken from the document analysis and provides information on salary level. The information can be aggregated and developed into company-level indicators on salary levels.

Analysis procedure

The combination of the four datasets strives to present a clear picture of each of the companies. It was possible to collect many different parameters and knowledge related aspects for each company. But it is not less true that the complexity and variety of sources can add error and ambiguity to the dataset. First an exploration of the different aspects of the knowledge management of the sample was carried out through the analysis of different contingency tables (see Annex III). Many companies could not provide all the necessary information which created gaps in values for some variables thus resulting in a very fragmented picture for some characteristics. The major problem, however, was the large number of variables describing the knowledge-intensive companies understudy.

The main (first) dataset had a total of more than 180 variables for the 18 companies under study. It was necessary, therefore, to reduce the data to a manageable and understandable set of variables. In order to do so, 43 relevant variables were selected as indicators for eight theoretically identified constructs in the knowledge-intensive company: (1) Size of the company, (2) workforce's stability, (3) workforce's experience, (4) professional orientation of the company, (5) tacit orientation of the recruitment process, (6) monetary reward system, (7) communication intensiveness and (8) investment in information technologies (IT).

In a similar way, seven indicators were used to grasp the knowledge creation effort and the demand for training of the companies: (1) training estimated time per employee each year; (2) average number of training events that each employee demands; (3) total training estimated cost per employee; (4) actual total training expenditure per employee; (5) actual expenditure as a proportion of the total estimated training cost; (6) total training cost per hour of training; and, (7) the company's average of the informal learning activities items.

These 50 indicators were recoded into binary variables using the median split method that determined low or high level of the attribute. This data reduction had the advantage of simplifying the sample into high achievers and low achievers for the different indicators selected. In other words, it divided the sample into companies that "*have*" certain characteristics (indicators) and companies that "*do not have*" them. It also "destroyed" the outliers, and in this way avoided problems in associative measures. The indicators were correlated using the Pearson correlation. The bivariate Pearson correlation presents an idea of how different indicators measuring the same construct of the company (such as size, communication activities, etc.) are related to each other.

A joint scale was created for each construct using the arithmetical average of all the different binary indicators of that specific construct. If an indicator had missing values, a scale without that indicator was created for that specific construct. Then, the arithmetical average of all the possible scales in that construct was calculated. In this way, the final scale for each construct had virtually no missing values. In addition, this procedure ameliorates any biases created for companies with no missing values. As a general rule, indicators with more than four cases of missing values were not included in the composition of the scales. These scales were then used in order to relate the different constructs.

Creating the scales, as described above, has the advantage of summarizing a-priori theoretically related variables and creating a comparable scale. However, it is important to note that each scale implies that all the indicators have a similar weight. This means that the different indicators that measure a construct are treated equally. For example, if we have a construct with three indicators, there are 2^3 possible profiles (000, 001, 010, 100, 110 011, 101, 111), while the scale will have only 4 possible values. In the scale the profiles 001, 010 and 100 have a similar score (Score= $1/3 = 0.33$). This means that companies with similar scores in a scale might actually have a slightly different knowledge-enabling environment. To some degree the study is assuming that all the components of the knowledge-enabling environment are equally important.

Another characteristic of the constructs' scales is that they have only a few specific possible scores. The scores in each scale depend on the number of indicators used to calculate the scale; the higher number of indicators a construct is composed of, the higher the number of possible scores the scale can represent. For example, in a construct with three indicators, the scale will have four possible values. If the construct has two indicators, the scale will have only three possible values. Despite this problem, it is possible to study these construct-scales through the median split method. This provides a clear view of the extent to which each company is above or below the median in each of the constructs. These scales, recoded using the median split method, were related to indicators on effectiveness, innovation as well as training.

Finally, in order to relate all the different constructs an entropy analysis was conducted. This provided a better definition of the relationship between the different constructs within the knowledge-enabling environment.

The next two chapters look specifically at the knowledge enabling environment and training for the companies in the study using the data and methods described above. These analyses are followed by a final chapter which presents the overall summary and conclusion.

PART IV RESULTS

CHAPTER 7: EXPLORATORY ANALYSIS OF THE KNOWLEDGE-ENABLING ENVIRONMENT

7.1 Introduction

This chapter presents findings from the document analysis, interviews and questionnaires in order to provide a description and an exploration of the selected companies and their working arrangements. A total of 18 companies were studied 12 in consultancy and 6 in education. The business activity most represented (as classified in NACE rev. 1) is "advertising", with four companies. Three companies are dedicated to each of the three activities: "architectural and engineering activities and related technical consultancy", "adult education" and "financial and law consultancy". Two companies are dedicated to provide "primary education" and "secondary education". "Technical testing and analysis" and "labor recruitment" are represented by one company each (see Table 7.1).

Small companies are the main focus of this study; however, some companies that are categorized as small enterprises by the ESF database really belong to larger enterprises. Larger companies are defined by the European Commission (2002c) as conglomerates when the total number of employees is more than 500. Although the companies under study that belong to these corporations are technically independent entities (they have independent budgets, independent recruitment and selection processes, independence in the organization of their work, etc.), it is obvious that certain limitations associated with small companies do not affect them as much as the companies that do not belong to a larger corporation. Table 7.1 shows that only three of the companies participating in the study are independent SMEs that belong to a larger parent corporation. All three cases are in the consultancy field. Thus the majority of companies in the study are not associated with larger parent firms. Also interesting is that eight companies have other locations within Sweden: six in consultancy and two in educational services. Of these eight companies, only "Company 2" has offices outside of Sweden. Therefore, the vast majority of companies operate solely within Sweden.

The companies under study have an average monetary turnover of around 21.3 million SEK: 21.7 million SEK in consultancy and 20.7 million SEK in education. The range goes from Company 58 which reported a turnover of almost 50 million SEK to Company 26 which reported less than 6 million SEK.

A general description of the companies can be found in the Annex III. The brief description of each company shows the different types of company activities and interests. These differences pose major challenges for the analysis since it is often difficult to come up with suitable comparisons and groupings for the various companies. As the next section summarizes, this variety is translated into heterogeneity of the companies' characteristics in each of the variables considered.

7.2 Descriptive analysis of the knowledge enabling environment

7.2.1 Heterogeneity in the selected knowledge intensive companies

The different variables selected show a very heterogeneous and complex picture of the 18 companies under study in relation to their knowledge-enabling environment (see Chapter 4 for a list of aspects and Annex III for data in each aspect). Tables AIII.1 to AIII.16 in Annex

Table 7.1: Company characteristics

Company identifier	Activity	Part of a large corporation	Number of offices in Sweden	Number of offices in other countries	Monetary turnover, 2002 (in million SEK)
Consultancy		**0.25****	**4***	**4***	**21.7***
58	Legal, accounting, tax, management consultancy	No	0	0	49.8
87	Legal, accounting, tax, management consultancy	No	0	0	12.4
94	Legal, accounting, tax, management consultancy	No	3	0	25
2	Architectural and engineering activities	Yes	13	50	..
98	Architectural and engineering activities	Yes	8	0	24
110	Architectural and engineering activities	No	0	0	13.3
11	Technical testing and analysis	Yes	19	0	..
49	Advertising	No	0	0	9
82	Advertising	No	0	0	..
83	Advertising	No	2	0	31.5
106	Advertising	No	2	0	7
24	Labor recruitment	No	0	0	23
Education		**0****	**1***	**0***	**20.7***
26	Primary education	No	0	0	5.2
71	Primary education	No	0	0	..
33	Secondary education	No	3	0	60
30	Adult and other education	No	0	0	12
55	Adult and other education	No	0	0	16.3
68	Adult and other education	No	3	0	10
All		**0.17****	**0***	**0***	**21.3***

*Is an average

**Proportion of companies part of a large corporation

III show that companies vary considerably within the different aspects presented. For most of the indicators, the standard deviations are high and the ranges are also relatively high.

Roughly, the sampled companies can be described as Swedish companies that in some cases have other offices within Sweden, but in most cases have only one or two offices. Only a few companies are part of a larger corporation with a large number of offices and only one company has offices in other countries. On average, companies in the study had 19 employees in 2001 and this figured increased to 25 employees in 2003. Women comprise 47 % of their workforce. Their employees are, for the most part, full time workers and professionals; and only a few are support staff members. In the majority of cases, the manager of the company is a professional in the strict sense of the term, and in nine of the cases s/he is the owner of the company. Also noteworthy is that most of the companies have their employees work in teams, and more specifically, in cross-functional teams, which in theory is the best way to promote innovation (see Chapter 4).

From the respondent questionnaires, it seems that the companies are composed mainly of Swedish employees with an average age of 41 years. There, however, is a good deal of variability both between companies and within companies. Variability also exists in the relevant work experience that employees have both within and between companies. The company with the highest average in this indicator is Company 55 with an average of 20 years experience. In contrast, Company 24 and 71 have an average of five years. The educational attainment in the companies under study is also relatively heterogeneous. In general terms, however, one can say that companies seem to have employees with high educational attainment (level 5 in the ISCED97).

The process of recruiting new employees also presents important differences among the 18 companies. In general, companies tend to use regular advertising methods to announce vacancies, such as notices at the unemployment office or in newspapers; although consultancy companies also use contacts for this purpose. Selection procedures almost always call for one or two interviews and companies tend to be interested mainly in the social skills of the candidates. However, it is also important that the candidate has experience. Once someone new is recruited, about half of the companies provide guidance through a mentor or some kind of standardized program.

On average employee turnover in the last year for all the companies was three percent. There are, however, major differences between the firms. There are companies which gained almost half of their workforce in the last year as well as companies that lost almost 20% of their workforce. In looking at employee turnover using a two year reference period, comparing the number of employees in 2001 and 2003, most of the companies gained employees. While there is still a high degree of variability, the average for the whole sample shows that in the two years there was a workforce net gain of 13%. It is interesting to note that over two years the companies tended to grow, while in a year perspective the employee turnover was more balanced with more companies losing employees.

In many cases, the monetary reward system of the companies uses a bonus system together with individually stipulated salaries which means that the salary is set independently of the employee's position. The average salary per hour is around 160 SEK. Again there are major differences among companies as well as within companies. The standard deviation in the whole sample is 65 SEK with a range of more than 450 SEK difference.

Another important aspect in the knowledge-enabling environment is communication patterns. Companies tend to have information meetings every week where all employees share information. Scheduled meetings among professionals are not very common. Employees that responded to the questionnaire tend to spend more time in regular informal meetings than in formal meetings. The general meetings are usually described as useful as is also the case with informal meetings. Around half of the companies have a newsletter which, in most of the cases, is published on the web page. Finally, the main manager is the most common gatekeeper for information. A gatekeeper is the person at the company who locates information that is relevant for organizational processes. S/he might be in charge of looking for new developments in the field or important changes in the law.

Also related to communication patterns is investment in information technologies (IT). Virtually all companies use the Internet and have an intranet to connect their different computers. Databases are also a common tool within the 18 companies but, in most cases the database is related to customer invoicing. While there is substantial variability in the number of computers per employee, in general the majority of companies have at least one computer per employee. There are also major differences in the investment in IT but in few cases is it higher than two percent of the total monetary turnover of the company.

7.2.2 Similarities and differences between consultancy and educational companies

There is high variability in most of the variables presented both within consultancy and education; in this way one could say that in general they are equally heterogeneous. Educational companies tend to have the most extreme cases in all the measures, while consultancy companies, although heterogeneous, are less divergent.

One of the major differences between consultancy and educational companies is company size. There are no educational companies that belong to bigger corporations, and only two (33%) have other offices within Sweden. In terms of monetary turnover, on average, consultancy companies and educational companies are similar but educational companies present more extreme cases and therefore a higher range than consultancy. In general consultancy companies have more offices in other parts of Sweden. Consultancy companies had on average 18 employees in 2001 and 20 in 2003, while educational companies had 21 and 36 employees in 2001 and 2003 respectively. Consultancy companies had on average 40% women in their workforce, while education had 59%. This proportion roughly corresponds with the Swedish gender distribution in consultancy, but the gender distribution for Sweden in educational services is higher than the one presented in the companies under study (see Figure 5.16 in Chapter 5).

There are also differences in the type of contracts that educational and consultancy companies have with their employees. On average, 87% of the workforce in consultancy companies is full time while only 64% is employed full time in educational companies. Similarly, educational companies have less permanent employees (83% versus. 95% in consultancy), and less permanent part time employees (37% versus. 52% in consultancy). Educational companies also lost more employees in the last year: 11% of their workforce versus 8% in consultancy. Questionnaire responses, however, show that educational employees have been in the company longer, in relation to when the company was started, than consultancy employees. Thus, it seems that consultancy companies have more stable arrangements for employees, while education companies have longer term relationships with some of their employees. It could be that questionnaire respondents in education are a self-selected sample of the "loyal" employees to the company. In terms of employee age, it is interesting to note that consultancy and education do not differ very much. Educational companies have slightly older respondents, with fewer years of experience on average in the area. Educational employees also tend to have higher educational attainment.

Both educational and consultancy companies tend to use teams in their companies. Consultancy companies seem to use cross-functional teams more than in education. Cross-functional teams refer to companies that are organized in groups of people with different expertise and competencies. In the case of education, it refers to groups of teachers from different subjects working together with the same kids at the same time in the classroom (see Chapter 4). In both sectors around half of the cases have a middle manager, and almost all companies have a manager that is a professional worker.

In advertising for available positions, educational companies almost exclusively use the traditional government unemployment office, while in consultancy advertising methods are more varied. In addition to advertising vacancies through the unemployment office, consultancy companies use their contacts and people they know to find suitable candidates. Both sectors mainly use interviews as the procedure to select employees. The most common selection criterion is social skills, 75% in consultancy and 80% in education. However, consultancy companies often use "fits in the company" while educational companies do not use this criteria. Experience and educational certificates are also used in approximately half of the companies in both sectors.

It is more common for educational companies to have some kind of standardized procedure when a new employee is hired. However, in both sectors about half of the companies use mentors.

With regard to employee turnover, educational companies lost three percent of their employees in the last year while consultancy companies gained five percent. On the other hand, in the last two years, consultancy companies workforce grew seven percent while educational companies increased by 26%. Educational companies have the most extreme cases in the last two years, both in terms of companies that lost and gained employees.

In terms of monetary reward systems, both sectors usually use an individual basis to determine salaries. Educational companies mainly use experience as the criteria for determining salary level while consultancy often use external authority. Consultancy companies have, on average, a higher salary level. More consultancy companies have bonuses than educational companies. In most of the cases bonuses are provided based on end or year profits. Half of the companies in both sectors provide bonuses for groups within the company. A bonus, in most cases, is based on work contribution and consists of additional salary for the employee.

In terms of communication activities, consultancy companies tend to have meetings once a week while in educational companies this is the case in around half of the firms. Few companies have additional scheduled meetings for professional workers. About half of the companies in both sectors have newsletters. Educational companies have a manager as the main informational gatekeeper, while in consultancy firms it varies between different actors: a regular professional worker, each employee, the manager or the project leader. With regards to meetings, the respondents to the questionnaire do not show major differences between the two sectors. In general the majority of people have meetings for less than five hours a week both for regular and informal meetings. Educational employees seem to spend slightly more time in meetings. Employees in both sectors spend more time in informal meetings than in regular meetings. Respondents seem to have similar views in both sectors with regards to the perceived usefulness of meetings.

In terms of distribution of information there are no major differences between the sectors in any of the indicators. Respondents in both sectors tend to write and read a similar amount of documents and they receive a similar number of emails as well as telephone calls both from customers and colleagues. Educational companies seem to receive slightly fewer emails but compensate with having more telephone calls. In terms of reading and writing at work both sectors have similar percentages of respondents from the different educational levels.

Finally, in line with the finding of differences in email usage of educational and consultancy companies, consultancy companies have more computers per employee than educational companies. However, education has the most extreme cases ranging from companies with more than two computers per employee to companies with one computer for ten employees. Internet is present in all companies and only one educational company does not have intranet. Databases are more common in consultancy companies, although it is likely that educational companies have some sort of database with all the clients (students) but these are often not considered as databases since they only have basic information on the clients. However, educational companies seem to spend relatively more on IT than consultancy companies.

7.3 Exploratory analysis of the knowledge-enabling environment: eight enabling constructs

The previous section described the different aspects of the knowledge-enabling environment in the 18 companies under study. This section explores further the similarities and differences between companies. In order to better explore the knowledge-intensive environment it was necessary to simplify the data collected. In order to do so, a few variables were selected in order to try to capture eight different aspects or constructs of the organization, namely: (1) Size of the company (*size*); (2) workforce's stability (*stability*); (3) workforce's experience (*experience*); (4) professional orientation of the company (*professionalism*); (5) tacit orientation of the recruitment process (*recruitment*); (6) monetary reward system (*reward system*); (7) communication intensiveness (*communication*); and, (8) investment in IT (*IT*). In total, 43 variables were used for the analysis of the eight aspects. Interval type variables were transformed into binary variables (dummy variable) using the median split method. Each of the resulting binary indicators, therefore, identifies if the company is above (having a value "1") or below (having a value "0") the median of the 18 companies under study in that specific indicator (see Chapter 6). Other variables were recoded to fit a binary structure. There were also several variables that were dichotomous already and did not require any data editing. The 18 companies were, thus, described with 43 binary indicators referring to eight different constructs of their knowledge-enabling environment.

The different indicators within each of the eight constructs were correlated in order to find underlying principals within each construct in the sample. Table 7.2 shows the different indicators used to capture the eight constructs considered in the knowledge-enabling environment (see also Annex IV). The first aspect that has been described extensively in the literature as important for providing competence development opportunities and affecting the management of knowledge is the size of the company (see e.g. Boudard, 2001; Earl and Gault, 2003). Traditionally the size of a company refers to the number of employees on the company payroll. Turnover is also an important aspect in determining the size of the company (Holliday, 1995, p. 5). The bivariate Pearson correlation among the six selected indicators seems to show that size in the selected companies has two main but relatively independent characteristics that are labeled: (1) "company expansion" and (2) "volume". "Company expansion" refers to companies that tend to have more than one office in Sweden. "Volume" refers to the number of employees and the monetary turnover of the company (see Table IV.1 and IV.2 in Annex IV).

The second aspect within the knowledge-enabling environment tries to capture information about the stability of the workforce in the companies. The bivariate Pearson correlations between the indicators show that the sample has two different components in the construct stability. First are companies that tend to have full time employees and have permanent arrangements for employment. This can be called "permanency". Second are companies that had: a high proportion of employees who left the company in the last year; tended to have less part-time permanent employees; and, their workforce had been with the company for fewer years. This can be called "loyalty". It is interesting to note that number of years in the company is not closely related to having full time employment (see Tables IV.3. and IV.4 in Annex IV).

Third, in terms of workforce experience, there is high heterogeneity among the selected companies. Companies with older employees tend to have lower educational attainment but their workforce has more experience. But these relationships are very weak (see Tables IV.5 in Annex IV).

The fourth construct, *professionalism*, is with no doubt one of the most difficult to grasp. It tries to show to what degree the companies are organized around and composed of professional workers. The indicators are meant to show what companies are more "professional" in their orientation than others. The Pearson correlations show that there is a moderate relationship between having a manager that is a professional and having cross-functional teams and a middle manager. But this is mainly due to the fact that only company68 has a manager that is not a professional. The same applies in the correlations of having a specific person for human resources, where only Company 58 has a person dedicated to human resource issues. The only relatively interesting association is between having cross-functional teams and the ratio of professional workers ($r= 0.41$). This shows that companies with higher proportions of professional workers tend to work in cross-functional teams (see Tables IV.6 and IV.7 in the Annex IV).

The fifth construct deals with recruitment policies. The indicators were again recoded to fit into a binary structure. The underlying principle in recoding these variables is the level of tacit orientation of the different recruitment procedures. For example, "method of advertisement" was binary recoded: the variable took the level 1 if the company uses contacts

Table 7.2: Indicators for the constructs of the knowledge-enabling environment

Size	Median
• Part of a large corporation	
• Number of offices in Sweden	0
• Number of offices in other countries	0
• Monetary turnover (in million SEK)	19
• Number of employees in 2001*	21
• Total number of employees in 2003	15
Stability	
• Percentage of full-time employees	88%
• Percentage of permanent employees	100%
• Percentage of permanent part-time employees	45%
• Percentage of employees lost in the last year (inversed scale)	10%
• Respondent's number of years in the company in relation to companies starting date	43%
Workforce's experience	
• Average respondent's age	42 years
• (a5) Average numbers of years working in related area	12 years
• Percentage of employees with tertiary education degree (more than 3 years)	40%
Professionalism indicators	
• Professional as a manager of the company	
• Main manager owns the company (totally or partially)	
• Having cross-functional teams	
• Having a middle manager	
• Specific person for human resource function	
• Number of professionals as a percentage of the total n. of employees	85%
Recruitment policy	
• Method for advertising available positions: Through contacts	
• Method of selecting employees: interviews	
• Criteria for personnel selection: Social skills	
• Criteria for personnel selection: Fitting into the company	
• Having a mentor for new employees	
• Policy for newly employed	
Reward system	
• Salary level	165 SEK/h.
• Salary determination individually	
• Bonus within the company	

for recruitment and level 0 in all the other categories. In a similar way, the "method of selecting employees" was codified in terms of using a standardized method (a test or an outsourced company) or not. The value 1 refers to companies that use interviews which are more tacit oriented than a standardized method. Also, from the list of selection criteria, the ones related to tacit aspects of the recruitment process, such as "social skills" or "fitting into

Table 7.2 (cont'd): Indicators for the constructs of the knowledge-enabling environment

Communication intensiveness	Median
• Percentage of respondents with more than 5 ...	
...hours in informal meetings	23%
...hours in regular meetings	0%
...work related written materials in one week	15%
...work related materials in one week	36%
...telephone calls per day from other colleagues	11%
...emails per Day from other colleagues	9%
• Having regular meetings every week	
• Professionals having an scheduled meeting	
• Having a Newsletter	
IT investment	
• Number of computers per employee	1
• Investment in IT per employee in 2002	7407 SEK
• Investment in IT as a percentage of the total monetary turnover, 2001	7 per MSEK
• Investment in IT as a percentage of the total monetary turnover, 2002	8 per MSEK
• Investment in IT as a percentage of the total monetary turnover, 2003	6 per MSEK

the company" were selected to measure the tacit orientation of the process. Finally, the policy used with new recruits is also an important aspect of the recruitment policies. Companies that have a mentor system will be more tacit oriented than those that do not. "Having a specific plan for someone that is recruited" supposes an explicit plan and therefore less tacit orientation. Considering all these six indicators, there are no Pearson correlations above 0.5 among them. There is however, moderate correlation between advertising through contacts and having interviews as the selection procedure (r = 0.43); although this relationship could be due to the univariate distribution of the two variables since there are few cases that are not tacit oriented in both variables. There is also a negative association between having a mentor and having a plan for new recruits (r = -0.41), which means that companies without an explicit plan might compensate by having a mentor system. (see Table IV.8 in Annex IV)

The monetary reward system is explored using three indicators. There are two clear components in the reward system of a company: (1) salary level and (2) corporate approach to salary determination. The first component refers to the salary per hour of each employee; this is heavily influenced by the service that the company provides. Corporate approach to salary determination includes the two indicators "having bonuses" and "salaries determined on individual basis". The indicator: "salaries determined on individual basis" refers to salaries that are set individually, independent of the position the person holds (1= individually determined salaries) (see Table IV.9). The Pearson correlation between the three indicators seems to point to that companies compensate for not having an individual salary determination with having a bonus system (see Table IV.10 in Annex IV). In general, companies that determine salaries individually do not provide bonuses. The differences between consultancy and education are clear in this construct of *reward system*. The univariate distributions for the three indicators of the construct differ considerably. Educational companies have low salary levels (except in the case of Company 30). In addition, only two companies in education provide bonuses. Also interesting is the fact that all the companies that have high salaries in consultancy provide bonuses, while the only educational company that has high salaries does not provide bonuses. Companies that have low salaries tend to provide bonuses, but this is more common in consultancy than in education (see Tables IV.9 and IV.10).

Communication was measured in two main ways. On the one hand the frequency of meetings that companies have, and on the other hand, the frequency of oral and written communication between employees. It has seven indicators (see Table 7.2 and Table IV.11). The bivariate Pearson correlation between the seven indicators shows that not having scheduled meetings among professional workers is compensated through other means of communication among professionals. It seems that this is mostly accomplished through reading materials (see Table IV.12). Because of this, the indicator "having scheduled meetings among professionals" was recoded into an inverted scale, in a way that correlates positively with the other variables, strengthening the communication activity. In other words, not having regular scheduled meetings among professional workers is considered positive in relationship to overall company communications. This will be used later on when connecting the different constructs.

Information technology is mainly studied from an investment point of view. All the other variables related to IT present low variability (see Annex III Table III.16) making it very complicated to discriminate between companies. Investment in 2001 and 2003 had eight missing values each (44% of the sample), and although they are presented in the tables because they are interesting, they were not considered in the analysis. The indicators of the construct "information technology investment" seem very much related to each other. Companies that have more computers per employee invest more in IT per employee and as a percentage of the total turnover (see Table IV.13 and IV.14).

7.4 Relating the enabling constructs

7.4.1 Relationships among the different construct indicators

The previous section explored the different identified knowledge-enabling constructs. Eight aspects were presented and explained: size, stability, workforce's experience, professionalism, tacit orientation of the recruitment process, monetary reward system, communication patterns and IT investment. The intention of this section is to explore the relationship between these eight different aspects. This will provide an illustration on how these small companies are creating their knowledge-enabling environment. First, correlations between the different indicators will be presented. It is not possible to present all the correlations among the 43 different indicators due mainly to space constrains. The section presents a summary of the most interesting relationships among indicators.

The first interesting relationship appears between the constructs of *size* and *IT*. Most of the size indicators relate negatively to investment in IT. In other words, the bigger and the more offices a company has, the less it invests in IT. This is surprising since these companies would need a higher investment in order to maintain connectivity. Also interesting to note is the negative relationship between the "volume" of a company, in terms of employees and monetary turnover, with the use of interviews for the recruitment process. Companies with more employees tend to outsource the process of recruitment or use standardized tests instead of interviews. On the other hand, companies that are spread over several offices around the country use contacts more often. Bigger companies also tend to have lower salary levels. These relationships can be explained because of the differences between consultancy companies and educational companies. Consultancy companies have more geographic locations than educational companies, and they have, in general, higher salaries and more recruitment through contacts. It is therefore likely that the differences are due to a different approach by each sector, rather than due to *size* per se.

The construct *stability* has two main components; the first is "permanency" and the second "loyalty". As could be expected, the two components are positively related with experience indicators; the more years one has worked in a company, the more experience one has gained. This is especially clear with the indicator "respondents' average age". In addition, *stability* is negatively related with determining salaries individually, which means that companies that determine salaries individually tend to have more permanent and "loyal" employees. It also seems that companies with more permanent employees have less communication activities and these activities are shorter. Finally, companies with more permanent employees seem to invest more in IT, but companies where employees have been with the company longer, tend to invest less in IT. This can be explained because in the sample, companies that invest in IT are adult educational companies that tend to have a substantial number of non-permanent employees.

The construct *experience* had three individual indicators that were not found significantly related. The three indicators (respondents experience in the area, high percentage of respondents with high educational attainment and high respondent's average age) have a variety of relationships with other indicators. The three of them have a negative relationship with having a high number of phone calls among employees. This is especially the case if employees are older and have more experience. Companies with high experience in their workforce tend to have lower salaries. This could be explained partly because the sector "legal, accounting, tax, management consultancy" has high salaries but the workforce in this sector has low experience. The second indicator seems to be negatively related to the ratio of professional workers of the company. Companies that have fewer professionals seem to have more educated people. This could be explained because educational companies tend to have a higher proportion of employees with high educational attainment, and they have fewer professionals. On the other hand, high educational attainment in the workforce is positively related to the different indicators in *communication* as well as with high investments in IT. The third indicator, respondent's average age, correlates negatively with having a middle manager. Companies with older employees seem to use mentors but in general they do not have a standardized program when a new employee is recruited. Also in companies with older employees salaries are not usually determined individually and in general, there is less overall communication.

The construct *professionalism* was composed of three main indicators: having cross-functional teams; having a middle manager; and, the proportion of professional workers in the company. In general terms, the more professionalism that the company has, the less communication there is in the company. This corresponds with the Sveiby's description of the archetypical professional worker (Sveiby, 1997). However, having cross-functional teams correlates positively with some *communication* indicators, specially the ones referring to literacy practices at work. It seems that in companies where employees work with colleagues with different expertise the individuals have to read more in order to understand each other better. This is in line with the findings that relate knowledge management success projects with having cross-functional teams. It might be that the composition of such teams enforces communication and exchange of written materials.

The Pearson correlations also seem to show that having cross-functional teams and a high number of professionals can create an environment where bonuses are provided. However, if there is a middle manager there may not be any bonuses and the salaries will probably be lower. Companies with cross-functional teams will tend to have employees that use their literacy skills at work a lot, while if the company has a middle manager, less written communication will probably be required.

The construct of *recruitment* was constructed with six independent indicators. These indicators differ in the way they relate to other indicators. In general, the six indicators correlate negatively with the salary indicators, except in the case of using fitting into the company as a criterion for selection, which correlates positively with salary level and having a bonus system. This is probably the case because it is only consultancy companies that use this criterion and they are the ones with higher salaries and provide bonuses to their employees. Companies that use contacts as a way of recruitment seem to spend less time in regular meetings and their employees have less reading of written materials. Using interviews in the selection process has a positive relationship with investment in IT as well as with informal meetings among professionals. Having a mentor correlates positively with the different *communication* indicators, except with meeting informally among professional workers. Finally, having a standardized method for assimilating a new recruit correlates positively with investment in IT.

Higher scores in *communication* indicators seem to be associated with higher investment in IT infrastructure, as could be expected. At the same time, more communication in the company seems to be associated with less retention of human capital.

7.4.2 Overall scales for the knowledge-enabling constructs and their relationships

The previous section looked into the relationship among indicators of the eight different constructs: (1) Size of the company (*size*); (2) workforce's stability (*stability*); (3) workforce's experience (*experience*); (4) professional orientation of the company (*professionalism*); (5) tacit orientation of the recruitment process (*recruitment*); (6) monetary reward system (reward system); (7) communication intensiveness (*communication*); and, (8) investment in IT (*IT*) (see Table 7.2). Going a step further, this section examines the relationship between these eight constructs. To this end, a scale for each of the constructs was created. The scale in each construct is the arithmetical average of its binary indicators. Therefore, each construct can be placed within a scale from 0 to 1, where 1 means the company is above the median in all the construct indicators, and 0 the opposite. The handling of missing values and the limitations of the created scales were described in Chapter 6. It is important to mention that the scales in each construct provide an overall picture of each construct with a similar weight for each indicator. This means that a score of 0.5 might mean slightly different things in different companies. The construct scales were also divided in low and high following the median split method.

Table 7.3 shows whether the companies can be considered high or low in relation to the median in each construct scale. The last column shows the overall knowledge intensive scale (*KISall*). The knowledge intensive scale was created using the constructs presented above excluding *size*. The assumption is that the overall knowledge intensive scale measures how knowledge-friendly each company is. In other words, companies that score high on the knowledge intensive scale have a richer knowledge-enabling environment than companies in the sample with lower scores. It is important to remember that the scales refer specifically to these 18 companies and cannot be related to other non-studied companies.

Table 7.4 shows the Pearson correlation among the different scales for each construct. Only one moderate relationship was found and exists among *experience* and *stability* (r =0.49). As could be expected, companies with people that have more experience are companies that have a more stable environment for the employee. The table also shows that companies with more professionals tend to determine the salary in a less individualized way (r=- 0.40). Companies that are more tacit oriented in their recruitment processes seem to have a more stable (r = 0.27) and more experienced (r=0.33) workforce. *Communication* correlates positively with investment in IT (r=0.29), which seems to indicate that more communication implies more investment in IT. Finally, although the relationship is weak, it seems that companies high in their professional orientation have less communication among their members (r =-0.22). This could be explained in two ways, professional workers need less communication among themselves since they all share certain codes or as Sveiby (1997) indicated, the people in professional roles are not usually very communicative. Other weak relationships exist among stability of the workforce and individual salary determination (r =- 0.22), *communication* (r = -0.24) and investment in IT (r =-0.22). This seems to show that companies that have more stable arrangements for employees have a less individualize reward system, have less communication between employees and less investment in IT.

Table 7.3: Knowledge-enabling constructs scales binary recoded through the median split method by company and sector

Company ID	Size	Stability	Experience	Professionalism	Recruitment	Reward system	Communication	IT	KISall
Median	0.43	0.4	0.5	0.56	0.65	0.5	0.48	0.55	0.57
Consultancy	0.50*	0.50*	0.50*	0.58*	0.58*	0.25*	0.58*	0.45*	0.50*
58	High	High	Low	Low	Low	Low	High	.	Low
87	Low	Low	Low	Low	High	Low	High	High	Low
94	High	High	High	Low	High	Low	High	Low	High
02	High	Low	Low	High	Low	High	Low	Low	Low
110	Low	High	High	High	High	Low	Low	High	High
98	High	High	High	High	High	Low	Low	Low	High
11	Low	High	High	Low	High	High	High	Low	High
106	Low	High	High	High	High	Low	Low	High	High
49	Low	Low	Low	High	Low	Low	High	High	Low
82	Low	Low	Low	Low	Low	High	High	High	High
83	High	Low	Low	High	Low	Low	Low	Low	Low
24	High	Low	High	High	High	Low	High	Low	Low
Education	0.50*	0.33*	0.50*	0.17*	0.33*	0.50*	0.33*	0.50*	0.50*
26	Low	High	Low	Low	Low	Low	Low	Low	Low
71	Low	Low	High	Low	Low	High	Low	Low	Low
33	High	Low	High	High	Low	Low	High	High	High
30	Low	Low	Low	Low	High	Low	Low	Low	Low
55	High	High	High	Low	Low	High	Low	High	High
68	High	Low	Low	Low	High	High	High	High	High

* Proportion of companies above the median

Table 7.4: Pearson correlations of the knowledge-enabling constructs (above 0.20)

	Size	Stability	Experience	Professionalism	Recruitment	Reward system	Communication	IT
Size	1.00							
Stability		1.00						
Experience		0.49	1.00					
Professionalism	0.22		0.22	1.00				
Recruitment		0.27	0.33		1.00			
Reward system		-0.22		-0.40	-0.24	1.00		
Communication		-0.24		-0.22			1.00	
IT		-0.22					0.29	1.00
KISall		0.38	0.56		0.33	0.24		0.42

An entropy analysis was also carried out to determine further relationships among the knowledge-enabling environment constructs. As the Pearson correlation indicates, the only significant relationship at a five percent level is between *stability* and *experience* of the workforce. These two constructs, therefore are somehow underlying a similar principle. Probably the main factor is the respondent's age, since this is strongly associated with the number of years in the company, and the possibility of having a contract on permanent basis. All the rest of the constructs do not show significant relationships. This means that they are relatively independent of each other.

7.4.3 Summary of construct relationships

The 43 different indicators, which try to grasp the knowledge-enabling environment, present a very complex picture of the companies. No major patterns of association can be found, and in most of the cases the associations are always below 0.7. Accordingly, a-priori theoretically related indicators, within each of the constructs, are not always closely related. This weakens the relationship among the eight constructs of the knowledge-enabling environment.

Many of the relationships between indicators in the constructs *size, stability, experience* and *recruitment* seem to be related to the service that the companies are providing. It seems, therefore, that certain knowledge-enabling characteristics are associated with the activity of the company, as could be expected. The data, however, presents some interesting relationships that are not easily associated with the activity of the company which could be studied further. For example, stability of the workforce (*stability*) seems to be associated with less communication among employees (*communication*). Or, in other words, the more communication within a company the less stable its workforce seems to be. This could be related to the idea of creative chaos that Nonaka and Takeuchi (1995) propose. According to Nonaka and Takeuchi (1995), certain amount of instability increases the communication among the employees that in turn, creates more insights and knowledge creation. Also interesting is that older people tend to communicate less with colleagues. More *professionalism* within the company is also associated with lower levels of communication among employees. While organizing work in cross-functional teams and having a mentor seem to be related to a higher level of communication. This could be in line with the Sveiby's characterization of professionals in knowledge-intensive companies (Sveiby 1997) and with the research on knowledge management effectiveness (see e.g. Davenport and Prusak, 1998) as well as the characterization of a knowledge creating company in Nonaka's work (see e.g. Noanaka and Takeuchi, 1995).

In the overall construct scales, one could argue that the sample does not present a clear strong relationship among the different constructs. It seems that each construct is relatively independent from each other, except in the case of workforce's stability and experience. This can be explained because each construct is composed of different components and each seems to behave in a different way. Or in other words, the companies have certain knowledge-enabling characteristics but do not have others. Accordingly, one could argue that companies do not have a clear pattern for managing their knowledge. Taking into account the eight constructs, no company stands out as being above the median in all the construct scales (see table 8.3). Companies 30, 26, and 83 are among the ones with more constructs below the median. In other words, these are among the ones that are, theoretically at least, less knowledge intensive. In summary, the analysis seems to indicate that these 18 companies are quite different from one another despite the fact that some of them carry out similar services

The scales for each of the eight constructs present a very similar distribution in both sectors. Despite the fact that the median was calculated for both sectors, the overall scale for knowledge intensiveness shows that both sectors have an equal proportion of companies above and below the median. This shows that consultancy and educational companies do not seem to differ in their level of knowledge intensiveness measured through the composite scale of all the constructs. In relation to each of the constructs, consultancy seems to present a slightly higher proportion of companies above the median except in the case of salary determination. Education presents a rather low proportion of companies above the median in *professionalism, stability* and *communication*. It seems that educational companies are comparatively less oriented towards professionals, having more support staff members than consultancy. They also tend to provide employment on a less permanent basis than consultancy.

7.5 Profiles in relation to certain effectiveness indicators

In this section, to finalize the exploration of the knowledge-enabling environment, the thesis tries to relate the knowledge-enabling constructs created in the previous section with certain indicators that try to capture the results of a knowledge-enabling environment which are referred to here as effectiveness indicators. They try to capture to what extent the knowledge-enabling environment is effective in promoting collaboration, retaining employees and expanding the workforce, creating innovation, and generating benefits. These indicators are grouped into: Collaborative Climate Index (CCI); employee turnover; innovation; and, monetary profit.

Table 7.5: Bivariate Pearson correlation between construct scales and effective measurements (above 0.20)

	Kisall	*CCI*	*Employee turnover*	*Product innovation*	*% of profit*	*Profit per employee*
Size			0.33	0.26		
Stability	0.38				0.24	0.38
Experience	0.56					
Professionalism			0.22	-0.47		
Recruitment	0.33	-0.33			0.29	
Reward system	0.24	0.24	-0.24	0.60		
Communication				0.26	-0.43	
IT	0.42					

Collaborative Climate Index

The first effectiveness indicator is the Collaborative Climate Index. Sveiby and Simon (2002) developed the Collaborative Climate Index (CCI) to study to what extent company employees collaborate with each other (see Chapter 3). It is interesting to relate the different constructs of the knowledge-enabling environment with the Collaborative Climate Index. The assumption is that higher levels of collaborative climate will be related with higher levels of knowledge intensiveness in each company and probably with each of the constructs. However, Table 7.5 shows somewhat the contrary. The Pearson correlation shows that there are no significant relationships among the knowledge enabling environment constructs and the CCI. CCI only presents two correlations above 0.20; a negative relationship with *recruitment* (r = -.33) and a positive relationship with *reward system* (r= 0.24). This seems to indicate that there might be other factors not grasped in the construct scales that are influencing the collaborative climate. In other words, it seems that the different knowledge-enabling characteristics of the working environment are not strongly related to the level at which employees collaborate (as measured by the CCI). It seems that companies that recruit using more tacit oriented strategies have less collaboration among their employees and that if they have a more individually oriented reward system the employees tend to be more collaborative.

Employee turnover 2003

The second indicator of the effectiveness of the company is related to the retention or growth of human capital. It was possible to collect data on employee turnover in the period from 2001 to 2003 at the time of the interview. In this way, employee turnover shows to what extent the company workforce had grown or contracted in these two years. Employee turnover therefore can be positive, if the company gained employees or negative, if the company lost employees. The variable was re-codified into a binary variable with the median split method (median = 9 %).

Employee turnover between 2001 and 2003 presents moderate positive relationships with the construct scale *size* (r=0.33), and weak and positive with *professionalism* (r=0.22), while it has a negative correlation with *reward system* (r=-0.24). It is surprising that there is no relationship with *stability* or *experience*. This could be explained because the *stability* and *experience* constructs are composed of other indicators that are not specifically related to employee turnover, but rather to the types of company contracts. It seems, therefore, that providing stable contract arrangements does not seem to guarantee a more permanent workforce. This is somewhat in line with Takeuchi and Nonaka's (2004) idea that companies have to manage the paradox of constant change while maintaining stability.

Innovation

The third effectiveness indicator refers to the innovation activity of the company. Companies were asked if they had developed a new service or product in the last year. In the case of educational companies, innovation refers to offering a new course. Thus, the indicator was binary coded, registering as 1 if the company had a product innovation or as 0 if they did not. It is important to note, that certain companies providing services in primary education have a small range of possibilities to create new courses. There are two missing values. In total, there were ten companies that had product innovation: six in consultancy and four in education. It seems that educational companies provide relatively speaking more new services than consultancy companies.

The Pearson correlation between the knowledge-enabling constructs and the binary coded indicator for innovation ("product innovation" in the table) is presented in Table 7.5. Product innovation seems to have a moderate correlation with individual salary determination (r=0.60). It is weak and positively related to *communication* (r=0.26) and *size* (r=0.26). On the other hand, companies that are more professionally oriented seem to have less product innovation (r= -0.47). Accordingly, it seems that individualized rewards help product innovation. At the same time, as most of the literature has shown (see Chapter 3) more communication among employees seems also to be related to more innovation. *Size* is also associated with more innovation, which could be due to the ability of bigger companies to dedicate part of their workforce to the production of new services. Finally, more professionalism is associated with less innovation. This could be explained by assuming that the professional role is concentrated on delivering specific products and thus not leaving much time or energy to be spent on creating new products especially if there is no support personnel. This goes against the theoretical assumption that innovative companies are mainly composed of professionals. It might be that when there is a high level of professionalism, professionals are able to think about new services if the company is able to provide sufficient support.

Profit

Finally, effectiveness of the company in monetary terms are explored. Profit refers to the monetary benefits of the company; in rough terms, it can be defined as money generated by a company's activity after all operating expenses have been met. Here, company profits are related to their turnover in order to make the profit comparable between companies. This ratio is used as an indicator for how well the companies had done in the last year. It is important to mention that educational companies are non-profit organizations in Sweden and therefore any profit has to be re-invested into the company. The interview tried to isolate profits before these re-investments were made.

It was possible therefore to calculate profit as a percentage of monetary turnover in 14 companies in 2002 (there are four missing values for monetary turnover). This is referred in the tables as "% of profit". Companies had an average profit of five percent of their monetary turnover in 2002 (std. dev. 8%). As could be expected, consultancy companies had a higher average profit at seven percent (std. dev.10%) versus. two percent (std. dev. 3%) in education. It was possible also to calculate the profit per employee ("profit per employee" in the Table 7.5). The average for the whole sample came to almost 90000 SEK of profit per employee. For the 12 consultancy companies the average was more than 125000SEK per employee, while in education the average was almost 4000 SEK per employee. This difference is not really significant in statistical terms (0.05 level of significance) due mainly to the low number of cases and the high standard deviations. The two indicators, profit as a proportion of total monetary turnover and profit per employee, were re-codified using the median split method in order to be able to relate them to the knowledge-enabling constructs.

In relation to the knowledge-enabling scales, profit as a percentage of turnover correlates weakly and positively with *stability* (r=0.24) and with tacit orientation of the recruitment process (r=0.29). It is negatively related to *communication* (r=-0.43). If one looks at the profit per employee (which provides some measure of the effectiveness of each employee) there is a moderate relationship with *stability* (r=0.38). Thus, it seems that companies that are more communicative are less profitable, and that companies that are more stable have more profits.

7.6 Summary and Synthesis

This chapter has provided a description and an exploration of the knowledge-enabling environment of the companies under study. The major conclusion from the descriptive analysis is that companies present a high degree of variability in the different aspects studied. Companies differ considerably in the composition of their workforce, the way they select and recruit employees, in the way they provide bonuses, in the way they structure their work, in their communication activities, and their investment in IT.

This heterogeneity in the different aspects is translated into a complex picture when looking at the different knowledge-enabling constructs. Seven different constructs of the knowledge-enabling environment together with size were built with different indicators in order to capture the knowledge intensiveness of the company. This resulted in the eight construct scales. The exploration of the relationship among the indicators showed that within each construct there were a variety of aspects that did not always "behave" in a similar way. Or in other words, it seems that the companies did not have a set of consistent actions for the management of knowledge. Accordingly, the scales created for each construct as a summary of their approach toward knowledge do not present strong relationships. Only workforce stability and workforce experience seem to be significantly related. The others present some interesting but relatively weak relationships.

In relation to certain effectiveness indicators, it is obvious that the relationships cannot be too strong mainly due to the variety of factors that might be influencing the measures. It is interesting to note, however, that product innovation seems to be associated with individual stipulation of salaries. This is in line with the idea that individualized reward promotes higher incentives for innovation. Product innovation is negatively related to professionalism within the company. It seems that companies with more professionals provide less new services. Also interesting, and to certain degree unexpected is that higher levels of communication are associated with less profit as a percentage of the total turnover. It is difficult to explain such a relationship since there are many factors that might affect profit and many reasons for having high levels of communication. This put into question whether encouraging more communication among employees is a positive strategy for increasing companies' competitive advantage. In a similar vein, a collaborative climate among employees does not seem much related to the different knowledge-enabling constructs. This could be because there might be other factors not grasped in the scales that affect the collaborative climate. Another explanation could be that the indicator's variability within each construct weakens any other relationship.

In conclusion one could say that each of the eighteen companies is relatively unique in the way they manage their knowledge. Consultancy and education, although they differ in certain aspects, do not present major differences in their knowledge-enabling environment. Educational companies seem to have less professional orientation. They seem also to have less communication, stability and tacit orientation of the recruitment process. The next chapter looks into the learning arenas since both the knowledge-enabling environment and the learning arenas are part of the knowledge management processes of a company

CHAPTER 8: EXPLORATORY ANALYSIS OF THE TRAINING ACTIVITIES

8.1 Introduction

The previous chapter presented the knowledge-enabling environment for the companies under study using seven different constructs related to the general management of knowledge, and the additional construct of size. However, the creation of knowledge which is one of the main aspects of company knowledge management, was not studied directly. The main objective of a knowledge-enabling environment is precisely the promotion and continuous upgrading of employee skills and competencies in order to foster innovation and competitiveness. To this end, training activities are seen as key to the development of skills. Thus, this chapter explores the topic in the context of the selected companies planned training activities. Data was obtained from interviews with contact persons from each company in the sample and from company documents. The bulk of material analyzed was obtained from documents pertaining to activity analyses that companies conducted within Measure 1.1 of Objective 3 of the Swedish ESF Council (see Chapter 5).

Companies training needs, rather than actual training activities, are the focus of this chapter. This limited focus is attributed to the fact that gathering information on training was difficult for a number of reasons. First of all, some companies did not have a special budget for training and as such, determining the actual cost of training would have been difficult. Additionally, the lack of central records on what training was purchased was also a problem, even if in a few cases the relevant training specifications were available through invoices sent to the Swedish ESF Council. Finally, the program under Objective 3 was still in progress at the time of data collection.

Thus the training needs specified are assumed to constitute the basis for actual training in the companies. They provide a good picture of what companies perceive as necessary in order to remain competitive. In other words, the main focus of this chapter and hence of the study is the demand for training. Even though the employees might not actually attend all the proposed training activities, training plans constitute the perceived need for training in order to remain competitive and grow. This is, therefore, an excellent and unique opportunity to study the demand for training in knowledge intensive companies.

This chapter is structured in the following way. First, several indicators on formal and non-formal training activities planned by the companies are presented as well as planned training events, their contents and duration. In addition, figures for participants in training, estimated training costs and training subject areas are presented. Then informal learning activities, using information from the questionnaires, is discussed. After this descriptive analysis, specific indicators comparable among companies are related to each other. Finally, the chapter explores the relationship among knowledge creation indicators and the knowledge enabling constructs as well as their relationship to certain effectiveness indicators. In order to do so, the knowledge-creation indicators are transformed into binary variables using the median-split method.

8.2 Non-formal and formal training activities

8.2.1 Training events

Training plans represent the desires of a company, in the ideal situation, for all necessary training activities for all their employees in order to remain competitive. It represents, therefore, a perfect situation to study the demand for training that companies have and their support for lifelong learning. Training events refer to each training activity that a company has planned as the result of their competence analysis plan. They are directed towards the development of their employee's competencies, or in other words, they constitute a form of human capital investment. The training events would be equivalent to vocational training courses, as defined by the European Commission (2002b) in the European Continuous Vocational Training Survey (CVTS), except that this publication excludes initial Vocational Education and Training (VET) in its definition which is not necessarily the case in this study. The figures are, therefore, only partially comparable with the CVTS.

The number of training events was registered from company documents. In some cases if an event was a repetition of another one, with the same subject and same number of participants, only one training event was registered. Thus, certain training events had several sessions which might have resulted in an underestimation of training events. Table 8.1 shows the number of training events planned for each company. The number of training events a company plans for indicates the training effort of that company. There are in total 491 training events registered, 329 in consultancy and 162 in education. The number of events ranges from companies that plan for only 10 events, such as company 33, to Company 55 that planned for 56 events. However, companies differ in the number of years for which their plans are made. For instance, Company 11 and 98 planned for two years, while Company 24 planned for three years. Therefore, the total number of events per company is divided by the number of years in the company training plan since this gives a better estimation of the reported needs. Thus, on average each company planned 22 (std. dev. 12) events per year; consultancy companies planned for 23 (std. dev. 13) events on average; and education planned for an average of 21 (std. dev. 9) events.

The total time planned for training was extracted mainly from company documents. Time was calculated as the sum of all the training hours of each employee; thus if an employee is to go to three courses of ten hours each course, the number of hours registered would be thirty. Using this method, the total number of man-hours planned for training is estimated at 1935 (std. dev. 1202) per company per year. On average, educational companies plan for 2712 (std. dev. 1287) man-hours per year while for consultancy services the average is 1418 (std. dev. 859). The average depends on the number of employees the training is planned for. As already noted, the training is planned for all employees, since this was a condition to access training assistance from the ESF council. However, in order to compare companies it is more meaningful to present training time planned per employee.

The number of hours of training per employee is calculated by dividing the total number of hours of training that each company has planned by the number of employees. Here the correction for years is also made and thus the figures refer to training time per employee each year planned. The 15 companies with data in this variable have an average of 111 (std. dev. 71) hours of training per employee each year. This means that companies plan for almost three weeks of full-time training for each of their employees. This ranges from 20 hours in Company 58 to 287 hours of training for each employee in one year in Company 71. The average for consultancy companies is 91 (std. dev. 61) hours while the number of hours for educational companies is 140 (std. dev. 79) per employee. The variability in both sectors is considerable; the range in consultancy is 191 while in education it goes up to 223 hours.

Table 8.1: Training events and training time by company

Company ID	Number of years planned for training	Number of training events per year	Total training time per year (in hours)	Total training time per employee and year (in hours)	Average total training time per course in hours (std. dev.)	
Consultancy		23*	1418*	91*	**21***	(40)
58	1	49	424	20	14	(12)
87	1	11	2534	211	87	(185)
94	1	44	3026	98	24	(11)
2	1	26	.	.	.	.
98	2	8	806	34	18	(10)
110	1	32	1270	85	16	(7)
11	2	20	1279	85	20	(14)
49	1,5	12	696	70	15	(14)
82	1	21	.	.	.	.
83	1	27	.	.	.	.
106	1	15	1626	163	18	(6)
24	3	10	1099	55	13	(17)
Education		21*	2712*	140*	**34***	(53)
26	1,5	19	2160	120	11	(10)
71	1	25	3157	287	45	(31)
33	1	10	3320	158	56	(121)
30	1	16	892	64	12	(16)
55	1,5	37	2098	84	42	(74)
68	1	17	4642	129	60	(32)
All		22*	1935*	111*	**25***	(46)

* Is an average

** Is an average calculated using all the courses not clustered by company

Course length differs from company to company. The average number of hours per course for all companies is 25 (std. dev. 46). This means that companies planned, on average, for courses lasting more than three full time working days. Consultancy services tend to have shorter courses, with an average of 21 (std. dev. 40) hours while courses for educational companies are on average 34 (std. dev. 53) hours long. An ANOVA of the two groups shows that the length of the courses in education and consultancy is statistically different at a 5% confidence level (n= 349 training events, see TableIV.15 in the Annex IV.15).

8.2.2 Number of participants or the demand for training

When studying training, training participation indexes are usually seen as indicators of the demand for training. In this particular study, however, participation rates are irrelevant because the training is planned for all employees, since this was a condition of the ESF-council. The training needs are therefore stipulated for all the employees in the company; however, each employee will demand a different number of courses. It was possible to obtain the number of training places that each employee has generated, or in other words, the average number of training events each employee demands (see Table 8.2). The average number of courses demanded per employee is 7 (std. dev. 3). It ranges from two in Company 98 to 15 in Company 83. In consultancy the average is 7 (std. dev. 3) courses while in education it is 6 (std. dev. 4). The two extreme cases are in education, which explains why the standard deviation is higher in this sector.

Table 8.2: Aspects of training participation by company

Company ID	Number of training courses that each employee demands	Training events (with information on participation)	Number of participants per course		SPECIFICITY INDEX CODIFIED		
			Training participants per year and event (Std. dev.)**	Training participants as a percentage of total number of employees (Std. dev.)**	From 0 to 0.49	From 0.50 to 0.99	all employees
Consultancy	**7***	**318**	**6** (7)**	**0.35** (0.41)**	**235**	**47**	**36**
58	8	47	3 (6)	0.16 (0.26)	42	4	1
87	5	9	7 (5)	0.60 (0.46)	4	1	4
94	4	44	3 (3)	0.10 (0.08)	44	0	0
2	9	26	7 (6)	0.35 (0.29)	18	8	0
98	2	16	7 (8)	0.29 (0.35)	13	3	0
110	6	32	3 (4)	0.18 (0.24)	29	1	2
11	7	39	6 (6)	0.37 (0.38)	26	8	5
49	7	18	6 (4)	0.61 (0.40)	7	6	0
82	4	18	4 (4)	0.25 (0.21)	14	4	12
83	15	26	14 (10)	0.57 (0.44)	13	1	4
106	8	12	7 (3)	0.70 (0.32)	4	4	5
24	5	31	9 (8)	0.38 (0.38)	21	7	3
Education	**6***	**160**	**6** (6)**	**0.32** (0.35)**	**121**	**30**	**9**
26	13	38	9 (7)	0.50 (0.38)	19	15	4
71	7	24	3 (3)	0.30 (0.32)	19	3	2
33	5	10	11 (6)	0.50 (0.26)	4	5	1
30	4	15	4 (3)	0.26 (0.19)	13	2	0
55	6	56	4 (6)	0.15 (0.23)	51	3	2
68	3	17	6 (9)	0.16 (0.24)	15	2	0
All	**7***	**478**	**6** (7)**	**0.31** (0.34)**	**356**	**77**	**45**

* Is an average

** Is an average calculated using all the courses not clustered by company

The number of participants in each course indicates the specificity of the courses in relation to company needs. The assumption is that if a course has one participant then only the need of that individual is satisfied, and s/he is likely to receive training with employees from other companies. On the other hand, the more participants from one company the greater the number of company employees involved, and the more "specific" the training is for that company (i.e., the training is "company-specific"). The distinction between general and specific training is important according to the human capital theory (see Becker, 1962, 1993). Table 8.2 shows the average number of company participants per course. The companies sampled, as a total and for each sector individually, have an average of 6 (std. dev. 7) participants per course. The range of participants per course falls between about three per course in Company 110 to 14 participants per course in Company 83.

It is important to relate this number to the total number of employees that each company has. This indicator, labeled "specificity index", is the proportion of employees that attend the same training event. It is more accurate in determining the specificity of the courses in each company than the average number of participants per course since it relates the participants in each course with the total number of employees. The smaller the difference between the average number of employees per course and the number of employees of the company, the more "company-specific" the courses are. A score of 1 in the specificity index means that all employees go together to the same courses within a given company. If the number is closer to 0 each employee goes to a different course. This index is interesting because it may indicate a possible level of course-sharing among companies. For example, if the majority of employees of a company attend the same course (i.e., the specificity index is high) it is likely that the course is tailored to that specific company. In addition, one could argue that since courses attended by higher number of employees of the same company will be more company-specific, the courses may not be transferable to other competitors. Also, employees who take the same courses are very likely socializing, and they will likely create more similar mental models (see Chapter 2).

There are 356 (74 %) training events where less than half of the employees participate. In 77 events (16 %) more than half of a company's workforce participates. All employees participate in 45 (9%) events distributed among 12 (67%) companies. The specificity index average for all the training events is 0.31 (std. dev. 0.34). This indicates that on average around 31% of the employees of each company attend the same courses. Consultancy has an index of 0.35 (std. dev. 0.41), while in education the specificity index is 0.32 (std. dev. 0.35). Company 106 in education presents the highest specificity of the courses, 70% of their employees on average go to the same courses.

8.2.3 Training costs

The data on the cost of training is extracted from both documents and interviews. Data from documents come from company plans submitted to the Swedish ESF Council. Anticipated expenses are based upon a needs assessment for each company in the ideal situation where all members of a company would attend training. Actual budgets for training for training that each company reported in the last three years come from interviews.

The total estimated cost of training in the sample is around 12.1 million SEK per year. The costs break down into 44 % (around 5.3 million SEK) allocated for labor costs, 41% (around 5.0 million SEK) for direct costs and 14% (more than 1.7 million SEK) for other costs. The 11 consultancy companies (65% of the total number of companies) estimate a total annual training cost of more than 8.8 million SEK, which constitutes 73% of the total estimated yearly cost for all companies in the sample. Table 8.3 shows the average of the total estimated cost for training by company. Each company has an average calculated cost of 712000 (std. dev. 458000) SEK per year. Labor costs average around 293000 (std. dev. 242000) SEK, direct costs average 312000 (std. dev. 449000) SEK and other costs average 100000 (std. dev. 193000) SEK per company.

Table 8.3: Aspects of the training costs

Company ID	Labor estimated cost per company (in 1000 SEK)	Direct estimated cost per company (in 1000 SEK)	Estimated non-specified/other cost per company (in 1000 SEK)	Total estimated cost per company (in 1000 SEK)	Total estimated cost per employee (in 1000 SEK)	Average training cost in the last three years (in 1000 SEK)	Actual training cost per employee (in SEK)	Actual training cost as a proportion of the planned training cost
Consultancy	**251***	**413***	**141***	**803***	**47***	**305***	**18544***	**0.39***
58	80	1883	9	1 972	94	400	33333	0.29
87	899	460	0	1 358	113	410	22593	0.19
94	563	758	0	1 321	43			
2		142	30	297	12	600	30000	
98	125							
110	211	486	248	944	63	300	18750	0.66
11	202	256	0	458	31	92	5667	0.40
49	112	156	41	309	31			
82	0	0	583	583	34	161	5943	0.39
83	144	0	595	739	31	146	6677	0.13
106	211	166	42	419	42	345	34500	0.82
24	209	233	0	442	22	292	9433	0.22
Education	**377***	**127***	**28***	**544***	**30***	**301***	**7379***	**0.43***
26	261	54	98	455	20	148	8714	0.35
71	456	243	37	737	67		.	
33	540	128	0	668	32	733	10667	0.90
30	16	84	14	249	18	30	2500	0.12
55	450	156	19	609	24	187	7480	0.31
68	541	95	0	541	18	406	7532	0.47
All	**293***	**312***	**100***	**712***	**41***	**304***	**14556***	**0.40***

* Is an average

The estimated cost depends mainly on the number of employees the company has, since a large proportion of the cost is made up of labor costs. Thus in order to compare companies it is necessary to look at the cost per employee and company each year planned is 41000 (std. dev. 28000) SEK. Consultancy companies have an average of total estimated cost per year of 803000 (std. dev. 540000) SEK which constitutes an estimated investment of around 47000 (std. dev. 31000) SEK per employee. Educational companies, on the other hand, have an average total estimated cost of 544000 (std. dev. 192000) SEK which comes to an average of 30000 (std. dev. 19000) SEK per employee.

Table 8.3 also presents the actual company investment in training for the last three years or the last year available. Not all companies were able to provide these figures, so in some cases approximations were requested. The sum of the average cost budgeted for training in the last three years, where data from 14 companies is available, is more than 4.2 million SEK. On average, companies invested around 304000 (std. dev. 198000) SEK in training in the last three years. Consultancy companies invested an average of 305000 (std. dev. 158000) SEK and educational companies 301000 (std. dev. 277000) SEK.

In order to compare different companies, it is more accurate to provide the actual investment in training per employee. This was only possible for the year 2002 since the number of employees in the last three years was not known. Thus for 2002, the average budgeted cost per employee was around 15000 (std. dev. 12000) SEK. The range goes from company 30 which budgeted 2500 SEK per employee to Company 106 which invested more than 34000 SEK. In consultancy the average expenditure on training is almost 19000 (std. dev. 12000) SEK, while in education it is little more than 7000 (std. dev. 3000) SEK.

There is data from 13 companies on both the budgeted cost of training and the estimated cost of all training needs in similar years. This allows for comparison between what a company would do in an ideal situation (what they propose to the ESF) with what the company actually did in the relevant year. The actual budgeted cost as a proportion of the total estimated cost in the relevant year is presented in Table 8.3. On average companies budgeted for around 40% of their training needs in the 13 companies for which there was data. It ranges from company 33 fulfilling 90% of their training needs (cost-wise) to company 30 investing only 12% of what they perceived as necessary. It is important to keep in mind that this is assuming that the ESF plans really do estimate all the training needs that the company has. It could be that companies only apply for a part of their training needs, in which case the proportion would appear bigger since the total actual cost would include training activities not included in the ESF plan. This, however, seems quite unlikely in light of the results, since the proportions are in general below 50%. Consultancy companies invest around 39% of their planned training while educational companies invest around 43%.

Training cost of the courses

The training cost per course is on average 32000 (std. dev. 45) SEK. The cheapest training event is an advertisement for on-the-job training in Company 26 that cost 400 SEK while the most expensive is a leadership-training event that costs 291000 SEK in Company 87. In consultancy, courses cost on average 35000 (std. dev. 44) SEK, while in education the average cost is 28000 (std. dev. 46000) SEK. The courses for consultancy are much more expensive in terms of direct costs at 22000 (std. dev. 29000) SEK compared to 9000 (std. dev. 11000) SEK in education. Educational companies, on the other hand, have higher labor costs at 21000 (std. dev. 39000) SEK compared to 15000 (std. dev. 30000) SEK in consultancy. Although the total estimated cost per course is not statistically significantly different at a 5% confidence level (probably due to the high standard deviations of the two groups), the direct cost is statistically different between the two sectors at a 1% level. This indicates that the overall cost of the courses is statistically similar but that consultancy companies pay higher direct costs than educational companies. This could be explained because educational companies might prefer to have more internal training events, where the majority of the cour-

Table 8.4: Estimated training cost per course

	Training events (with information on cost)	Labor training cost of the course each year	(Std. dev.)	Direct cost of the course each year	(Std. dev)	Other training cost of the course each year	(17)	Total training cost of the course each year	(44)	Total estimated cost per hour (in SEK)
Consultancy	264	15**	(30)	22**	(29)	6**	(17)	35**	(44)	609**
58	48	5	(06)	39	(42)			41	(44)	1703
87	11	82	(90)	42	(51)			123	(111)	585
94	44	13	(13)	17	(22)			30	(34)	471
2										.
98	16	16	(16)	20	(20)	4	(5)	37	(33)	525
110	31	7	(11)	16	(23)	8	(14)	30	(40)	806
11	39	10	(10)	13	(14)			23	(23)	351
49	18	9	(13)	15	(9)	3	(5)	26	(24)	505
82	18					32	(25)	32	(25)	.
83	27	48	(17)			22	(37)	27	(37)	.
106	12	16		15	(7)	4	(4)	19	(8)	200
24										.
Education	127	21**	(39)	9**	(11)	2**	(6)	28**	(46)	252**
26	38	9	(11)	5	(11)	4	(7)	14	(19)	215
71	25	18	(22)	10	(13)	1	(7)	29	(41)	254
33	10	54	(74)	13	(14)	0	(0)	67	(77)	228
30	16	9	(21)	7	(5)	1	(3)	16	(23)	405
55	21	29	(47)	12	(11)	2	(6)	38	(59)	332
68	17	32	(59)			0	(0)	32	(59)	116
All	391	18**	(34)	19**	(26)	5**	(15)	32**	(45)	467**

** Is an average calculated using all the courses not clustered by company

se costs are labor costs. Another reason is that education has a higher number of participants per course, thus their labor cost is higher since the number of employees influences the overall cost of the courses considerably.

Because of this, the cost per hour is a better parameter to compare companies and sectors. The cost on average for each hour of training in both sectors is 467 SEK (std. dev. 550); the direct cost is on average 328 (std. dev. 542) SEK per hour while the labor cost is on average 166 (std. dev. 74) SEK. The ANOVA between the two sectors shows that all hourly costs are statistically different at the 1% level (see Table IV.16 in Annex IV). Consultancy averages a total cost per hour of 609 (std. dev. 660) SEK, while education has an average of 252 (std. dev. 158) SEK per hour. The major difference is registered at the direct cost per hour where consultancy companies pay on average 401 (std. dev. 621) SEK while educational companies pay 151 (std. dev. 150) SEK on average. The difference in labor cost per hour is not as high: 182 (std. dev. 82) SEK for consultancy and 144 (std. dev. 53) SEK for education. This confirms that educational employees have lower salary levels, but the labor cost of their training is higher because more employees participate in each training event. It is important to note, however, that Company 58 in consultancy presents a very high cost per hour. This can affect the average of the whole consultancy group. However, the results are the same after redoing the ANOVA without Company 58.

Comparison with Swedish companies

As already indicated, it is possible to partially compare certain figures from the study with the general Swedish context using CVTS. However, it is important to keep in mind that CVTS represent actual figures of training and that CVTS might consider fewer courses than the present study. However, the comparison can be used to indicate roughly how accurate the estimated cost is with respect to the real cost. Also, the actual investment in training of 14 companies can be compared with the CVTS figure. Table 8.5 shows information on CVTS. For the last three years, these 14 companies had an average expenditure on training of around 304000 SEK. In CVTS2 the total cost per company in Sweden is around 167000 SEK for companies with 10 to 49 employees. This difference might be due to the fact that CVTS2 has a higher proportion of companies with fewer employees than our sample.

It is more interesting to compare the cost per participant and per employee in CVTS with the actual cost per employee in our sample. The total cost per training participant for Sweden is around 15000 SEK and the total cost per employee is around 9000 SEK (see Table 8.3). In the studied sample the actual investment in training per employee is around 15000 SEK. However, the total estimated cost per employee in the sample goes up to almost 41000 SEK. This clearly shows that, in general, companies would need a major increase in investment in training to cover their perceived needs. It also shows that the investment per employee is higher in the studied companies than for the average Swedish company.

Table 8.5: Aspects of training costs in Sweden in CVTS, 1999

	Labor cost per company (in 1000 SEK)	Other course cost (in 1000 SEK)	Total cost per company (in 1000 SEK)	Cost per employee (in 1000 SEK)	Total cost per participant (in 1000 SEK)	Total cost per hour
From 10 to 19	52	47	99	7	11	391
From 20 to 49	119	133	252	8	14	447
From 50 to 249	314	400	713	7	13	509
All training companies in Sweden	381	451	832	9	15	488

Source: European Commission, 2002b.

The cost per hour of training in all of Sweden is 488 SEK, while in the 18 companies the total estimated cost per hour is on average 467 SEK, which shows that the estimations are quite accurate (see Table 8.4). The difference between consultancy and education in this specific parameter was at a 1% level of significance. While it is not possible to compare consultancy and education in CVTS, it is possible to narrow the comparison to their service category; in the case of consultancy, "activities auxiliary to financial intermediation" and in the case of education "other services".

Consultancy averages a total estimated cost of 609 SEK per hour which is almost equal to the average in its sector in Sweden (610 SEK per hour). Education, on the other hand, averages 252 SEK per hour while its service family in Sweden averages 542 SEK per hour. This could be explained because "other activities" includes many other services that might have higher associated costs than the educational sector. In any case, it is clear that educational companies seem to have a lower training cost per hour than the majority of the sectors in Sweden.

It can be concluded that the estimated costs seem accurate since the costs per hour are relatively similar to the costs per hour in the Swedish context. The companies under study seem to invest around 54 % more per employee in training than companies in CVTS in Sweden. This could be explained by the extra help provided by the ESF. Meanwhile, the estimated cost per employee to fulfill all training needs is far higher than the actual investment.

8.2.4 Training subjects

Purpose of the training

The final features of training reviewed here are the purpose and the subject matter of the courses planned by the companies. Understanding the subject matter and purpose of company training will assist the exploration of how companies might or might not have similar training demands or needs.

The subject matter of the courses outlined below was determined by the course title and, in some cases, a description of the course content. There are two different codes used in this section. First, Table 8.6 refers to seven categories that relate to the purpose of the training event in relation to the professional role within the company. Second, Table 8.7 refers to the subject matter of the training events.

In terms of the information on training events in relation to the professional role within the company, seven categories were used inspired by Sveiby's personnel categories (see Chapter 4). They were categorized according to type of training: leadership skills, professional skills, support activity skills, ESF planning, and customer capital skills. The category labeled "leadership" deals with training that is directed toward improving leadership skills and normally targeted at managers and project leaders. "Professional" refers to training that is related to the professional activity that the specific company is involved with. It is training for teaching or for consultancy activities, accordingly. "Support" refers to training that is directed toward support activities, which includes training to learn software programs or the use of computers in general. It also includes training for certain administrative routines such as creating invoices and the like. In some cases it is quite difficult to categorize training as professional or support, since certain activities in areas such as auditing are very closely related to administrative training. When in doubt, the activity was registered as support and therefore this category might be overestimated and the category for professional role might be underestimated.

The category "ESF plan" refers to training activities related to ESF Measure 1.1 such as completing competence analyses. Finally, "customer capital" refers to training activities directed towards the promotion of customer relationships such as seminars with customers or the like.

Table 8.6: Training events and total training time by purpose and sector

Purpose of training	Number of events						Average training time (in hours)			Total time of training yearly (In hours)					
	Consultancy	%	Education	%	Both sectors	%	Consultancy	Education	Both sectors	Consultancy	%	Education	%	Both sectors	%
Customer capital	14	4	10	6	24	5	5	10	15	558	3	796	04	1354	04
ESF plan	14	4	6	4	20	4	14	6	20	1202	7	1998	11	3200	09
Leadership training	42	13	16	10	58	12	37	16	53	3823	2	1638	09	5461	15
Other training activities	18	5	2	1	20	4	14	2	16	1061	6	40	00	1101	03
Work improvement conditions	7	2	1	1	8	2	7	1	8	912	5	48	00	960	03
Professional training	152	46	86	53	238	48	97	67	164	6067	35	10263	56	16330	46
procon	152	46	0		152	31				6067	35		.		
protea	0		86	53	86	18						10263	56		
Support training	82	25	41	25	123	25	53	30	83	3760	22	3619	20	7379	21
supadm	21	6	4	2	25	5	11	4	15	252	1	196	01		01
supoth	4	1	1	1	5	1	4	0	4	312	2		0		
supIT	57	17	36	22	96	20	38	26	64	2785	16	3539	19		18
supITge	11	3	10	6	24	5	9	9	18	573	3	2238	12		08
supITpro	9	3	6	4	15	3	5	1	6	658	4	384	02		03
supITsp	24	7	13	8	37	8	16	12	28	1064	6	377	02		04
supITweb	13	4	7	4	20	4	8	4	12	490	3	540	03		03
All training events	**329**		**162**		**491**		**227**	**132**	**359**	**17383**		**18402**		**35785**	

Table 8.6 shows the number of events and hours by type of training, purpose and sector. Since 29% of the training events do not have training time registered both training events and total training time is presented. The training events are not as informative as the training time but they are more comprehensive since they show all the training needs. A total of 49% of all the training events are directed towards professional training, while 25% are directed towards support training and 12% directed towards leadership training. Both sectors show a major interest in professional training, followed by interest in training for support activities. The distributions are very similar for training events, although educational companies have relatively more professional training than in consultancy services.

In terms of total training time the patterns are relatively similar. Some 46% of the total training time is directed towards professional training. Educational companies are more focused on this type of training, 56% versus 35% in consultancy. In consultancy companies an important share of time is dedicated to other training objectives besides professional and support. The major difference between consultancy and education is in leadership training. Consultancy companies spend 22% of their time in leadership training while in education 9% of the total time is dedicated to leadership. On the other hand, educational companies devote more time to ESF competence analysis planning.

Support training is mainly directed towards computer related training. General training for computers (supITge) refers to training with the title "computer training". Training support IT professional (supITpro) refers to the training on certain computer software that is used in that specific service sector. It is considered support training since the individual does not develop professional knowledge although it is very closely related to the professional job that the individual does. Support IT training specific (supITsp) refers to training on a specific computer program such as word processor, or other similar types of software. Support training for web (supItweb) refers to training activities directed towards web design or learning how to use the Internet. Computer use training accounts for 19% of all the training events planned and 17% of the total training time estimated. Educational companies spend slightly more time and events directed towards computer training: 22% of the events and 19% of the training time in education versus 18% of the events and 16% of the training time in consultancy. For all the companies, 5% of all training events and 8% of the total training time is directed towards general computer training.

The distribution of training time by subject and company is presented in Table IV.17 in Annex IV. Company 68 provides 13% of the training time estimated for all companies, while it only provides a 3% of the training events. The opposite is the case for Company 49 which provides 10% of the training events and only 1% of the training time. This can be explained because Company 49 has many training events with no training time estimated. It is important, therefore to note that there is a big difference between what training events might show and what training time is indicating. In general, training time corresponds with training events, but in some cases they differ substantially.

Looking at how each company distributes their training events and time, one could say that there is no clear pattern. Companies differ in their interests, although overall, as already indicated, professional training is the most common training area, both in time and events. In terms of time, Companies 33 and 24 spend more than 10% of their time in customer capital activities. Company 30 is the one that, relative to its total time, directs the most time towards ESF competence analysis (43%), although it is just registered as one training event. In terms of training for leadership skills, Company 87 directs 54% of its estimated training time. In "work improvement conditions", Company 106 directs 15% of its time, where no other company spends more than 10%. Professional training is the most common training purpose; six companies plan for more than 50% of their training time for this purpose. Company 11 is the one with the highest proportion of training time estimated for this purpose at 78%. Finally, Company 106 is the one that directs the most training towards support purposes with 47% of its time.

Subject classification: ISCED classification

Training events were also codified with the ISCED 97 fields of education and training classification (EUROSTAT, 1999). The fields where determined from the course title and the description if available. The ISCED 97 is a classification with three hierarchical levels; the second level is used here. In the codification of education training events if possible, the subjects where not codified as "teacher training and education science" (code 14 in the ISCED 97) because this would not provide any additional information. When used, this category only refers to training in pedagogy or similar subjects.

Business administration was the subject of most interest to the companies (see Table 8.7). For all the companies 37% of their estimated training time was dedicated to business administration. It was most common in both consultancy (37% of training time) and education (28% of training time). Computing was the second most common subject also in both sectors. Educational companies plan for 24% of all their time for computer training while for consultancy the figure is 18%. The third most common subject in the overall sample, above the 10% line of estimated time, was "teacher and educational science". This is not surprising since 40% of the companies and more than 50% of the total estimated time for training falls within the educational sector. However, surprisingly, companies in sectors "labor recruitment" and "technical testing and analysis" also dedicate some time to "teacher and educational science."

The rest of the subjects are related in some way to the type of activity the company carries out. Sector "architectural and engineering activities" has 27% of its estimated time for "architectural and building science". Sector "technical testing and analysis" has 53% of its time dedicated towards "engineering and other related subjects". Sectors "legal activities", "advertising" and "labor recruitment" are all among the sectors that are mainly interested in business administration and computing.

In the educational sector, teacher training and educational science consume 15% of the estimated time for primary schools, 48% for the secondary school and 28% for the adult education sector. Computing is also an important subject for all the educational sectors.

Table 8.7: Total estimated training time by subject (ISCED 97) and sector

	Consultancy		Education		TOTAL	
	Time (in hours)	%	Time (in hours)	%	Time (in hours)	%
Business and administration	7406	43	5744	31	13150	37
Computing	3290	19	4203	23	7493	21
Teacher training and educational science	112	1	4944	27	5056	14
Unspecified	865	5	742	4	1607	5
Personal skills	1139	7	459	3	1598	5
Engineering and engineering trades	1352	8	0	0	1352	4
Arts	252	1	722	4	974	3
Security services	912	5	48	0	960	3
Humanities	565	3	256	1	821	2
Architecture and building	780	5	0	0	780	2
Others	710	4	1284	7	1994	6
All subjects	17383	100	18402	100	35785	100
N. of valid companies	9	75	6	100	15	83

8.3 Informal learning

Chapter 3 indicated that informal learning plays a crucial role in lifelong learning. Chapter 2 argued for the importance of tacit knowledge in developing innovation. Informal learning is probably the main means of acquiring tacit knowledge, if informal learning is considered as the process of unconsciously acquiring new knowledge through our daily activity, just by doing. However, this type of informal learning is very complicated to grasp and to measure. This is why it was decided to follow the European definition of informal learning (see Chapter 3, Table 3.1).

The questionnaire included seven items related to informal learning. The employees where asked to determine how often they engaged in seven different activities on a five point Likert-scale from "never or almost never" to "very often". Averaging the scores in all seven activities (see Chapter 6 for a justification of using averages from Likert-scales), for all 18 companies resulted in an average of 3.37 (std. dev. 0.29). All companies except three (Company 2, 11 and 26) scored higher than three, which could be considered a neutral point in terms of informal learning engagement. One could argue that in general, employees of the companies (at least the ones that responded) have a certain engagement in informal learning activities. Company 68 and Company 83 have the highest average score at 3.54 for the seven activities. Activity d2: "going on guided tours to museums or galleries" and d7: "learning by reading job-related news on the Internet" were the least engaging for employees. Activity d2 averages a score of 2.73 (std. dev. 0.46) and d7 averages 2.94 (std. dev. 0.78). Activity d6, "Learning by myself trying things out, doing things for practice, trying different approaches to do things" is the activity with the highest average score, 3.97 (std. dev. 0.49). The activity d1 refers to "read manuals, reference books, journals or other written materials not part of a

Table 8.8: Respondent's informal learning activities by sector

	Consultancy			Education			Both sectors		
	N	Mean*	Std. Dev.	N	Mean*	Std. Dev.	N	Mean*	Std. Dev.
d1 Read manuals, reference books, journals or other written materials but not as part of a course.	105	3.66	0.45	58	3.94	0.31	163	3.75	0.42
d2 Went on guided tours at a museum, art gallery or other such cultural facilities	106	2.68	0.41	59	2.82	0.58	165	2.73	0.46
d3 Used media- assisted products to learn such as computers, video, television, tapes that were NOT part of a course.	105	2.86	0.42	59	3.50	0.61	164	3.07	0.56
d4 Asked my colleagues for help when I have a problem in my work	106	3.68	0.37	59	3.74	0.27	165	3.70	0.34
d5 Learned by watching, getting help or advice from others - but NOT from course instructors	104	3.41	0.33	57	3.38	0.34	161	3.40	0.32
d6 Learned by myself trying things out, doing things for practice, trying different approaches to do things	105	3.84	0.53	55	4.24	0.29	160	3.97	0.49
d7 Learned by reading job-related news on the Internet.	106	3.07	0.54	59	2.67	1.15	165	2.94	0.78
Average of all the informal learning activities	102	3.31	0.26	54	3.47	0.35	156	3.37	0.29

* Averages and std. dev. are calculated from the companies' average scores

course". It averages 3.75 (std. dev. 0.42) for the whole sample. Activity d3, "use media-assisted products to learn such as computer, video, television, tapes that were NOT part of a course" has an overall average of 3.07 (std. dev. 0.56). The activity d4, "ask my colleagues for help when I have a problem in my work" scored 3.70 (std. dev. 0.34) on average for all the companies. Activity d5, "learnt by watching, getting help or advice from other- but NOT from course instructors", scores on average for all the companies 3.40 (std. dev. 0.32). Thus it seems employees appear to engage the most in learning by doing (activity d6).

Overall, educational and consultancy companies do not differ statistically in their engagement in informal learning: however, it seems employees in educational companies engage more in certain learning activities. This is the case for activity d1 "read manuals, reference books, journals or other written materials not part of a course". The average in consultancy is 3.66 (std. dev. 0.45) while in education it is 3.94 (std. dev. 0.31). They are statistically different at 5% if one uses each questionnaire independently (n = 162 questionnaires). This means that employees in education seem to read more as a learning activity. Activity d3, "using media-assisted products to learn not part of a course" also presents a statistical difference between the sectors at a 1% level (n = 163). In d3, consultancy companies average 2.86 (std. dev. 0.42) while educational company employees present a higher average, 3.50 (std. dev. 0.61). Activity d6, "Learning by myself, trying things out, doing things for practice, trying different approaches to do things", also presents a statistically significant difference between sectors at the 5% level. Consultancy companies average a total of 3.84 (std. dev. 0.53) points while educational average 4.24 (std. dev. 0.29) (n= 159).

8.4 Patterns, similarities and differences within the learning arenas

8.4.1 Summary of the descriptive analysis

The previous three sections described the plans and activities directed toward the creation of knowledge for the companies under study. This section presents how the different aspects of knowledge creation efforts are related to each other. The study focused mainly on formal and non-formal training activities, since the measurement of informal learning is so much more complicated. The predominant focus is on company determined estimated training needs. From this perspective, each employee needs an estimated average of seven courses and around 111 hours (almost 3 working weeks) of training to remain competitive. This is translated into a total estimated cost per employee of 712000 SEK. The actual investment in monetary terms is around 40% of this total estimated cost. An average of about 31% of the employees in each company attends the same courses. The average duration of each course is 26 hours. Consultancy and education do not differ statistically in these parameters with one exception; educational employees attend longer courses.

The overall cost of the training courses does not differ in the two sectors, but the cost per hour is higher and statistically different at the 5% level in consultancy. Consultancy companies pay a higher direct cost, while educational companies pay a higher labor cost since more employees go to each course.

In terms of training purpose, the most important is directed towards professional training and secondly to support roles. Educational companies have a higher proportion of time and events for these training purposes than consultancy companies. Looking at the subject area, both sectors have a high percentage of training dedicated to business administration as well as computer science and use. After these two general subjects, the training is usually geared toward the area of company activity.

Finally, some attention was given to informal learning engagement. Employees seem to engage regularly in informal learning activities, especially in reading manuals and other written materials as well as in trying new things. Educational companies appear to have employees that report higher levels of engagement in informal learning in reading manuals that are not part of a course, in using media assisted products that are not part of a course and in trying new things. In these three items educational employees scored statistically higher than consultancy employees at a 5% level of significance.

To sum up, one could argue that educational and consultancy companies seem to be quite similar in terms of their demand for learning. There are not major differences between sectors except in the case of the cost of the courses, where consultancy has much higher direct costs and education has higher labor costs. Also educational companies seem to have slightly more engagement in informal learning among their employees.

8.4.2 Relationships among specific indicators for knowledge-creation

From the previous descriptive analysis, eight indicators were chosen as those which would allow comparison between the companies and to capture the companies' knowledge creation efforts. The seven indicators are: (1) training estimated time per employee each year ($trTemp$, median = 85 hours); (2) average number of training events that each employee demands ($trPemp$, median = 6 courses); (3) total training estimated cost per employee ($trCTemp$, median = 30903 SEK); (4) actual total training expenditure per employee ($trActemp$, median = 9074 SEK); (5) actual expenditure as a proportion of the total estimated training cost ($trActPer$, median = 0.35); (6) total training estimated cost per hour of training ($trctT$, median = 378 SEK); and, (7) the company's average of the informal learning activities items ($d17$, median = 3.45). All the indicators are continuous variables and therefore it is possible to correlate them without having to follow the median-split method. However, it is important to keep in mind that the Pearson correlation can be biased because of outliers in the sample.

The Pearson correlation among the knowledge-creation indicators (see Table 8.9) shows that estimated training time per employee ($trTemp$) correlates positively with actual training expenditure per employee ($trActemp$) ($r = 0.69$) and with actual training expenditure as a proportion of the total estimated cost ($trActPer$) ($r = 0.51$). The total estimated training cost

Table 8.9: Bivariate Pearson correlations of the knowledge creating indicators (above 0.20)

	trTemp	trPemp	trCTemp	trActemp	trActPer	trctT	d17
Yearly training estimated time per employee (trTemp)	1.00						
Average number of training events that each employee demands (trPemp)		1.00					
Total training estimated cost per employee (trCTemp)	0.37		1.00				
Actual total training expenditure per employee (trActemp)	0.69		0.73	1.00			
Actual expenditure as a proportion of the total estimated training cost (trActPer)	0.51			0.33	1.00		
Total training estimated cost per hour of training (trctT)	-0.48		0.60		-0.53	1.00	
Company's average of the informal learning activities items (d17)		-0.34		-0.29			1.00

per employee (*trCTemp*) correlates positively with actual training expenditure per employee (*trActemp*) (r = 0.73) and with the total estimated training cost per hour (*trctT*)(r = 0.60). Company 58 which has high scores in both indicators probably strengthens this last correlation. The estimated training cost per hour (*trctT*) correlates negatively with the actual training expenditure as a proportion of the total estimated cost (*trActPer*) (r = -0.53) and with the estimated training time per employee (*trTemp*) (r = -0.48). Also interesting, although the correlation is weaker, is that the number of training events that each employee demands (*trPemp*) correlates negatively with informal learning engagement (*dl7*) (r= -0.34). That Company 26 has a high average for employees' training demand and low engagement in informal learning might influence this correlation.

A factor analysis of these indicators reveals three components that explain 86% of the variance (see Table IV.19 and IV.20 in Annex IV). The first component includes all the indicators that relate to training time and cost per employee. It is referred to as (A) the training effort per employee in each company. The second component includes the actual training expenditure as a proportion of the total estimated cost and the total training cost per hour. They represent the two poles of the dimension. It is referred to as (B) the monetary effort in training of the company. Finally, the third includes number of training events demanded per employee and engagement in informal learning activities. The former is positively related to the component and the latter is negatively related. This dimension is referred as (C) the demand for formal learning.

These components appear to show, as seems logical, that companies where employees demand more time for training, estimate more cost per employee and spend more per employee. In addition, if the cost per hour of training is high, companies tend to spend less on training. Finally, it seems that employees demand less training events if their engagement in informal learning is high. Also interesting is that higher estimated training time and cost per employee is associated with having higher employee's demand for training. In general terms, the sample seems to show that the indicators relate positively to each other, except in the case of informal learning engagement and cost per hour that are negatively related to some of the other indicators.

Generally, the indicators behave in a similar way in education and consultancy. Only with regard to the indicator of informal learning engagement do the two sectors differ in some relationships. While in consultancy the relationship of informal learning engagement with all the rest of indicators is positive or around zero, for education most of the relationships with this indicator are negative.

8.5 The training arenas and the enabling constructs

After looking at the relationships among the different indicators of the creation of knowledge in the selected companies, it is possible to study its relationship with the knowledge-enabling environment aspects presented in Chapter 7. The assumption is that the overall knowledge-intensiveness of a company should correlate positively with the knowledge-creation effort of the company.

The indicators for the demand for training and informal learning were transformed into binary scales using the median split method (see Table 8.10) so that they could be seen in relationship to the knowledge-enabling constructs presented in Chapter 7 (see Table 7.3). The Pearson correlations of these relationships are presented in Table 8.11. The first interesting correlation occurs between actual expenditure per employee (*trActemp*) and experience of the workforce; companies seem to invest more per employee the more experienced the workforce is (r = 0.58). In addition, higher actual expenditure per employee (*trActemp*) seems to be associated with having more tacit orientation in the recruitment process (r = 0.43). There is also a positive relationship between actual investment per employee and stability of the workforce (r = 0.32).

Total training estimated cost per hour (*trctT*) and the individual stipulation of the salary (*reward system*) level are negatively correlated (r = -0.63). Thus, it seems that companies that determine salaries in a more individualized way choose "cheaper" courses. Individual stipulation of the salary level is associated positively with actual training expenditure as a percentage of the total estimated training cost (*trActPer*) (r=0.39), the more investment the more likely it is that the salaries are stipulated individually. Actual investment in training as a proportion of the total estimated cost (*trActPer*) correlates positively with communication intensiveness (r = 0.41) and with investment in IT (r = 0.55) as well as with the overall knowledge intensiveness scale (*kisall*) (r=0.55). Informal learning engagement (*dl7*) is negatively related to the stability of the workforce (r =- 0.34) but positively related to IT investment (r = 0.42). So companies which have more new technologies demand more informal learning from their employees. It also seems reasonable that there is less informal learning in companies where employees have been working for a long time and have more stability.

Finally, it is interesting that employee demand for training (*trPemp*) is negatively correlated with *size* (r= -0.33), *communication* (r = -0.33), tacit orientation of the recruitment process (*recruitment*) (r = -0.33), and the overall knowledge intensive scale (*kisall*) (r=-0.33). Training time per employee (*trTemp*) also has a negative correlation with *professionalism* (r = -0.33).

These relationships seem to show that higher investment in training is associated with an overall higher level of knowledge intensiveness. It appears that employees demand more learning in companies where the knowledge-enabling environment is poorer. More surprising

Table 8.10: Knowledge-creation indicators binary recoded through the median split method by company and sector

Company ID	trTemp	trPemp	trCTemp	trActemp	trActPer	trctT	dl7
Consultancy	0.44	0.70	0.60	0.67	0.50	0.75	0.42
2	.	High	.	High	.	.	Low
11	High	High	Low	High	High	Low	Low
24	Low	Low	Low	High	Low	.	High
49	Low	High	.	Low	High	High	Low
58	Low	High	High	.	.	High	Low
82	.	Low	High	Low	High	.	High
83	.	High	Low	Low	Low	.	High
87	High	Low	High	High	Low	High	High
94	High	Low	High	High	Low	High	Low
98	Low	Low	Low	.	.	High	Low
106	High	High	High	High	High	Low	High
110	Low	High	High	.	.	High	Low
Education	0.67	0.33	0.33	0.20	0.40	0.17	0.67
26	High	High	Low	Low	Low	Low	Low
30	Low	Low	Low	Low	Low	High	High
33	High	Low	High	High	High	Low	High
55	Low	Low	Low	Low	Low	Low	High
68	High	Low	Low	Low	High	Low	High
71	High	High	High	.	.	Low	Low
All	0.53	0.50	0.50	0.50	0.43	0.50	0.50

Table 8.11: Bivariate Pearson correlation between knowledge-enabling constructs and knowledge-creation indicators (above 0.20)

	trTemp	trPemp	trCTemp	trActemp	trActPer	trctT	d17
Size		-0.33					
Stability				0.32			-0.34
Experience				0.58			
Professionalism	-0.33						
Recruitment		-0.33		0.43			
Reward system					0.39	-0.63	
Communication		-0.33		0.41			
IT			0.46		0.55		0.42
kisall		-0.33			0.55		
CCI							-0.33

is the fact that informal learning engagement is weakly or negatively related to knowledge intensiveness, except in the case of IT investment. This appears to indicate that employees will demand more formal training and try to engage more in informal learning activities in companies where the knowledge-enabling environment is poorer. IT investment seems to be a motor for a positive orientation towards creation of knowledge.

Similarities and differences in consultancy and educational companies

It is important to note that most of the above relationships can be explained by the different characteristics of the knowledge-creation environment in each sector (see Table 8.10). In this way, education has a higher proportion of companies above the median in training time per employee (*trTemp*) and in informal learning engagement (*d17*), but a lower proportion of companies in all the rest. The only indicator in knowledge-creation that balanced with similar proportions in both sectors is the actual expenditure in education as a proportion of the total estimated cost (*trActPer*).

Most of the relationships outlined for both sectors, however, are maintained when considering education and consultancy separately (see Table V.21 in Annex IV). Both sectors present similar negative relationships between training courses demanded per employee (*trPemp*) and tacitness of the recruitment process and communication intensiveness. Training courses demanded per employee (*trPemp*) is also negatively correlated with the overall knowledge intensive scale (*kisall*). Both sectors present positive correlations between actual training expenditure as a proportion of the total estimated cost (*trActPer*) and investment in IT (*IT*), and between the former and the overall knowledge intensiveness scale (*kisall*). This is also the case between investment in IT (*IT*) and informal learning activities (*d17*). The main differences between the two sectors are in the relationship between actual training expenditure per employee (*trActemp*) and tacit orientation of the recruitment process, where consultancy presents a negative relationship while education presents a positive one. This is also the case in professionalism with training time per employee (*trTemp*) and estimated training cost per employee (*trCTemp*). Consultancy and education also differ in the relationship between size and actual total expenditure in training as a percentage of the total estimated cost (*trActPer*), where consultancy presents a negative correlation and education a positive one.

Thus, in general, there are a lot of similarities in education and consultancy in the directions of the relationships among knowledge-creation indicators and knowledge-enabling environment constructs. These similarities appear when considering both sectors together.

The differences appear mainly related to professionalism, where consultancy is more negatively related to the knowledge-creation indicators. That is to say, the more professionalism the less knowledge creation that seems to appear in consultancy companies; while this is generally the opposite in education. It is also interesting to note that educational companies have more positive relationships between informal learning activities and the knowledge-enabling constructs, while in the case of consultancy the relationships are either very weak or negative. Likewise relationships in the overall sample are often weak due to the bias created by the large number of consultancy companies in the sample.

8.6 Knowledge-creation indicators in relation to certain effectiveness indicators

The binary recoded indicators for knowledge-creation were related to the selected company effectiveness indicators. Actual expenditure in training as a percentage of total estimated cost correlates positively with the profit per employee (r= 0.54). This seems to indicate that the companies with higher investments in training obtain higher revenue per employee. However, if companies invest more in training per employee they seem to obtain less profit as a percentage of the total monetary turnover (r =-0.31). Training cost per hour is negatively related with product innovation in the last year (r = -0.37). This is probably due to the differences between education and consultancy in terms of product innovation. Consultancy companies have higher salaries which make training costs higher and they have less product innovation. Another interesting and surprising relationship appears between informal learning activities and the Collaborative Climate Index. Companies that have an overall high collaborative climate seem to have less informal learning engagement by their employees (r =- 0.33). This is somewhat surprising since some of the questions on collaborative climate are closely related to informal learning activities.

In conclusion, it seems that the indicators on knowledge-creation have weak or negative relationships with the indicators on effectiveness. However, to some degree, companies that invest more in training seem to get higher revenues from their employees. The relationship between effectiveness and knowledge creation is mainly explained by the difference in the sectors.

Table 8.12: Pearson correlation among knowledge-creation and effectiveness indicators (above 0.20)

	trTemp	trPemp	trCTemp	trActemp	trActPer	trctT	dl7
CCI	-0.20				-0.24		-0.33
Employee turnover							
Product innovation		-0.26		0.24		-0.37	
% of profit	-0.24	0.29		-0.31	0.21		
Profit per employee		0.29			0.54		

8.7 Summary and Synthesis

This chapter explored through analysis and comparison the companies' perceived needs for continuous competence development. From the study of formal and non-formal training needs, one of the major conclusions is that despite investing more in training than their average Swedish counterparts, the companies under study invest only around 40% of what would be needed to fulfill their perceived needs. The companies mainly provide training for professional purposes and the subjects of interest are usually associated with the activity in which the company is engaged. However, the training needs do not seem very specific. Both sectors plan an goodly proportion of training events and time for general computer training and business administration. Education and consultancy do not present major differences in terms of educational needs. Where they do differ is in the cost of training; consultancy has higher direct costs and education pays higher labor costs per course. Educational companies tend to plan for longer courses with more employees involved.

In terms of informal learning, employees seem to engage regularly in informal learning activities. Educational companies present a workforce more engaged in informal learning activities than consultancy companies.

Seven indicators were selected in order to grasp the overall knowledge-creation effort of the company: (1) estimated training time per employee each year; (2) number of training events that each employee demands; (3) total estimated training cost per employee; (4) actual total training expenditure per employee; (5) actual training expenditure as a percentage of the total estimated training cost in the relevant year(s); (6) total training cost per hour; and, (7) the company's average of the informal learning activity items. These seven indicators were divided into three factors: (A) the training effort per employee; (B) monetary effort in training of the company; and, (C) the demand for formal learning. (A) The training effort per employee is composed of indicators (1) estimated training time per employee, (3) the estimated training cost per employee and, (4) the actual training expenditure per employee. (B) Monetary effort in training of the company is captured in a dimension where indicators (5) actual training expenditure and (6) estimated training cost per hour present a negative association. Finally, (C) the demand for formal learning is also captured in a dimension where indicators (2) the demand for training per employee and (7) the informal learning engagement present a negative relationship. It seems, thus, that employees demand more training if their engagement in informal learning is low. This, although logical, goes against the assumption of the "long-arm of the job" where more informal learning is generally associated with higher demand for formalized training.

The chapter also explored the relationship between the knowledge enabling-environment and the demand for training, or in other words, between the enabling environment and the creation of knowledge. The knowledge-enabling constructs do not present strong relationships with the knowledge-creation indicators. It seems that in general, the overall scale of intensiveness correlates positively with the investment in training but negatively with the demand for training. This goes against the assumption that a knowledge-intensive environment should encourage the demand for learning. To some degree, it seems that employees compensate poor knowledge-enabling conditions with higher demand for learning and through engaging in informal learning activities. IT investment is associated positively with most of the knowledge-creation indicators.

Finally, the knowledge-creation indicators present a weak relationship with the effectiveness indicators; only actual training investment as a proportion of the total estimated training cost seems to be positively associated with employee effectiveness. It is surprising that, in general, the knowledge-creation indicators relate negatively to the Collaborative Climate Index.

To conclude, it is important to mention that differences between consultancy and education seem to be steadier in the knowledge-creation, than in the knowledge-enabling environment. This might explain, for example, why informal learning is negatively related with many of the indicators.

PART V CONCLUSIONS AND FURTHER RESEARCH

CHAPTER 9: CONCLUSIONS

9.1 Summary of the findings

This study started by stating that knowledge differs from information and that tacit knowledge and explicit knowledge are different and they require different types of business processes in order to be managed. The dissertation defends the idea that knowledge has to be both understood as content and as mental structure and that it constantly changes through our interaction with the environment. Thus, knowledge and learning are impossible to separate. In the learning process information is transformed into knowledge, while in the teaching process knowledge is translated into information.

Organizations, in general, and knowledge-intensive organizations, in particular, are more than ever faced with the necessity of continuously updating their employee's knowledge; or in other words, they have to promote constant learning. In policy terms, this is referred to as making organizations into "learning organizations" and making employees into "lifelong learners". In this way, organizations are meant to provide formal training as well as informal learning opportunities.

The purpose of this study was to explore the management of knowledge in relation to the demand for training in small, private knowledge-intensive business. The dissertation illustrates a hypothetical model for managing knowledge through the exploration of 18 selected companies. The model is divided in three main parts: the knowledge-enabling environment, learning arenas, and the use of knowledge. The exploration of the two first parts constitutes the core of the thesis. In addition, the connection of the knowledge-enabling environment and the learning arenas with the use of knowledge is explored through the analysis of certain effectiveness measurements. The knowledge-enabling environment refers to the specific daily business activities that in theory create conditions for the creation of knowledge. Learning arenas refer to planned company activities specifically directed towards learning; they refer, thus, to the processes directed specifically towards the creation of knowledge. The main focus of the study has been the demand for training where training was planned for all employees. Some attention has also been placed on informal learning activities.

Data on demand for training was available because all the selected companies participated in the Priority 1, "Competence development for employees", of Objective 3 of the European Social Fund Council in Sweden: "Supporting the adaptation and modernization of education, training and employment policies and systems". In Measure 1.1 of Priority 1, companies are obliged to analyze their business activity and provide an estimation of their entire workforce's training needs. This data, therefore, provides a unique opportunity to study training demand in SME companies. As such, this also implies that the data come from particular types of companies that are specifically interested in promoting their employees' knowledge. Because of this, one must be careful in making generalizations from the results. It is also important to note that the companies operate in Sweden, where the conditions for research, innovation and training are more ideal than in many European countries.

The knowledge-enabling environment

The major conclusion from the descriptive analysis of the 18 companies is that despite the similarities in the services they provide, companies present a high variability in the different aspects studied. Companies differ considerably in the composition of their workforce, the way they select and recruit employees, the way they provide bonuses, the way they structure their work, in their communication activities, and in their investment in IT. Based on this descriptive analysis, an exploration of the most important aspects of the knowledge-enabling environment was undertaken. These aspects were captured by seven constructs which were created and used together with the construct of size. These eight constructs are: (1) size of the company; (2) workforce stability; (3) workforce experience; (4) professional orientation of the company; (5) tacit orientation of the recruitment process; (6) monetary reward system; (7) communication intensiveness; and, (8) investment in IT. These constructs, with the exception of size, were grouped in an overall scale to measure the knowledge intensiveness of a company.

Analysis of the eight constructs shows that companies present a high degree of variability in their knowledge-enabling environment. Each company, thus, has a unique way of managing their knowledge; it was not possible to identify similar patterns among the companies. The relationship between the knowledge-enabling constructs was relatively weak. Only workforce stability and experience showed a positive significant relationship. The weak or non-relationship among knowledge-enabling constructs might, in part, be due to a seeming inconsistency between the different indicators within each construct. Another way of saying this is that the constructs are composed of aspects that each company uses differently. One could say that each company is unique in their approach to managing knowledge.

The relationships between the construct indicators of size, stability of the workforce, experience, and tacit orientation of the recruitment process can be explained by the service the company provides: consultancy or education. However, other relationships do not appear to be associated with the company activity and thus further exploration might be worthwhile. For example, the data shows that higher stability among employees is associated with lower communication intensiveness. This can be related to the idea of creative chaos defended by Nonaka and Takeuchi (1995). They suggest that less stability generates more communication among employees which in turn can create more innovation and insights. Also interesting to note is that the study indicated that companies with higher professionalism have less communication among employees which is in line with the characterization of professional workers presented by Sveiby (1997). It was also found that having cross-functional teams and a mentor system is associated with having a higher level of communication in a company which is in line with Nonaka and Takeuchi's characterization of a knowledge creating company (see Nonaka, 1991, Nonaka and Takeuchi, 1995). The seven constructs for a knowledge-enabling environment have a similar distribution in both sectors, or in other words, consultancy and education generally have similar knowledge-enabling environments.

The learning arenas

In relation to learning arenas, the study emphasized the demand for training. The study focused mainly on formal and non-formal training activities, specifically on company identified estimated training needs. The average estimate for each employee was seven courses and around 111 hours (almost 3 working weeks) of training. The 18 companies studied invest more in training than the average for Swedish companies. However the companies only invest around 40% of their total estimated training costs in monetary terms. On average around 31% of the employees attend the same courses in each company. The average duration of each course is 26 hours. Consultancy and education do not differ in estimated training time, cost or participation, except in the case of course duration where educational employees attend longer courses. The overall cost of the courses does not differ in the two sectors, but the cost per hour is higher in consultancy. Consultancy companies pay higher direct costs, while educational companies pay higher labor costs since more employees go to each course. The study of the purpose and subject matter of the training events indicate that the training is mainly directed towards professionals, which is in consonance with their workforce composition. Companies also seem to plan for general rather than specific training. It might be that the planned training is rather general because an external body, the ESF Council in Sweden, helps finance the training. This would be in line with economic theories within the human capital framework (Becker, 1962, 1993). Some attention was also given to informal learning engagement. Employees seem to engage regularly in informal learning activities, especially in reading manuals and other written materials that are not part of a course as well as in trying new things.

Seven indicators were selected in order to grasp the overall knowledge-creation effort of a company: (1) estimated training time per employee each year; (2) number of training events that each employee demands; (3) total estimated training cost per employee; (4) actual total training expenditure per employee; (5) actual training expenditure as a percentage of the total estimated training cost in the relevant year(s); (6) total training cost per hour; and, (7) the company's average of the informal learning activity items. These seven indicators were grouped into three main factors: (A) the training effort per employee, composed of (1), (3), and (4); (B) monetary effort in training of the company, composed of (5) and (6) negatively associated; and, (C) the demand for formal learning, composed of (2) and (7) negatively associated. The analysis indicated that companies that estimate more training events, estimate higher costs and invest more per employee. It also showed that companies invest less if the cost per employee is higher. And finally, employees seem to demand more formal training if they are less engaged in informal learning. This last relationship seems to indicate that formal learning compensates for lower levels of informal learning engagement or vice versa.

The differences between consultancy and education in the knowledge creation indicators are clearer than in the knowledge-enabling constructs, as could be expected from the descriptive analysis of the training demand. Education and consultancy only have a similar proportion of companies below and above the median in (5) actual training expenditure as a percentage of the total estimated training cost in the relevant year(s). The differences in the other indicators might be partially explained by the high salary levels that consultancy companies have in comparison to educational companies. This explains why consultancy companies have more companies above the median in (3) estimated training cost per employee, (4) actual expenditure per employee, and (6) training cost per hour. They also have a high proportion of companies above the median in (2) number of training events that each employee demands. This is associated with lower levels of informal learning engagement. It seems, therefore, that employees in education engage more in informal learning activities, while in consultancy companies, employees seem keener on participating in more formalized learning activities. However, it is interesting to note that generally the associations between the knowledge-creation indicators in education and consultancy have similar directions.

The relationship between the knowledge-enabling constructs and the knowledge-creation (or learning arenas) indicators is weak. This could in part be due to the differences between the consultancy and education sectors. However, generally, in both sectors the working-environment characteristics that theoretically promote learning, that is the knowledge-enabling environment, do not necessarily promote a higher demand for learning. This is contrary to the primary assumption of this dissertation that the existence of knowledge-enabling characteristics will be related to a higher demand for training. On the other hand, it also seems that companies that have more stability and more experience in their workforce invest more in training. This is in line with previous findings on the demand and supply for learning. Also in line with previous studies on the demand for learning is that higher IT investment seems to be associated with higher levels of training demand and investment in knowledge creation activities.

The use of knowledge

Finally, the dissertation explored the relationship between knowledge-enabling environment and the knowledge creation aspects with specific business effectiveness indicators such as: the Collaborative Climate Index, employee turnover, product innovation, percentage of profit and profit per employee. These relationships must be considered carefully, since there are likely to be numerous potentially explanatory intervening variables. However, the study might indicate certain directions for future research. It is interesting to note that product innovation is associated with individual stipulation of salaries. This is in line with the idea that individualized reward promotes higher incentives for innovation. Product innovation is negatively related to professionalism within a company. Since, higher levels of professionalism is associated with less support staff in the company, it seems that having fewer support members in the company might reduce the free time for professionals have to develop new services. Also noteworthy is that a collaborative climate among employees does not present a clear association with the knowledge-enabling constructs and presents a negative association with the knowledge-creation indicators. This could be explained by there being other factors not grasped in the scales that are somehow affecting the collaborative climate. Profit per employee is positively related to actual expenditure in training. This points to there being a positive relationship between effectiveness and training. However, communication intensiveness seems to be negatively associated with companies' profitability.

Generalization of these results must be done cautiously. It is important to keep in mind that the 18 companies can only be an illustration of the possible theoretical relationships presented in Chapter 4. The data collected comes from a particular set of companies in particular circumstances. It is not clear that this demand for training is representative of what companies might demand if not associated with the receipt of training assistance from an external source. In addition, it is not clear to what extent these companies are archetypical of a knowledge-intensive SME company in Sweden. It is, however, very likely that they represent companies interested in the promotion of employee's skills development.

The results seem to indicate that knowledge-intensive companies manage their knowledge in different, unique ways and that there are no strong relationships among the different aspects explored. In other words, companies differ in their knowledge-enabling environments, which complicate any determination as to what extent knowledge-enabling environments affect the demand for training and knowledge creation. With regard to the sectors, education and consultancy, they are relatively similar in their knowledge-enabling environments but differ considerably in their knowledge creation activities.

9.2 Theoretical model re-visited

This study used a hypothetical model for knowledge management in SMEs in Sweden. The model presented in Chapter 4 was used as a "map" to guide the exploration of knowledge management in 18 companies. The model was based on the conceptualization of knowledge described in Chapter 2. This model integrates different perspectives related to knowledge management in organizations as presented in Chapter 3. In this way, the model presents an interesting proposal for looking at each company's specific daily business activities from knowledge-enabling and knowledge-creation perspectives. The model contributes to the development of the emergent knowledge management field. It integrates different disciplines and insights from various areas. Especially interesting is the attempt to integrate the life-wide dimension of learning into the proposals for knowledge management. Knowledge management has usually been studied from a management or economic perspective, but there are few attempts to look at it from a learning perspective. In this way, the model can have some political usefulness in terms of integrating knowledge management with the mainstream educational policy idea of lifelong learning.

The empirical results have shown that the a-priori theoretically related indicators within each of the knowledge-enabling constructs are relatively independent from each other. Accordingly, the internal validity of such constructs is uncertain in this empirical example, and therefore the usefulness of the constructs is questionable. It might be necessary to divide the knowledge-enabling environment into "smaller bits" that have more internal consistency. The problem in doing so is the high degree of complexity, due to the large number of variables required and the amount of variability within each variable, thus making interpretation of the results extremely difficult. The median-split method has proved to be a valuable tool for simplifying complex data into binary indicators which allows for easier analysis. However, it might be that too much information is missed in the process which creates problems when trying to interpret the results. With a larger number of companies, a *logit* analysis could be feasible which would make the analysis more powerful.

The empirical results do illustrate the importance of IT infrastructure in driving both formal and informal learning. Higher levels of human capital as well as higher stability are associated with higher levels of training demand. Also interesting is that a knowledge enabling environment does not seem to necessarily promote informal learning activities.

9.3 Further research and recommendations

This exploratory study has shown certain directions in the management of knowledge in SMEs that need to be further developed in order to prove additional external validity. In essence, the results put into question the idea that a knowledge-enabling environment fosters demand for training. Survey data (such as IALS or CVTS) seem to indicate that company size and literacy practices at work relate positively to the demand for training. However, the small sample studied here does not appear to necessarily follow this trend. Further testing of these results is recommended in a larger sample and in other business sectors.

The results indicate that informal learning and formal learning activities seem to have a compensatory relationship. This relationship has to be analyzed further. In addition, higher informal learning engagement relates negatively with an overall collaborative climate. In this vein, further studies on how the collaborative climate relates to informal learning would be interesting. Do people who engage in more intentional informal learning have less interest in sharing their knowledge and in collaborating? Do they have less interest or time to engage in formal training?

The study has also shown the importance of IT investment in driving the demand for both formal and informal learning. This seems to be the case because people have to learn to use IT equipment. If this is the case, it is important to study to what extent learning associated with IT can enhance effectiveness.

From the exploration of the 18 companies, it seems advisable for companies to create a more explicit plan for managing knowledge. In this way, companies might be able to make their different business processes work in a similar direction, creating a truly knowledge-intensive company. However, it is important to link this knowledge-intensive environment with company effectiveness and survival in order to justify it. Further studies for determining what characteristics are associated with effectiveness are necessary. The present results provide neither clear relationships between the knowledge-enabling environment and effectiveness, nor between the knowledge-creation arenas and effectiveness.

Another interesting aspect to be further developed is to what extent these findings would be replicated in another country with less interest in lifelong learning. As Chapter 5 has showed, Sweden is among the countries with highest rates of training participation and investment in R&D. It is not clear to what extend the results are associated with the business culture in Sweden and how the relationships would hold up in other countries.

From a policy perspective, the study seems to indicate that the demand for training in small companies is high. The results seem to point to the idea that it might not be easy to fulfill SME demands for competence development. The analysis of the subject matter indicates the importance of providing business administration and leadership training. Another important subject for training is in the area of IT. Finally, also noteworthy is that the perceived training demands are often rather general, which might open a door for governments to consider providing general training at low cost to a variety of business services.

REFERENCES

Aguirre, J.L., Brena, R., and Cantu, F.J. (2001). Multiagent-based knowledge networks, *Expert Systems with Applications*, 20, pp. 65-75.

Ahmed, P. K., Kok, L.K., and Loh, A. Y. E. (2002). *Learning through knowledge management.* Oxford: Butterworth-Heinemann.

Alexander, P. A. (2003). Can we get there from here? In P.A. Alexander (ed.) Expertise, *Educational Researcher*, 32, pp. 3-4.

Allavi, M. and Tiwana, A. (2003). Knowledge management: The information technology dimension. In M. Easter-Smith and M. A. Lyles (eds), *Handbook of organizational learning and knowledge management*, pp. 105-121. Oxford: Blackwell Publishing.

Allen, T. J. (1977). *Managing the flow of technology: Technology transfer and the dissemination of technological information within the R&D organization.* Cambridge, MA: MIT Press.

Andriessen, D. (2004a). IC valuation and measurement: Classifying the state of the art, *Journal of Intellectual Capital*, 5, pp. 230-242.

Andriessen, D. (2004b). *Making sense of Intellectual Capital: Designing a method for the valuation of intangibles.* Oxford: Elsevier Inc.

Andriessen, D. (2006). On the metaphorical nature of intellectual capital: A textual analysis, *Journal of Intellectual Capital*, 7, pp. 93-110.

Andriessen, D. and Stam, C.D (2004). *The intellectual capital of the European Union. Measuring the Lisbon Agenda.* Amsterdam: Center for Research in Intellectual Capital, INHOLLAND University and de Baak, Management Center VNO-NCW. Retrived October 2005 from: http://www.intellectualcapital.nl/artikelen/ICofEU2004.pdf.

APQC (2000). *Successfully Implementing knowledge management.* Houston: APQC.

Ardichvili, A. (2001). Lev Semynovich Vygotsky, 1896-1934. In J. Palmer (ed.), *Fifty modern thinkers on education: From Piaget to the present day*, pp. 33-37. Florence, KY, USA: Routledge.

Argyris, C. (1991). Teaching smart people how to learn, *Harvard Business Review*, 69 (3), pp. 99- 109.

Argyris, C. (1993). *On organizational learning (First edition).* Oxford: Blackwell Business.

Argyris, C. (1999). *On organizational learning (Second edition).* Oxford: Blackwell Business.

Argyris, C. (2004). Double-loop learning and implementable validity. In H. Tsoukas and N. Mylonopoulos (eds), *Organizations as knowledge systems : knowledge, learning, and dynamic capabilities*, pp. 29-46. Houndmills: Palgrave: Mcmillan.

Argyris, C. and Schon, D. A. (1974). *Theory in practice increasing professional effectiveness.* San Francisco: Jossey Bass.

Argyris, C. and Schon, D. A. (1978). *Organizational learning: A theory of action perspective.* Reading, Massachusetts: Addison-Wesley Publishing company.

Argyrous, G. (1997). Statistics for social research. New York: Palgrave Macmillan.

Aspin, D.N. and Chapman, J. D. (2000). Lifelong Learning: Concepts and Conceptions, *International Journal of Lifelong Learning* 19, p. 2-19.

Aspin, D.N. and Chapman, J., (2001), Towards a philosophy of lifelong learning. In D. N. Aspin, J. Chapman, M. Hatton and Y. Sawano (eds), *International handbook of lifelong learning*, pp. 3-35. London: Kluwer Academic Publishers.

Aspin, D.N. and Chapman, J., Hatton, M., Sawano, Y. (2001), Introduction and overview. In D. N. Aspin, J. Chapman, M. Hatton and Y. Sawano (eds*), International handbook of lifelong learning*, pp. 3-35. Boston: Kluwer Academic Publishers.

Atkinsson, P. and Coffey, A. (1997). Analysis documentary realities. In D. Silverman (ed.), *Qualitative research: Theory, method and practice*. London: SAGE Publications.

Ausubel, D. P. and Robinson, F. G. (1969). *School learning: And introduction to educational psychology.* London: Holt, Rinehart and Wiston.

Barkham, R. Gudgin, G. Hart, M. and Hanvey, E. (1996). *The determinants of small firm growth: An interregional study in the United Kingdom 1986-90.* London: Jessica Kingsley Publishers .

Barney, J. (1991). Firm resources and sustained competitive advantage, *Journal of Management*, 17, pp. 99-120.

Becker, G. S. (1962). Investment in human capital: A theoretical analysis, *Journal of Political Economy*, 70, pp. S9-S49.

Becker, G. S. (1993). *Human Capital. A Theoretical and Empirical Analysis, with Special Reference to Education (Third edition).* Chicago: University of Chicago Press.

Bender, S. and Fish, A. (2000). The transfer of Knowledge and the Expertise: the continuing need for Global Assigments, *Journal of Knowledge Management*, 4, pp. 125-137.

Bilderbeek, R., Den Hertog, P., Marklund, G. and Miles, I. (1998). *Services in Innovation: Knowledge-Intensive Business Services as Co-Producers of Innovation* (Project Report S3). Retrieved *February, 5th, 2002 from: http://fssl.man.ac.uk/PREST/Download/finalrp3.pdf.*

Bixler, C.H. (2005). Developing a foundation for a successful knowledge management system. . In M. A. Stankosky (ed.), *Creating the discipline of knowledge management*: The latest in University Research, pp. 51-66. Oxford: Elsevier.

Blacker, F. (1995). Knowledge, knowledge work and organizations: An overview and interpretation, *Organization studies*, 16, pp. 1021-1046.

Blacker, F. (2002). Epilogue: Knowledge, knowledge work and organizations: An overview and interpretation, Organization studies. In C. Wei Choo and N. Bontis (eds), *The strategic management of intellectual capital and organizational knowledge*, pp. 63-64. Oxford: Oxford University press.

Blumer, H. (1969). *Symbolic Interactionism: Perspective and Method.* Berkeley: University of California Press.

Boeree, C.G. (2002). *Jean Piaget: 1896-1980.* Retrieved January 2005 at: http://www.ship.edu/~cgboeree/piaget.html.

Boiral, O. (2002). Tacit Knowledge and Environmental Management, *Long Range Planning*, 35, pp. 291-317.

Boisot, M. (2002). The creation and sharing of knowledge. In C. Wei Choo and N. Bontis (eds) (eds), *The strategic management of intellectual capital and organizational knowledge.* , pp. 65-76. Oxford: Oxford University press.

Bontis, N. (1998). Intellectual Capital: An exploratory study that develops measures and models, *Management decision*, 26, pp. 63-76.

Bontis, N. (2001). Assessing knowledge assets: A review of the models used to measure intellectual capital, *International Journal of Management Reviews*, 3, pp. 41 –60.

Bontis, N. and Fitz-enz, J. (2002). Intellectual capital ROI: A casual map of human capital antecedents and consequents, *Journal of Intellectual Capital*, 3, pp. 223-247.

Bontis, N., Crossan, M.M. and Hulland, J. (2002). Managing and organizational learning system by aligning stocks and flows, *Journal of Management Studies*, 39, pp. 437- 469.

Bontis, N., Dragonetti, N.C., Jacobsen, K., and Roos, G. (1999). The knowledge toolbox: A review of the tools available to measure and manage intangible resources, *European Management Journal*, 17, pp. 391-402.

Boström, A.K. (2003). *Lifelong learning, intergenerational learning and social capital: From theory to practice.* Studies in Comparative and International Education. No. 61. Stockholm: Institute of International Education, Stockholm University.

Boudard, E. (2000). What are the main predictors of recurrent education? A five country comparative model. In M. O'Dowd and I. Fägerlind (eds.), *Mapping European comparative education research perspectives: The PRESTiGE TMR Network.* Studies in Comparative and International Education No.52, pp.147-167. Stockholm: Institute of International Education.

Boudard, E. (2001). *Literacy Proficiency, Earnings, and Recurrent Training: A Ten Country Comparative Study.* Studies in Comparative and International Education, No. 57. Stockholm: Institute of International Education, Stockholm University.

Boudard, E. and Rubenson, K. (2003). Revisiting major determinants of participation in adult education with a direct measure of literacy skills. In R. Desjardins and, E. Boudard (eds). Literacy Proficiency, *International Journal of Educational Research*, 39, pp. 265 –281.

Brooking, A. (1997). The management of intellectual capital, *Long Range Planning*, 30, pp. 364-365.

Brooking, A. and Motta, E (1996). A taxonomy of intellectual capital and a methodology for auditing it, *17th Annual National Business Conference.* Ontario: McMaster University, Hamilton.

Brown, P. (2001). Skill formation in the Twenty-First century. In P. Brown, A. Green and H. Lauder *High skills: Globalisation, competitiveness, and skill formation,* pp. 1-56. Oxford: Oxford University Press.

Bryman, A. (1988). Introduction: Inside accounts and social research in organizations. In A. Bryman (ed.), *Doing research in Organizations.* London: Routledge

Buchler, J. (ed.) (1955). *Philosophical writings of Peirce.* New York: Dover.

Bulmer, M. (ed.) (2004). *Questionnaires. Volume I.* London: SAGE Publications.

Burnes, B., Cooper, C., and West, P. (2003). Organisational learning: The new management paradigm? *Management Decision*, 41, pp. 452-464.

Butler, J., Cameron, H. and Miles, I. (2000). *Grasping the nettle: Final report of a feasibility study concerning a program for research into measurement and validation of intangible assets.* Manchester: Center for Research on Innovation and Competition (CRIC) and policy research in Engeneering, Science and Technology (PREST), University of Manchester.

Butler, T. and Grace, A. (2005). Beyond knowledge management: Introducing learning management systems, *Journal of Cases on Information Technology*, 7, pp. 53-70.

Carmel, D. (2005). Effective knowledge management for professional services. In M. Rao (ed.), *Knowledge management tool and techniques: Practicioners and experts evaluate KM solutions*, pp. 384-393. London: Elsevier.

Carr-Hill, R., Carron, G. & Peart, E. (2001). Classifying out-of-school education. In K. Watson (ed.), *Doing Comparative Education Research: Issues and problems*, pp. 331-353. Oxford: Symposium Books.

CEDEFOP and EURYDICE, (2001). *National actions to implement lifelong learning on Europe.* Brussels: EURYDICE.

Chase, R.L. (1997a) The knowledge-based organization: An international Survey, *The Journal of knowledge management*, 1, pp. 38-49.

Chase, R. L. (1997b). Knowledge management benchmarks, *The Journal of Knowledge Management*, 1, pp. 83-92.

Chauvel, D. and Depres, C. (2002). A review of survey research in knowledge management: 1997-2001, *Journal of Knowledge Management*, pp. 207-223.

Chapman, M. (2001). Social anthropology and business studies: Some considerations of method. In D.N. and Hirsch, E. (eds), *Inside organizations: Antropologist at work*. Oxford: Berg.

Chi, M.T., Glaser, H.R. and Farr, M. J. (eds.), (1988). *The nature of expertise*. Hillsdale, NJ: Erlbaum.

Cleveland, H. (1985). *The knowledge executive: Leadership in an information society*. New York: Truman Tally books, E.P. Dutton.

Cohen, L. and Manion, L. (1994). *Research methods in education (4th edition)*. London: Routledge.

Coleman, D. (1999). GroupWare: Collaboration and Knowledge Sharing. In J. Lebowitz (ed.), *Knowledge Management Handbook*. Orlando: CRC pres LLC.

Coleman, J.S. (1990). Foundations of Social Theory. Cambridge, MA: Harvard University Press.

Coleman, J.S. (1971). Resource for social change. New York: Wiley.

Colletta, N.J. (1994). Formal, nonformal, and informal education. In T. Husén, and T. N. Postlethwaite (eds), *International encyclopedia of education (Second edition)*, pp. 2364-2369. Oxford: Pergamon Press and Elsevier Science.

Converse, J.M. (1984). Strong arguments and weak evidence: The open/closed questioning controversy of the 1940s, *Public Opinion Quarterly*, 48, pp. 267 – 282.

Coombs, P. (1973). *New paths to learning*. New York: International Council for Education and Development.

Coombs, P. and Ahmed, M. (1974). *Attacking rural poverty: how non-formal education can help.* Baltimore: John Hopkins University Press.

Council of the European Union (1977a). 77/803/EEC: Council Decision of 20 December 1977 on action by the European Social Fund for migrant workers, *Official Journal of the European Communities* L 337, pp.0012 - 0013

Council of the European Union (1977a). 77/804/EEC: Council Decision of 20 December 1977 on action by the European Social Fund for women, *Official Journal of the European Communities* L 337, p. 0014.

Council of the European Union (1977c). 77/802/EEC: Council Decision of 20 December 1977 amending certain Decisions adopted pursuant to Article 4 of Decision 71/66/EEC on the reform of the European Social Fund, *Official Journal of the European Communities* L 337, pp. 0010 – 0011.

Council of the European Union (1978). Council Regulation (EEC) No. 3039/78 of 18 December 1978 on the creation of two new types of aid for young people from the European Social Fund, *Official Journal of the European Communities* L 361, 23/12/1978 P. 0003 – 0004.

Council of the European Union (1993a). Council Regulation (EEC) No. 2081/93 of 20 July 1993 amending Regulation (EEC) No 2052/88 on the tasks of the Structural Funds and their effectiveness and on coordination of their activities between themselves and with the operations of the European Investment Bank and the other existing financial instruments, *Official Journal of the European Communities* L 193, pp. 0005 – 0019.

Council of the European Union (1993b). Council Regulation (EEC) No. 2082/93 of 20 July 1993 amending Regulation (EEC) No 4253/88 laying down provisions for implementing Regulation (EEC) No 2052/88 as regards coordination of the activities of the different Structural Funds between themselves and with the operations of the European Investment Bank and the other existing financial instruments, *Official Journal of the European Communities* L 193, 31/07/1993 P. 0020 – 0033.

Council of the European Union (1993c). Council Regulation (EEC) No. 2084/93 of 20 July 1993 amending Regulation (EEC) No 4255/88 laying down provisions for implementing Regulation (EEC) No. 2052/88 as regards the European Social Fund, Official *Journal of the European Communities* L 193, 31/07/1993 P. 0039 – 0043.

Council of the European Union (1999). Council Regulation (EEC) No. 1784/1999 of the European Parliament and of the Council of 12 July 1999 on the European Social Fund, *Official Journal of the European Communities* L 213 , 13/08/1999 P. 0005 – 0008.

Council of the European Union (2004). Education and Training 2010, *Official Journal of the European Union*, C104, pp.1-19.

Creswell, J.W. (1998). *Qualitative inquiry and research design*. London: Sage publications.

Curry, J. (1997). The Dialectic of Knowledge-in-Production: Value Creation in Late Capitalism and the Rise of Knowledge-Centered Production, *Electronic Journal of Sociology*, 2.

Cyert, R.M. and March, J. G., (1963). *A behavioural theory of the firm*. Engelwood, NJ: Prentice-Hall.

Daun, H. (2003). *World system, globalization and educational change*. Yellow report. Stockholm: The Institute of International Education, Stockholm University.

Davé, R. (1976). Foundations of lifelong education: Methodological aspects. In R. Dave, (ed.), *Foundations of Lifelong Education*, pp. 11-56. Oxford: Pergamon.

Davenport, T.H., and Prusak, L. (1998). *Working Knowledge. How organizations manage what they know*. Boston, MA: Harvard Business School Press.

Demarest, M. (1997). Understanding Knowledge Management, *Long Range Planning*, 30, pp. 374-384.

Denzin, K. (1978). *The research act: a theoretical introduction to sociological methods*. New York : McGraw-Hill.

Desjardins, R. (2003). Determinants of Economic and Social Outcomes from a Life-wide Learning Perspective in Canada, *Education Economics*, 11, pp. 12-38.

Desjardins, R. (2004). *Learning for well-being: Studies using the International Adult Literacy Survey*. Studies in Comparative and International Education, N. 65. Stockholm: Institute of International Education.

Desjardins, R., Murray, T. & Tuijnman, A. (eds). (2005). *Learning a Living: First results of the Adult Literacy and Life Skills Survey*. Paris and Ottawa: OECD and Statistics Canada.

Desouza, K. C. (2003). Knowledge management barriers: Why technology imperatives seldom works, *Business Horizons*, 46 (1), pp. 25-29.

DfEE, (1998). *The learning age: A renaissance for a new Britain*. London: Department for Education and Employment.

Diakoulakis, I. E., Georgopoulos, N. B., Koulouriotis, D. E., and Emiris, D. M. (2004). Towrads a holistic knowledge management model, *Journal of Knowledge Management*, 8, pp. 32-46.

DiMattia, S., and Oder, N. (1997). Knowledge management: Hope, hype, or harbinger? *Library Journal*, 122, pp. 33-35.

Drake, K. (1997). Human Resource accountancy in enterprises: Recent practices and new developments. In Ernst and Young Center for Business Innovation and OECD (ed.), *Enterprise Value in the knowledge economy: Measuring performance in the Age of Intangibles*, pp. 7-37. Cambridge, MA.: The Ernst and Young Center for Business Innovation.

Drejer, I. (2001). Identifying innovation in a 'Service Economy', *Business Studies working paper 2001-9*. Copenhagen: Center for Economic and Business Research (CEBR).

Drucker, P. (1988). The coming of the new Organization, *Harvard Business Review*, 66, pp. 45-53.

Dutch Ministry of Education, Culture and Science (1998). *Lifelong learning: The national action program of the Netherlands*. The Hague: Dutch Ministry of Education, Culture and Science.

Dweck, C. S. (1999). *Self-Theories: Their Role in Motivation, Personality, and Development*. Philadelphia: Taylor & Francis

Earl, L. and Gault, F. (2003). Knowledge management: Size matters. In OECD and Statistics Canada, *Measuring knowledge management in the business sector: First steps*, pp. 169-186. Paris: OECD.

Easter-Smith, M. and Lyles, M. A. (eds) (2003a). *Handbook of organizational learning and knowledge management*. Oxford: Blackwell Publishing .

Easter-Smith, M. and Lyles, M. A. (2003b). Introduction: Watersheds of organizational learning and knowledge management. In M. Easter-Smith and M. A. Lyles (eds), *Handbook of organizational learning and knowledge management*, pp. 1-17. Oxford: Blackwell Publishing.

Edvinsson, L. (1997). Developing intellectual capital at Skandia, *Long Range Planning*, 30, pp. 366-373.

Edvinsson, L. and Åberg (2001). The IC multiplier and the importance of structural capital: A first investigation of enablers shaping intellectual capital. Paper presented at *the 4th Intangibles Conference on Advances in The measurement of Intangible (Intellectual) Capital*, May 17-18. New New York: Stern School of Business, New York University.

Edvinsson, L. and Malone, M. (1998). *Intellectual capital: the proven way to establish your company's real value by measuring its hidden brainpower*. London: Piatkus.

Edward, R., Ranson, S., and Strain, M. (2002). Reflexivity: towards a theory of lifelong learning, International, *Journal of Lifelong Education*, 21, pp. 525-536.

Elkjaer, B. (2003). Social learning theory: Learning as participation in social processes. In M. Easter-Smith and M. A. Lyles (eds), *Handbook of organizational learning and knowledge management*, pp. 39-77. Oxford: Blackwell Publishing.

Ellström, P.-E., Löfberg, A. and Svensson, L. (2005). Pedagogik I arbetslivet: Ett historikt perspektiv (Education within working life: A historical perspective), *Pedagogiska Forskning i Sverige*, 10, pp. 162-181.

Ernst and Young Center for Business Innovation and OECD (ed.) (1997). *Enterprise Value in the knowledge economy: Measuring performance in the Age of Intangibles*. Cambridge, MA: The Ernst and Young Center for Business Innovation, pp. 7-37.

European Commission (1982). *Commission communication to the council concerning the European Social Fund*. Luxemburg: Office for Official Publications of the European Communities.

European Commission (1987). Notification relating to the date of entry into force of the Single European Act, signed at Luxembourg on 17 February 1986 and at The Hague on 28 February 1986, *Official Journal of the European Communities* L 169.

European Commission (1993). *White Paper on growth, competitiveness, and employment: The challenges and ways forward into the 21st century*. Luxemburg: Office for Official Publications of the European Communities. Retrieved August 2002 from: *http://europa.eu.int/en/record/white/c93700/contents.html*

European Commission (1995). *Teaching and Learning-Toward the Learning Society. White Paper*. Luxemburg: Office for Official Publications of the European Communities.

European Commission (1998). *The European Social Fund, an overview of the programming period 1994-99*. Retrieved January 2002: from: *http://europa.eu.int/comm/employment_social/esf/en/public/overview/toc.htm*

European Commission (1999a). *Reform of the Structural Funds 2000-2006: Comparative analysis*. Luxemburg: Office for Official Publications of the European Communities.

European commission (1999b). *Continuing Training in Enterprises: Facts and Figures. A report on the results of the Continuing Vocational Training Survey carried out in the enterprises of the Member States of the European Union in 1994*. Luxembourg: EUROSTAT. Retrived November 2001t: *http://europa.eu.int/en/comm/dg22/leonardo/*.

European Commission (2000a). *Towards a European research area*. Luxemburg: Office for Official Publications of the European Communities.

European Commission (2000b). *A memorandum on lifelong learning*. Luxembourg: Office for Official Publications of the European Communities.

European Commission (2001a). *Making a European area of lifelong learning a reality*. Luxembourg: Office for Official Publications of the European Communities.

European Commission (2001b). *Communication on European Social Fund: Support for the European Employment Strategy*. Luxemburg: Office for Official Publications of the European Communities.

European Commission (2001c). *Towards a European Research Area. Key figures 2001. Special Edition. Indicators for benchmarking of national research polices*. Luxemburg: Office for Official Publications of the European Communities.

European Commission (2001d). *Building an innovative economy in Europe*. Luxemburg: Office for Official Publications of the European Communities.

European Commission (2002a). *A European area of lifelong learning*. Luxembourg: Office for Official Publications of the European Communities.

European Commission (2002b). *European social statistics: Continuing vocational training survey (CVTS2)*. Luxembourg: Office for Official Publications of the European Communities.

European Commission (2002c). *Glossary*. Retrieved from: *http://europa.eu.int/comm/employment_social/esf2000/glossary-en.htm#EES (August, 20th, 2002)*.

European Commission (2002d). *The European Social Fund: 2000-2006. Facts on Sweden*. Retrieved August 2002, from: *http://europa.eu.int/comm/employment_social/esf2000/ms/s-faf-en.pdf*.

European Commission (2003). *Statistics on Science and Technology in Europe. Data 1991-2002*. Luxemburg: Office for Official Publications of the European Communities.

European Commission (2004). *Innovation in Europe. Results for the EU, Iceland and Norway. Data 1998-2001*. Luxemburg: Office for Official Publications of the European Communities.

European Commission (2005a). *Progress towards the Lisbon objectives in education and training, 2005 report*. Commission staff working paper, Luxemburg: Office for Official Publications of the European Communities.

European Commission (2005b). *Task force report on adult education survey*. Luxemburg: Office for Official Publications of the European Communities.

European Commission (2005c). The ESF 2000- 2006: Sweden. In European Commission, *ESF 2000-2006: Europe investing in people*. Last Retrieved: March 2006 in: *http://europa.eu.int/comm/employment_social/esf2000/docs/sv_esf_en.pdf*.

EUROSTAT (1996). NACE rev. 1. *Statistical classification of the economic activities in the European Community*. Luxemburg: EUROSTAT.

EUROSTAT (1999). *Fields of education and training: Manual.* Luxemburg: EUROSTAT.

EUROSTAT (2001). *Report of the EUROSTAT task force on measuring lifelong learning.* Luxemburg: EUROSTAT.

Evans, S., Gonzalez, J. Popiel, S. and Walker, T. (2000). Whose capital is it? Trends in human capital, *Ivey Business Journal*, Jan./Feb., pp. 30-37.

Fägerlind, I. and Saha, L. (1989). *Education and national development.* Oxford: Pergamon Press.

Ferris, G.R., Hochwarter, W.A., Buckley, M.R., Harrel-Cook, G., and Frink, D.D. (1999). Human resources management: Some new directions, *Journal of Management,* 25, pp. 385-415.

Field, J. (2000). *Lifelong learning and the new educational order.* Trent: Trentham Books.

Field, J. (2001), Lifelong education, *International Journal of Lifelong Education,* 20, pp. 3-15.

Filius, R., Jong, J.A., and Roelofs, E.C. (2000). Knowledge management in the HRD office: a comparison of three cases, *Journal of Workplace Learning* 12, pp. 286-295.

Flavell, J. H. (1973/1963). *The developmental psychology of Jean Piaget.* London: Van Nostrand Reinfold.[

Flood, R. L. (1999). *Rethinking the Fifth discipline: Learning within the unknowable.* Routledge: London.

Fombrun, C., Tichy, N. M. and Devanna, M. A. (1984). *Strategic Human Resource Management.* New York: Wiley

Fong, P.S.W. (2003). Knowledge creation in multidisciplinary project teams: an empirical study of processes and their dynamic interrelations, *International Journal Project Management, 21, pp. 479-486.*

Fontana, A. and Frey, J. H. (2000). The interview: From structured questions to negotiated text. In N.K. Denzin, and Y.S. Lincoln (eds), *Handbook of qualitative research (2nd edition),* pp. 645-669. London: Sage Publications.

Foray, D. and Gault, F. (2003a). Measurement of knowledge management practices. In OECD and Statistics Canada, *Measuring knowledge management in the business sector: First steps,* pp. 11-26. Paris: OECD.

Foray, D. and Gault, F. (2003b). Conclusion. In OECD and Statistics Canada, *Measuring knowledge management in the business sector: First steps,* pp. 213-219. Paris: OECD.

Foss, N. J. and Mahnke, V. (2003). Knowledge management: what can organizational economics contribute? In M. Easter-Smith and M. A. Lyles (eds), *Handbook of organizational learning and knowledge management,* pp. 79-103. Oxford: Blackwell Publishing.

Frank, O. (2000). Structural Plots of multivariate binary data, *Journal of Social Structure, 1* . Retrieved from: http://www.cmu.edu/joss/index.html.

Frankfort-Nacmias, C. and Nachmias, D. (1996). *Research Method in the Social Sciences (Fifth Edition).* London: Arnold.

Frey, J. H. and Fontana, A. (1991). The group interview in social research, *Social Science Journal*, 28, pp. 175-187.

Fukuyama, F. (2000). *The Great Disruption, Human Nature and the Reconstitution of Social Order.* New York: Touchstone.

Fulmer, R.M. and Keys, J. B. (1998). A conversation with Argyris: The Father of Organizational Learning, *Organizational Dynamics*, 27. pp. 21-33.

Garber (1998). Descartes' method and the role of experiment. In J. Cottingham (ed.), *Descartes*, pp. 234-259. Oxford: Oxford University Press.

Garvin, D. A., (1993). Building a learning organization, *Harvard Business Review*, 71, pp. 78-91.

Geertz. C. (1973). *The interpretation of cultures.* New York: Basic Books.

Gibbons, S.L. (1994). *Kant's theory of imagination: Bridging gaps in judgment and experience. Oxford philosophical monographs.* Oxford: Claredon Press.

Gloet, M. and Berrell, M. (2003). The dual paradigm nature of knowledge management: Implications for achieving quality outcomes in human resource management, *Journal of knowledge Management*, 7, pp. 78-89.

Goldman, L. (1967/ 1971). *Immanuel Kant* (Translated from the French and German by Robert Black). London: NLB.

Grandberg, O. and Ohlsson, J. (2005). Kollektiv lärande i team: Om utvekling av kollektiv handlingsrationalitet (Collective Learning in teams: Development of collective rationality of action), *Pedagogiska Forskning i Sverige*, 10, pp. 227-243.

Gustavsson, B., (2002). What do we mean by lifelong learning and knowledge? *International Journal of Lifelong Education*, 21, pp. 13-23.

Guthrie, J., Johanson, U., Bukh, P.N., and Sanchez, P. (2003). Guest editorial: Intangibles and the transparent enterprise: New strands of knowledge, *Journal of Intellectual Capital*, 4, pp. 429-440.

Guthrie, J., Petty, R. and Johanson, U. (2001). Sunrise in the knowledge economy: managing, measuring and reporting intellectual capital, *Accounting Auditing & Accountability Journal*, 14, pp. 365-382.

Hagtröm, T. (2003). Introduction. In T. Hagström (ed.), *Adult development in Post-industrial Society and working life*. Stockholm lectures in Educology. Lecture Series No. 2, pp. 1-21. Stockholm: Department of Education.

Halal, E. W. (1998). The economics imperatives of knowledge: New organization for a new era. In E. W. Halal (ed.), *The infinite resource: creating and leading the knowledge enterprise*, pp. 1-29. San Francisco, CA: Jossey-Bass Publishers.

Hall, R. (1992). The strategic analysis of intangible resources, *Strategic Management Journal*, 13, pp. 135-144.

Hammerer, G. (1996). Intangible investment in Austria. Paper presented at the OECD workshop *"New indicators for the Knowledge-based Economy"*. Paris: OECD. (Unpublished paper)

Harris, K., Fleming, M., Hunter, R., Rosser, B., and Cushman, A. (1999). *The knowledge management scenario: Trends and directions* for 1998 –2003. London: Gartner.

Harrison, S. and Sullivan, P.H. (2000). Profiting from intellectual capital: Learning from leading companies, *Journal of Intellectual Capital*, 1, pp. 33-46.

Harrison, S.J. (2000). *Managing know-who based companies: A multi-networked approach to knowledge and innovation management*. Cheltenham: Edward Elgar.

Hasan, A. (1996). Lifelong Learning. In A.C. Tuijnman (ed.), *The international Encyclopedia of adult Education and Training (Second Edition)*, pp. 33-41. Oxford: Pergamon Press.

Hauschild, S, Licht, T. and Stein, W. (2001). Creating a knowledge culture, *The McKinsey Quarterly*, 1, pp. 74-81.

Hays, W.L. (1988). *Statistics (fourth edition)*. New york: Holt Rinehart and Wiston inc.

Hedberg, B. (1981). How organizations learn and unlearn. In P. Nystrom and U. Starbuck (ed.) *Handbook of Organizational Design*. Oxford University Press, pp. 3-27.

Hedlund, G. and Nonaka, I. (1991). *Models of knowledge management in the west and Japan*. Stockholm: Institute of International Business, Stockholm University.

Hellström, T., Kemlin, P. and Malmquist, U. (2000). Knowledge and Competence Management at Ericsson: Decentralization and Organizational Fit, *Journal of Knowledge Management*, 4, pp. 99-110.

Hillier, B. (1996). *Space Is the Machine: A Configurational Theory of Architecture*. Cambridge: Cambridge University Press.

Hislop, D. (2002). Mission impossible? Communication and sharing knowledge via information technology, *Journal of Information Technology*, 17, pp. 165-177.

Hislop, D. (2003). Linking human resource management and knowledge management via commitment: A review and research agenda, *Employee relations*, 25, pp. 182-202.

Holliday, R. (1995). *Investigating small firms: Nice work?* London: Routledge.

Hookway, C. (1985). *Peirce*. London: Routledge & Egan Paul.

Hunt, D. (2003). The concept of knowledge and how to measure it, *Journal of intellectual capital*, 4, pp. 100-113.

Hurwitz, J., Lines, S., Montgomery, B. and Schimidt, J. (2002). The linkage between management practices, intangibles performance and stock returns, *Journal of Intellectual Capital*, 3, pp. 51-61.

Husén, T. (1968). Lifelong learning in the educative society, *International review of applied psychology*, 17, pp. 87-99.

Husén, T. (1999). Reflections on recurrent education and lifelong learning. In A. C. Tuijnman, and T. Schuller (eds), *Lifelong learning policy research*, pp. 33-43. London: Portland Press.

Ichijo, K. (2004). From managing to enabling knowledge. In H. Takeuchi and I. Nonaka (eds), *Hitosubashi on Knowledge Management*, pp. 125-153. Singapore: John Wiley and Sons.

Illeris, K. (2003a). Learning changes through life, *Lifelong Learning in Europe*, 8, pp. 50-61.

Illeris, K. (2003b). Adult education as experience by the learners, *International Journal of Lifelong Education*, 22, pp.13-23.

Järvinen, A., and Poikela, E. (2001). Modelling reflective and contextual learning at work, *Journal of workplace learning*, 13, 282-289.

Jarvis, P. (2002). Active citizenship and the learning society, *Lifelong Learning in Europe*, 7, pp. 19-28.

Jasimuddin, S. M., Klein, J. H. and Connell, C. (2005). The paradox of using tacit and explicit knowledge: Strategies to face dilemmas, *Management decision*, 43, pp. 102-112.

Johannessen, J. A., Olsen, B. and Olaisen, J. (1999). Aspects of innovation theory based on knowledge management, *International Journal of Information Management*, 19, pp. 121-139.

Johanson, U. (1999). Mobilizing change: Characteristics of intangibles proposed by 11 Swedish firms. Technical paper presented at the *International Symposium, Measuring and Reporting Intellectual Capital: Experience, Issues, and Prospects*. Amsterdam, Technical meeting, 9-10 June.

Johanson, U., Mårtensson, M. and Skoog, M. (1999). Measuring and managing intangibles: Eleven Swedish qualitative exploratory case studies. Paper presented in *the International Symposium,*

Measuring and Reporting Intellectual Capital: Experience, Issues, and Prospects. Amsterdam, Technical meeting, 9-10 June.

Johanson, U., Mårtensson, M. and Skoog, M. (2001a). Measuring to understand intangible performance drivers, *The European Accounting Review*, 10, pp. 407-437.

Johanson, U., Mårtensson, M. and Skoog, M. (2001b). Mobilizing change through the management control of intangibles, *Accounting, Organization and Society*, 26, pp. 715-733.

Johnsson, L. (2003). Postformal thinking in the workplace. In T. Hagström (ed.), *Adult development in Post-industrial Society and working life*, pp. 153-185. Stockholm lectures in Educology. Lecture Series No. 2. Stockholm: Department of Education.

Junnarkar, B. (1997). Levering Collective Intellect by building organizational capabilities, *Expert Systems With Applications, 13*, pp. 29-41.

Kallen, D., (1979). Recurrent education and lifelong learning: Definitions and distinctions. In T. Schuller and J. Megary (eds), *World yearbook of education 1979: Recurrent education and lifelong learning*, pp. 45-54. London: Kogan Page.

Kant (1781/2003). The critique of pure reason (Translated by J.M. D. Meiklejohn). Retrieved, December 2003 from:
  http://www.ilt.columbia.edu/academic/digitexts/kant/pure_reason/pure_reason.txt.

Kaplan, R.S. and Norton, D.P. (1992). The balanced scorecard – Measures that drive performance, *Harvard Business Review*, 70, pp. 71-79.

Kaplan, R.S. and Norton, D.P. (1996). Using the balanced scorecard as a strategic management system, *Harvard Business Review*, 74, pp. 75-85.

Kaplan, R.S. and Norton, D.P. (2000). Having trouble with your strategy? Then map it, *Harvard Business Review*, 78, pp. 167-176.

Kaplan, R. S. and Norton, D. P. (2004). Measuring the strategic readiness of intangible assets, *Harvard Business Review*, 82, pp. 52-63.

Karmiloff-Smith, A. and Inhelder, B. (1974*).* If you want to get ahead, get a theor*y, Cognition*, 3, pp. 195-212.

Kaufmann, L. and Schneider, Y. (2004). Intangibles: A synthesis of current research, *Journal of Intellectual Capital*, 5, pp. 366-388.

Kenny, A. (2001). *The Oxford Illustrated History of Western Philosophy*. Oxford: Oxford University Press.

Kessels, J. and Keursten, P. (2002). The hanging relation between work and learning: Creating knowledge productive work environment, *Lifelong Learning in Europe*, 7, 104-114.

Khan, R.L. and Cannell, C.F. (1957). The formulation of questions. In R.L. Khan and C.F. Cannell, *The dymnamics of interviewing: Theory , technique, and cases*, pp. 106-130. New york: Jhon wiley & Sons.

Kim, D.H. (1998). The linking between individual and organizational learning. In D.A. Klein, (ed.), *The strategic Management of Intellectual capital*. Oxford: Butterworth-Heinemann, pp. 41-63.

Kjellström, C. (1999). *Essays on Investment in Human Capital*. Swedish Institute for Social Research-36. Stockholm: University Hereà.

Klein, A.D. (1998). The strategic management of intellectual capital: An introduction. In A. D. Klein (ed.), *The strategic Management of Intellectual capital*, pp. 1-11. Oxford: Butterworth-Heinemann.

Kohli, R. and Devataj, S. (2003a). Performance impact of information technology: Is actual usage the missing link? *Management Science*, 49, pp. 273-289.

Kohli, R. and Devataj, S. (2003b). A meta-analysis of structural variables in firm-level empirical research, *Information systems research*, 14, pp. 127-145.

KPMG (1998). *Knowledge Management: Research Report*. London: KPMG Management Consulting.

KPMG (2000). *Knowledge management: Research Report. Retrieved, October 2002, from:*
  http://www.kpmg.nl/Docs/Knowledge_Advisory_Services/KPMG%20KM%20Research%20Report %202000.pdf.

Kuhn, T.S. (1970). *The Structure of Scientific Revolution*, Chicago: Chicago University press.

Lazarsfeld, P. F. (1944). The controversy over detauled interviews: An offer for negotation. In Bulmer, M. (2004), *Questionnaires. Volume I*, pp. 149-169. London: Sage Publications.

Leader, G., (2003). Lifelong learning: Policy and practice in further education, *Education + Training*, 45, pp. 361-370.

Lear, J. (1988). *Aristotle: The desire to understand*. Cambridge, MA: Cambridge University Press.

Leech, S. A. and Sutton, S. G. (2002). Editorial: Knowledge management issues in practice: opportunities for research, *International Journal of Accounting Information Systems*, 3, pp. 60-73.

Leitch, C., Harrison, R., Burgoyne, J., and Blantern, C. (1996). Learning organizations: the measurement of company performance, *Journal of European Industrial Training*, 20, pp. 31-44.

Leonard, D. and Sensiper, S. (1998). The role of tacit knowledge in group innovation, *California Management review*, 40, pp. 112-132.

Leonard-Barton, D. (1995). *Wellsprings of knowledge: Building and sustaining the sources of innovation*. Boston, Mass.: Harvard Business School Press

Lesser, E.L. and Storck, J. (2001). Communities of practice and organizational performance, *IBM System Journal*, 40, pp. 831-841.

Lev, B. (2003), Intangibles at a crossroads, *Controlling*, 15, pp. 121-127.

Li, M. and Gao, F. (2003). Why Nonaka highlights tacit knowledge: A critical view, *Journal of knowledge management,* 7, pp. 6-14.

Liebowitz, J. (2000). *Building organizational intelligence: A knowledge management Premier*. London: CRC Press.

Liebowitz, J. (ed.) (1999). *Knowledge management handbook*. London: CRC Press.

Limón, M. (2001). On the cognitive conflict as an instructional strategy for conceptual change: critical appraisal, *Learning and Instruction*, 11, pp. 357-380.

Livingstone, D.W. (2000a). Researching expanded notions of learning and work and underemployment: Findings for the first Canadian Survey of informal learning practices, *International Review of Education*, 46, pp. 491-514.

Livingstone, D.W. (2000b). Exploring the Icebergs of Adult Learning: Findings of the First Canadian Survey of Informal Learning Practices, *Canadian Journal for the Study of Adult Education*, 13, pp. 49-72.

Livingstone, D.W. (2001). Expanding notions of work and learning: Profiles of latent power, *New Directions for Adult and Continuing Education*, 92, pp.19-30.

Livingstone, D.W. (2004). *2004 R.W:B. Jackson Lecture: The Learning Society: Past, Present and Future Views*. SSHRC Research Network on the Changing Nature of Work and Lifelong Learning (WALL), Working paper No. 4. Toronto: Center for the Study of Education and Work, University of Toronto.

Livingstone, D.W. (2005). *Basic findings of the 2004 Canadian learning and work survey*. Work and Lifelong Learning Research Network. Retrieved October 2005 from: *www.lifelong.oise.utoronto.ca/papers/WALLBasicSummJune05.pdf*

Loermans, J. (2002). Synergizing the learning organization and knowledge management, *Journal of Knowledge Management*, 6, pp. 285-294.

Louis, K. S. (1982). Multisite / multimethod studies: An introduction, *American Behavioral Scientist* 26, pp. 6-22.

Lowendahl, B. (1997) Strategic management of professional service firms. Copenhagen: Copenhagen Business School Press.

Lundquist, J. (2000). Intellectual Capital in information technology companies. A correlation study of IC Rating[TM] and variables measuring growth and profitability. Advanced course paper in Business Finance. Örebro: Örebro University.

Lundvall, B. Å. (2000). Understanding the role of education in the learning economy: The contribution of economics. In OECD, *Knowledge management in the learning society*, pp. 11-35. Paris: OECD.

Malhotra, Y. (2000). Knowledge management for e-business performance: Advancing information strategy to "Internet time, *Information Strategy: The Executive's Journal, 16*, pp.5-15.

Malhotra, Y. (2004). Why knowledge management system fail? Enablers and constraints of knowledge management in human enterprises. In K. Srikantaiah and M.E.D. Kening (eds), *Knowledge management lessons learned: what works and what doesn't*, pp. 87-112. Medford, N.J.: Information Today.

Manson, C., Castelman, T. and Parker, C. (2004). Knowledge management for SME-based regional clusters. *Proceedings of Twelfth CollECTeR Workshop on eCommerce May 7/8, 2004*. Adelaide: South Australia.

Markie, P. (1998). The cogito and its importance. In J. Cottingham (ed.), *Descartes,* pp. 140-173. Oxford: Oxford University Press.

Marr, B. (ed.) (2005a). *Perspectives on Intellectual Capital*. London: Elsevier.

Marr, B. (2005b). The evolution and convergence of intellectual capital as a theme. In B. Marr (ed.), *Perspectives on intellectual capital*, pp. 213-227. Oxford: Elsevier.

Marr, B. and Chatzkel, J. (2004). Intellectual capital at the crossroads: managing, measuring, and reporting of IC. In B. Marr and J. Chatzkel (eds), Intellectual capital at the crossroads: managing, measuring, and reporting of IC, *Journal of Intellectual Capital*, 5, pp. 224 –229.

Mårtensson, M. (2000). A Critical Review of Knowledge Management as a management tool, *Journal of Knowledge Management*, 14, pp. 204-216.

Martiny, M. (1998) Knowledge Management at HP Consulting, *Organizational Dynamics*, 27, pp. 71-77.

Mata, F.J., Fuerst, W.L., Barney, J.B. (December, 1995). Information technology and sustained competitite advantage: A Resource-Based Analysis, *MIS Quarterly, December 1995*, pp. 487-505.

Mavrinac, S. and Siesfeld, G.A. (1997). Measures that Matter: An Exploratory Investigation of Investors' information needs and value priorities. In Ernst and Young Center for Business

Innovation and OECD (ed.) *Enterprise Value in the knowledge economy: Measuring performance in the Age of Intangibles*, pp. 49-73. Cambridge, MA.: The Ernst and Young Center for Business Innovation.

Mayo, A. (2000). HR People in Know: Knowledge Management and the Role of HR, *People Management*, 6, pp. 61-63.

McAdam, R. and Reid, R. (2001). SME and large organization perceptions of knowledge management: comparisons and contrasts, *Journal of Knowledge Management*, 5, pp. 231-241.

McElroy, M.W. (2000). Integrating complexity theory, knowledge management and organizational learning, *Journal of Knowledge Management*, 4, pp. 195-203.

McElroy, M.W. (2003). *The new knowledge management: Complexity, learning, and sustainable innovation*. Burlington, MA: Butterworth-Heinemann.

Meissner, M. (1971). The long arm of the job: A study of work and leisure, *Industrial Relations, Journal of Economy & Society*, 10, pp. 239-260.

Mezirow, J. (2003). Issues in transformative learning. In T. Hagström (ed.), *Adult development in Post-industrial Society and working life*. Stockholm lectures in Educology. Lecture Series No. 2, pp. 49-66. Stockholm: Department of Education.

Miles, I. (2000). *New Jobs in the information society*. Retrieved: April 2002 from: *http://les.man.ac.uk/cric/Ian_Miles*.

Mincer, J. (1989). Human capital and the labour market: A review of current research, *Educational Researcher*, 18, pp. 27-34.

Mincer, J. (1997). The production of human capital and the life cycle of earnings: Variations on a theme, *Journal of Labor Economics*, 15, pp. S26-S47.

Moody, M. & Duff, A. (2000). Is that public knowledge? *Director*, 53, pp. 21-24.

Morley, M.J. and Garavan, T.N. (1995). Current themes in organizational design: Implications for human resource development, *Journal of European Industrial Training*, 19, pp. 3-13.

Mortensen, J. Eustace, C. and Lannoo, K. (1997). Intangibles in the European Economy. Brussels: Centre for European Policy Studies

Muldivie, A. and McDougall, M. (1990). *Human Resource Management in Practice*. Chartwell-Bratt. Lund. Sweden.

Mumford, M.D. (2000). Managing creative people: Strategies and Tactics for Innovation, *Human Resource Management Review*, 10, pp. 313-351.

Murnane, R.J., Willet, J.B., and Levy, F. (1995). The growing importance of cognitive skills in wage determination, *Review of economics statistics*, 77, pp. 251-266.

Nachmias, C. and Nachmias, D. (1996). *Research Methods in Social Sciences*. London: Edward Arnold,

National Agency for Education (2000). Lifelong learning and lifewide learning. Stockholm: The National Agency for Education in Sweden.

Neef, D. (1997). Human Resource Reporting: Elements of an Improved System of Knowledge Management. In Ernst and Young Center for Business Innovation and OECD (ed.) *Enterprise Value in the knowledge economy: Measuring performance in the Age of Intangibles*, pp. 1-7. Cambridge, MA: The Ernst and Young Center for Business Innovation.

Neef, D. (1999). Making the case of knowledge management: the bigger picture, *Management Decision*, 37, pp.72-78.

Neuman, W.L. (2000). *Social Research methods: Qualitative and quantitative approaches (fourth edition)*. London: Allyn and Bancon.

Newel, S., Robertson, M., Scarbrough, H. and Swan, J. (2002). *Managing knowledge work*. New York: Palgrave Macmillan.

Nisbet, J.D. and Watt, J. (1980). *Case Study. Rediguide 26*. Nottingham: University of Nottingham School of Education, UK.

Nonaka, I. (1988). Creating organizational order out of chaos: Self-renewal in Japanese firms, *California Mangement Review*, 30, pp. 57-73.

Nonaka, I. (1991). The knowledge creating company, *Harvard Business Review*, 69, pp. 96-104.

Nonaka, I. (1994). A dynamic theory of organizational knowledge creation, *Organizational Science*, 5, pp. 14-37.

Nonaka, I. and Konno, N. (1998). The concept of "ba", *California management review*, 43, pp. 40-54.

Nonaka, I. and Takeuchi, H. (1995). *The knowledge creating company*: How Japanese companies create the dynamics of innovation. Oxford: Oxford University Press.

Nonaka, I. and Toyama, R. (2002). A firm as a dialectic being: towards a dynamic theory of the firm, *Industrial and Corporate Change*, 11, pp. 995-1009.

Nonaka, I. and Toyama, R. (2004). Knowledge creation as a synthesis process. In H. Takeuchi and I. Nonaka (eds), *Hitosubashi on Knowledge Management*, pp. 91-125. Singapore: John Wiley and Sons.

Nonaka, I., Toyama, R. and Konno, N. (2000). SECI, ba and leadership: a unified model of dynamic knowledge creation, *Longe Range Planning*, 33, pp. 5-34.

Nonaka, I., Umemoto, K. and Senoo, D. (1996). From information processing to knowledge creation: A paradigm shift in business management, *Technology In Society*, 18, pp. 203-218.

O'Connor, D.J. and Carr, B. (1982). *Introduction to the theory of knowledge*. London: The harvester press limited.

O'Dell, C., Wiig, K. and Odem, P. (1999). Benchmarking unveils emerging knowledge management strategies, *Benchmarking: An international journal*, 6, pp. 202-211.

OECD (1973). *Recurrent education: A strategy for lifelong learning*. Paris: OECD.

OECD (1992). *Technology and the economy. The key relationships*. Paris: OECD.

OECD (1996). *Lifelong learning for all*. Paris: OECD.

OECD (1997). *Sustainable flexibility. A prospective Study on work, Family and Society in the Information Age*. Paris: OCDE.

OECD (1998). *Human Capital Investment. An International Comparison*. Paris: OECD.

OECD (2000). Knowledge management in the learning society. In OECD, *Knowledge management in the learning society. Education and Skills*, pp. 11-104. Paris: OECD.

OECD (2001a). *The well-being of nations: The role of human and social capital*. Paris: OECD.

OECD (2001b). *Science and Technology Scoreboard 2001*. Paris: OECD

OECD and HRDC (1997) Literacy for the knowledge society: Second Report of the International Adult Literacy Survey (Paris and Ottawa: OECD and HRDC).

OECD and Statistics Canada (2000). *Literacy in the information age: Final report on the international adult literacy survey*. Paris: OECD.

Oltra, V. (2005). Knowledge Management effectiveness factors: the role of HRM, Journal of Knowledge Management, 9, pp. 70-86.

Ordóñez de Pablos, P. (2002). Evidence of intellectual capital measurement from Asia, europe and the Middle East, *Journal of Intellectual Capital*, 3, 2002, pp. 287-302.

Ordóñez de Pablos, P. (2004). Measuring and reporting structural capital: Lessons from European learning firms, *Journal of Intellectual Capital*, 5, pp. 629-647.

Patton, M.Q. (1990). *Qualitative evaluation and research method (2nd edition)*. London: SAGE Publication .

Pavlov, I.P. (1904). Physiology of digestion. Nobel Lecture, December 12. In Elsevier Publishing Company (ed.), *Nobel lectures: Physiology or Medicine 1901-1921*. Amsterdam: Elsevier Publishing Company. Retrieved October 2004 from: *http://nobelprize.org/medicine/laureates/1904/pavlov-lecture.html*.

Pavlov, I.P. (1928). *Lectures on conditioned reflexes. Twenty-five years of objective study of the higher nervous activity (behavior) of animals* (Translated from the Russian by W. Horsley Gantt). New York: International Publishers.

Pelton, C. (1999). Share the knowledge, *Informationsweek*, 737, p.188.

Penrose, E. T. (1959). *The Theory of the Growth of the Firm*. Oxford: Basil Blackwell.

Perner, J. (1996). Cognitive development: Overview. In T. Husén and T. N. Postlethwaite (eds.), *International encyclopedia of education (Second edition)*, pp. 852-856. Oxford: Pergamon Press and Elsevier Science.

Peters, T. (1992). *Liberation Management: Necessary disorganization for the nanosecond nineties*. London: Macmillan London.

Philliphs, D.C. and Burbules, N.C., (2000) *Postpositivism and Educational Research*. Boston: Rowman & Littlefield Publishers.

Piaget, J. (1950). *The psychology of intelligence*. Florence, KY, USA: Routledge.

Piaget, J. (1975). *L'e´quilibration des structures cognitives. Proble`me central du de´velopment*. Paris: PUF (*The development of thought: equilibration of cognitive structures*. Eng. trans. New York: Viking Press).

Piaget, J. (1977). *The development of thought: Equilibration of cognitive structures*. Translated by Arnold Rosin. Oxford: Basil Blackwell.

Pintrich, P. R. and De Groot, E. V. (1990). Motivational and self-regulated learning components of classroom academis performance, *Journal of Educational Psychology*, 82, 33-40.

Pintrich, P. R., Marx, R.W., and Boyle, R. A. (1993). Beyond cold conceptual change: The role of motivational beliefs and classroom contextual factors in the process of conceptual change, *Review of Educational Research*, 63, pp. 167-199.

Plaskoff, J. (2003). Intersubjectivity and community building: learning to learn organizationally. In M. Easter-Smith and M. A. Lyles (eds), *Handbook of organizational learning and knowledge management*, pp. 161-184. Oxford: Blackwell Publishing.

Polanyi, M. (1962). Tacit Knowing: Its bearing on some problems of philosophy, *Reviews of Modern Physics*, 34, 601-616. Retrieved last on, May 2005, from:

http://www.culturaleconomics.atfreeweb.com/Anno/Polanyi%20Tacit%20Knowlng%20RMP%201 962.htm.

Polanyi, M. (1967). *The tacit dimension (Second Edition)*. New York: Anchor Books.

Polanyi, M. (1969). On body and mind, *The New Scholasticism, 43*, pp. 195-204.

Popper, K. R. (1976). *Unended Quest*, Glasgow : Fontana/William Collins Sons & Co. ,.

Pozo, J. I. (2003). *Adquisición de conocimiento (Knowledge acquisition)*. Madrid: Morata.

Psacharopoulos, G. (1994). Returns to investment in education : A global update. *World Development*, 22, pp. 1325-1343.

Quinn, J.B., Anderson, P., and Finkelstein, S. (1998). Managing professional intellect: making the most of the best. In A. D. Klein (ed.), *The strategic Management of Intellectual capital*, pp. 87-100. Oxford: Butterworth-Heinemann.

Quintas, P. Lefrere, P. and Jones, G. (1997). Knowledge management: A strategic agenda, *Long Range Planning*, 30, pp. 385-391.

Quintas, P. (2003). Managing knowledge in practice. In OECD and Statistics Canada, *Measuring knowledge management in the business sector: First steps*. Paris: OECD, pp. 385-391.

Ramboll Management (2005). Slututvärdering Växtkraft Mål 3: Final version. Stockholm: Ramboll management. (Ramboll Management (2005). *Final evaluation of the Objective 3*. Stockholm: Ramboll management.).

Rao, M. (2005a). The social life of KM tools. In M. Rao (ed.), *Knowledge management tool and techniques: Practicioners and experts evaluate KM solutions*. London: Elsevier, pp. 1-77.

Rao, M. (ed.) (2005b). *Knowledge management tool and techniques: Practicioners and experts evaluate KM solutions*. London: Elsevier.

Rivière, A. (1995). *La Psicología de Vygotski*. Madrid: Visor.[Rivière, A. (1995). The Vigotski's psychology. Madrid: Visor].

Robinson-Kaluzni, C. (2000). *Wealth of an Education: Social capital as a resource for human capital outcomes* (Unpublished M.A. thesis). Stockholm: Institute of International Education.

Rodriguez Perez, J. and Ordoñez de Pablos, P. (2003). Knowledge management and organizational competitiveness: a framework for human capital analysis, *Journal of Knowledge Management*, 7, pp. 82-91.

Román-Velazquez, J. (2005). An empirical study of organizational culture types and their relationship with success of knowledge management system and the flow of knowledge in the U.S. Government and non-profit sectors. In M. A. Stankosky (ed.), *Creating the discipline of knowledge management: The latest in University Research*. Oxford: Elsevier, pp. 66-92.

Romer, P. (1990) Endogenous Technological Change, *Journal of Political Economy*, 98, pp. S71-S102.

Roos, G. and Roos, J. (1997). Measuring your company's intellectual performance, *Long Range Planning*, 30, pp. 413-426.

Roos, G., Ferström, L. and Pike, S. (2004). Human resource management and business performance measurement, *Measuring Business excellence*, 8, pp. 28-37.

Rothwell, W. J., Prescott, R. K. and Taylor, M. W. (1998). *Strategic human resource leader: How to prepare your organisation for the six key trends shaping the future*. Palo Alto, CA: Davies Black Publishing.

Roy, S. (2003). *Navigating in the knowledge Era: Metaphors and stories in the construction of Skandia's Navigator*. Stockholm University school of business research report No. 2003: 1. Stockholm: School of Business, Stockholm University.

Rubenson, K. (1987). Participation in recurrent education: A research review. In H. G. Schuetze and D. Istance (eds.), *Recurrent education revisited: Mode of participation and financing*, pp. 39-67. Stockholm: Almqvist & Wiksell International.

Rubenson, K. (1997). Adult education and training: The poor cousin. An analysis of OECD reviews of national policies for education, *Scottish Journal of Adult Education*, 5, pp. 5-32.

Rubenson, K. (1999). Supply of lifelong-learning opportunities: Issues for research. In A. C. Tuijnman and T. Shuller, (eds), *Lifelong learning policy and research: Proceedings of an international Symposium*, pp. 109-121. London: Portland Press.

Rubenson, K. (2001a). Lifelong learning for all: Challenges and limitations of public policies. In Ministry of Education and Science in Sweden (ed.), *Adult lifelong learning in a Europe of knowledge, Ekilstuna, Sweden, 21-23 March 2001*. Stockholm: Ministry of Education and Science in Sweden, pp. 29-39.

Rubenson, K. (2001b), The Swedish adult education initiative: From recurrent education to lifelong learning. In D. N. Aspin, J. Chapman, M. Hatton and Y. Sawano (eds), *International handbook of lifelong learning*, pp. 329-339. London: Kluwer Academic Publishers.

Rubenson, K. (2003). Adult education and Cohesion, *Lifelong Learning in Europe*, 8, pp. 32-36.

Rubenson, K. and Schuetze, H.G. (1995). Learning at and through the workplace: A review of participation and adult learning theory. In D. Hirsch and D.A. Wagner (eds.), *What makes workers learn: The role of incentives in workplace education and training*. Series on Literacy, Research, Policy and Practice, pp. 95-116. Cresskill, NJ: Hampton press.

Rubenson, K. and Schuetze, H.G. (2000). *Transition to the knowledge society: Policies and strategies for individual participation and learning.* Vancouver, BC: British Columbia Press

Rubenson, K. and Xu, G. (1997). Barriers to participation in adult education and training: Towards a new understanding. In P. Bélanger and A. C. Tuijnman (eds), *New patterns of adult learning: A six country comparative study,* pp. 77-100. Oxford: Pergamon Press and Hamburg: UNESCO Institute of Education.

Saettler, P. (1990). *The evolution of American educational technology.* Inglewood, Colorado: Libraries Unlimited.

Salaman, G.; Cameron, S.; Hamblin, H.; Iles, P.; Mabey, C. and Thompson, K. (ed.) (1992). *Human Resource Strategies.* Sage Publications. London.

Sanchez, M. P., Chaminade, C. and Olea, M. (2000). Management of Intangibles: An attempt to built a theory, *Journal of Intellectual Capital,* 1, pp. 312-328.

Saussois, J.M. (2000). Presentation of Expert's reports on the Management of Knowledge. In OECD *Knowledge Management in the Learning Society,* pp. 107-114. OECD. Parish.

Savage, C. M. (1996). *Fifth generation management: Co-creating through virtual enterprising, dynamic teaming, and knowledge networking.* Oxford: Butterworth-Heinemann.

Schiller, S. (1999). *The intelligent enterprise: From a competence management perspective.* Gothenburg: BAS.

Schuetze, H. G. and Fujitsuka, T. (2002). Organization of knowledge transfers between universities and industry in North America, Europe and Japan. Daigaku Ronshu, 26, pp. 179 -194.

Schultz, T. (1961). Investment in human capital, *American Economic Review,* 51 (1), pp.1-17.

Senge, P. M, (1990). *The fifth discipline: The art and practice of learning organization.* New York: Doubleday Currency.

Senge, P. M., Kleiner, A., Roberts, C., Ross, R., Roth, G.; and Smith, B. (1999). *The dance of change: The challenge of sustaining momentum in learning organizations.* London: Nicholas Brealey Publishing.

Senge, P.M., Roberts, C., Ross, R.B., Smith, B.J. and Kleiner, A. (1994). *The fifth discipline fieldbook: Strategies and Tools for building a learning Organization.* London: Doubleday.

Shuell, T.J. and Moran, K.A. (1996). Learning theories: Historical overview and trends. In T. Husén and T.N. Postlethwaite (eds), *International encyclopedia of education (Second edition),* pp. 3340-3349. Oxford: Pergamon Press and Elsevier Science.

Shute, V.J. (1996). Learning processes and learning outcomes. In T. Husén and T. N. Postlethwaite (eds), *International encyclopedia of education (Second edition),* pp. 3315-3325. Oxford: Pergamon Press and Elsevier Science.

Silverman, D. (1993). *Interpreting qualitative data: Methods for analaysing talk, text and interaction.* London: Sage.

Skinner, B.F. (1953). *Science and Behavior.* New York: Macmillan, p. 153

Skinner, B.F. (1974). *About behaviorism.* New York: Alfred A. Knopf, INC.

Skirme, D.J. (1999). *Knowledge networking: Creating the collaborative enterprise.* Oxford: Butterworth-Heinemann.

Smith, A. (1784/1994). *The wealth of nations (Fifth edition).* New York: The modern library.

Smith, J. A. and Ross, W. D. (eds) (1908). *The works of Aristotle translated into English.* London: Oxford University Press.

Sole, D. and Edmondson, A. (2002). Bridging knowledge gaps: learning in geographically dispersed cross-functional teams. In C. Wei Choo and N. Bontis (eds), *The strategic management of intellectual capital and organizational knowledge,* pp.587-605. Oxford: Osford University press.

Sosa, E. and Kim, J. (eds) (2000). *Epistemology: an antology.* Oxford: Blackwell Publishers Inc.

Spender, J.C. (2002). Knowledge, uncertainty, and an emergency theory of the firm. In C. Wei Choo and N. Bontis (eds), *The strategic management of intellectual capital and organizational knowledge,* pp. 149-163. Oxford: Oxford University.

Spender, J.C., and Grant, R.M. (1996). Knowledge and the firm: Overview, *Strategic Management Journal,* 17, pp. 5–9.

Ståhle, P. (2002). Knowledge management as a learning challenge, *Lifelong Learning in Europe,* 7, pp. 10-19.

Stake, R.E. (2000). Case studies. In N.K. Denzin, and Y.S. Lincoln (eds), *Handbook of qualitative research (2nd edition),* pp. 645-669. London: Sage Publications.

Stankosky, M. (ed.) (2005a). *Creating the discipline of Knowledge Management: The latest in University Research.* London: Elsevier.

Stankosky, M. A. (2005b). Advanced in knowledge management: University research toward an academic discipline. In M. A. Stankosky (ed.), *Creating the discipline of knowledge management: The latest in University Research,* pp. 1-15. Oxford: Elsevier.

Starbuck, W.H. (1992). Learning by knowledge-intensive firms, *Journal of Management Studies,* 29, pp. 713-738.

Statistics Netherlands and EUROSTAT (1999). *Intangible investments: indicators for intangibles.* Voorburg and Luxemburg: Statistics Netherlands/ EUROSTAT.

Stegmüller, W. (1977). *Collected papers on epistemology, philosophy of science and history of philosophy.* Volume I. Dordrech-Holland: D. Reidel Publishing Company.

Stenhouse, L. (1982). The conduct, analysis and reporting of case study in educational research and evaluation, In R. Murphy and H. Torrance (eds) (1987), *Evaluating education: Issues and methods,* pp. 74-80. London: Paul Chapman Publishing.

Stewart, T.A. (1999). *Intellectual capital: The new wealth of organizations.* London: Currency Doubleday.

Stovel, M. and Bontis, N. (2002), Voluntary turnover: Knowledge management – friend or foe? *Journal of Intellectual Capital,* 3, pp. 303-322.

Sveiby, K.E. (1992). The know-how company: Strategy formulation in knowledge-intensive industries. In D.E. Hussey (ed.), *International Review of Strategic Management,* 3, pp. 167-186.

Sveiby, K.E. (1997). *The new Organizational Wealth: Managing and Measuring Knowledge-based Assets.* San Francisco, CA: Berrett-Koehler Publishers.

Sveiby, K.E. (2001). A knowledge-based theory of the firm to guide strategy formulation, *Journal of Intellectual Capital,* 2 (4), pp. 344-358.

Sveiby, K.E. (2002). *Methods for measuring intenagible assets.* Retrieved, November 2004 from: *http://www.sveiby.com/Portals/0/articles/IntangibleMethods.htm.*

Sveiby, K.E. and Simons, R. (2002). Collaborative Climate and effectiveness of knowledge work – an empirical study, *Journal of Knowledge Management,* 6, pp. 420-433.

Sveiby, K.E., and Lloyd, T. (1987). *Managing knowhow.* Bloomsbury, London.

Sveiby, K.E., Linard, K. and Dvorsky, L. (2002). Building a knowledge-based strategy: A system dynamics model for allocating value adding capacity. Research paper. Retrived October 2004 from: *http://www.sveiby.com/Portals/0/articles/sdmodelkstrategy.pdf*

Svensson, L. (2005). Arbetstagares lärandemiljöer i kunskapsintensiv verksamhet (Learning environments of employees in knowledge intensive work), *Pedagogisk Forskning i Sverige,* 10, pp. 195-208, 289-290.

Svensson, L., Brewster, C., Heraty, N., larsen, H.H., Kjellberg, Y., Madsen, P. L., Morley, M. and Tregaskis, O. (2002). *Final report: Learning environments of knowledge intensive company units in five European countries.* Retrieved, February 2006 from: *www.learningcitizen.uni-bremen.de/download.php?ID=193.*

Swedish ESF Council (2001). *Summary of the Swedish Objective 3: Single Program Document (SPD)* 2000-2006. August, 19th , 2002. Retrieved from:
   http://europa.eu.int/comm/employment_social/esf2000/ms/s-obj-3-doc-en.pdf .

Swedish Ministry of Finance and Ministry of Industry, Employment and Communications *(1999). Sweden's action plan for employment, 2000.* Stockholm: Government of Sweden. Retrieved November 2002, from: *http://www.sweden.gov.se/sb/d/108/a/1859;jsessionid=aFVFi7RjXjp_.*

Swedish Ministry of Finance and Ministry of Industry, Employment and Communications (2004). *Sweden's action plan for employment, 2004.* Stockholm: Government of Sweden. Retrieved November 2005, from: *http://www.regeringen.se/sb/d/2530/a/36642.*

Swedish National Board for Education, (2000), *Lifelong learning and lifewide learning,* Stockholm: Swedish National Board for Education.

Sweetland, S. R. (1996). Human capital theory: Foundations of a field of inquiry, *Review of Educational Research,* 66, 341-359.

Takeuchi, H and Nonaka, I. (eds), (2004a). *Hitosubashi on Knowledge Management.* Singapore: John Wiley and Sons.

Takeuchi, H. and Nonaka, I. (2004b). Knowledge creation and dialectics. In H. Takeuchi and I. Nonaka (eds), *Hitosubashi on Knowledge Management,* pp. 1-29. Singapore: John Wiley and Sons.

Tayles, M., Bramley, A., Adshead, N. and Farr, J. (2002). Dealing with the management of intellectual capital: The potential role of strategic management accounting, *Accounting, Auditing & Accountability Journal,* 15, pp. 251- 267.

Taylor, G. H. (1998). Knowledge companies. In W. E. Halal (ed.), *The infinite resource: Creating and leading the knowledge enterprise,* pp. 97-110. San Francisco: Jossey-Bass.

The Ernst & Young Center for Business Innovation and OECD (eds) (1997). *Enterprise Value in the Knowledge Economy.* Cambridge, M.A.:Ernst and Young Center for Business Innovation.

The Skandia Group (1994). Visualizing intellectual capital. In The Skandia Group, *Annual Report.* Stockholm: The Skandia Group.

Tsang (1997). Organizational learning and the learning organization: A Dichotomy between descriptive and perspective research, *Human Relations,* 50, pp. 73-89.

Tuijnman, A.C. (1989). *Recurrent Education, Earnings and Well-Being: A fifty-year longitudinal study of a cohort of Swedish men.* Acta Universitatis Stockholmiensis, Stockholm Studies in Educational Psychology, No. 24. Stockholm: Almqvist & Wiksell International.

Tuijnman, A.C. (1996). Recurrent Education. In A.C. Tuijnman, (ed.), *International Encyclopedia of Adult Education and Training (2nd edition)*, pp. 99- 107. Oxford: Pergamon Press.

Tuijnman, A.C. (1999). Research agenda for lifelong learning: A report by the task force of the International Academy of Education. In A.C. Tuijnman and T. Schuller (eds.), *Lifelong Learning Policy & Research: Proceedings of an International Symposium*, pp. 1-22. London: Portland Press.

Tuijnman, A.C. (2000). Measuring human capital: Data gaps and survey requirements. In K. Rubenson and H.G. Schuetze (eds.), *Transitions to the knowledge society*, pp. 396-410. Vancouver: University of British Columbia Press.

Tuijnman, A.C. and Boström, A.-K., (2002), Changing notions of lifelong education and lifelong learning, *International Review of Education*, 48, pp. 93-100.

Tuijnman, A.C. and Boudard, E. (2001). *Adult education in North America: An international comparative study*. Washington, DC: U.S. Department of Education, Office of Vocational and Adult Education.

Tuomi, I. (1999). Hierarchy for knowledge management and organizational memory, *Journal of Management Information Systems*, 16, pp. 103-117.

Tuomi, I. (2002). Towards the third generation of knowledge management, *Lifelong Learning in Europe*, 7, pp. 69-80.

Van Winkelen, C., Birchall, D. and Smith, G. (2004). A framework for comparing knowledge management practices. In E. Truch (ed.), *Levering corporate knowledge*, pp. 23-33. Aldershot, UK: Gower.

Vera, D. and Crossan, M. (2003). Organizational learning and knowledge management: Toward an integrated framework. In M. Easter-Smith and M. A. Lyles (eds), *Handbook of organizational learning and knowledge management*, pp. 122- 142. Oxford: Blackwell Publishing.

Villalba, E. (2004). *Knowledge management as a strategy for lifelong learning: A report for the European Social Fund Council in Sweden*. Yellow report series, No. 118. Stockholm: Institute of International Education, Stockholm University.

von Krogh, G. and Grand, S. (2002). From economic theory toward a knowledge-based theory of the firm: Conceptual building blocks. In C. Wei Choo, and N. Bontis, (eds), *The strategic management of intellectual capital and organizational knowledge*, pp. 163-185. Oxford: Oxford University Press.

von Krogh, G. and Roos, J. (1995). *Organizational epistemology*. London: Macmillan press ltd.

von Krogh, G. and Roos, J. (1996). Conversation Management for knowledge development. In G. von Krogh, and J. Roos, (eds), *Managing Knowledge: Perspectives on cooperation and competition*, pp. 218-225. London: SAGE Publications.

von Krogh, G. and Roos, J. and Slocum, K. (1996). An essay on corporate epistemology. In G. Von Krogh, and J. Roos, (eds), *Managing Knowledge: Perspectives on cooperation and competition*, pp. 157-183. London: SAGE Publications.

von Krogh, G., Ichijo, K., and Nonaka, I. (2000). *Enabling knowledge creation: How to unlock the mystery of tacit knowledge and release the power of innovation*. Oxford: Oxford University Press.

Vosniadou, S. (1996). Knowledge Representation and Organization. In T. Husén and T. N. Postlethwaite (Eds.), *International encyclopedia of education (Second edition)*, pp. 3151-3155. Oxford: Pergamon Press and Elsevier Science.

Vygotski, L.S. (1978). *Mind in society. The development of higher psychological processes*. Cambridge, Mass: Harvard University Press.

Watson, J.B. (1924). *Psychology: From the standpoint of a behaviorist*. Philadelphia: J.B. Lippincott Company.

Webber, A. (1993). What's so new about new economy, *Harvard Business Review*, 71, pp.24-42.

Wei Choo, C. and Bontis, N. (eds) (2002a). *The strategic management of intellectual capital and organizational knowledge*. Oxford: Oxford University Press.

Wei Choo, C. and Bontis, N. (2002b). Knowledge, intellectual capital, and strategy. In C. Wei Choo, and N. Bontis, (eds), *The strategic management of intellectual capital and organizational knowledge*, pp. 3-19. Oxford: Oxford University Press.

Weiler, H.N. (2001). Knowledge, politics, and the future of higher education: critical observations on a worldwide transformation. In Hayhoe, R. and Pan, J. (eds), *Knowledge across cultures: A contribution to dialogue among civilizations*, pp.25-43. Hong Kong: Comparative Education Research Center, the University of Hong Kong.

Whitaker, R. (1998). Managing context in enterprise knowledge processes. In A. D. Klein (ed.). *The strategic Management of Intellectual capital*, pp. 73-87. Oxford: Butterworth-Heinemann.

Wiig, K.M. (1993). *Knowledge management foundations: Thinking about thinking. How people and organizations create, represent and use knowledge*. Arlington, Texas: Schema Press.

Wiig, K.M. (1994). *Knowledge management: The central management focus for intelligent-acting organizations*. Arlington, Texas: Schema Press.

Wiig, K.M. (1995). *Knowledge management methods: Practical approaches to managing knowledge*. Arlington, Texas: Schema Press.

Wiig, K.M. (1997a). Knowledge Management: Where did it come from and where will it go? *Expert Systems with Applications*, 13, pp. 1-14.

Wiig, K.M. (1997b). Integrating intellectual capital and knowledge management, *Long Range Planning*, 30, pp. 399-405.

Wiig, K. M. (2000). Knowledge Management: An emerging discipline rooted in long history. In C. Despres and D. Chauvel (eds), *Knowledge horizons: the present and the promise of knowledge management*, pp.3-27. Woburn, MA: Butterworth-Heinemann.

Wiig, K.M., de Hoog, R, and Van der Spek, R. (1997). Supporting KM: A selection of methods and techniques, *Expert System with Applications*, 13, pp.15-27.

Wong, Kuan Yew and Aspinwall, E. (2004). Characterizing knowledge management in the small business environment, *Journal of Knowledge Management*, 8, pp. 44-61.

Wood, R. E. (2001) Implicit theories of managers: Do your assumptions help or hinder you? *AGSM*, 1, pp. 12-15.

Wundt, W.M. (1897). Outlines of Psychology (Translated by Judd, C. H.). York University, Toronto, Ontario. Retrieved February 2004, from: *http://psychclassics.yorku.ca/Wundt/Outlines/index.htm*.

Yahya, S. and Goh, W.K. (2002). Managing human resources toward achieving knowledge management, *Journal of Knowledge Management*, 6, pp. 457- 468.

Yin, R.K. (1993). *Applications of case study research*. Applied social research methods series. Volume 34. London: SAGE Publications.

Zuboff, S. (1988*). In the Age of the Smart Machine: The Future of Work and Power*. New York: Basic Books.

ANNEXES

ANNEX I: CODE BOOK

Table of contents for Annex I

Interview and document data

The knowledge enabling environment

VV	Label
General information	
idcomp	Company ID
idcomp2	
company	company
contact	Contact person for the project
sni	International Sector Number
sni2	International Sector Number, 2 digits
ESF plan	Start date of ESF plan
startc	When did the company started
big	Does the company belong to a bigger corporation?
1	Yes

	0	No
sucsu		N. of offices in Sweden
sucfo		N. of offices outside Sweden
chart		Structure/ chart of the company
layers		Number of tiers of the company
	1	No boss
	2	C. has a leading group/ leader and the rest workers (no sections)
	3	C. leading group (or a leader) + middle manager, leaders of the sections, and then employees
	4	C. leading group (or leader) + middle managers + responsible of subsections + employees
owo2		Ways of working codified
	1	Working individually
	2	Working in teams (people = section)
	3	Working teams, people different sections = cross-functional teams) in Schools: different subjects teachers = group in teams

Employee's characteristics

emptot	N. of total employees
empwom	N. of women employed
empmen	N. of men employed
emppart	N. of employees participating in the program
emptot2	N. of employees (SUM of FT, PT, TP)
empful	N. of permanent employees full time: FT
empprt	N. of permanent employees part time hired: PT
emptem	N. of temporal employees: TP
empptft	N. of permanent part time employees per full time employee (empprt/ empful)
emperft	Percentage of ft employees' (empful/emptot2)
empperm	Proportion of permanent employees as a percentage of the total number of employees (empful + empprt) / emptot2
emptemp	Proportion of temporally workers as a proportion of the total (emptem / emptot2)
empppt	Permanent part time of all part time' (empprt / (empprt + emptem))
empsup	N. of employees in support functions (no matter if part time or full time)
emppro	N. of employees in professional role
emplead	N. of project leaders
empman	N. of managers (people in positions responsible for others)
empund	Number of employees not determined (emptot2 - (empsup + emppro + emplead + empman))
emledman	Ratio n. of project leaders/ n. of managers
emsuppro	Ratio n. of support staff/ n. of professional workers
emledpro	Ratio n. of project leaders/ n. of professional staff
emprorat	Number of professional workers as a % of all employees (emppro/emptot2)
empcom	comments for numbers of employees
empnew	N. of employees for new employees
emplevr	N. of employees left voluntary because of retirement
empleoj	N. of employees left voluntary because going to other job
emplein	N. of employees left involuntary
empsic	N. of employees in sick leave or mama/papa ledig
emloss	N. of employees that left the company(emplevr + empleoj + emplein + empsic)
emgain	N. of employees gained in the last year (newemp- (sum of emp leaving))
emturn	Employee turnover (emgain/emptot2)
sicday	N. of sick days registered
manpro	Is the manager/ director of the company a professional worker?
	1	yes

	0	no
manown		Is the manager/ director of the company a owner of the comany?
	1	yes
	0	no
hrboss		Who is the one in charge of HR in the company?
Hrboscod		Who is in cahrge of human resources = Salary negotiations
	1	the manager/ owner/ director
	2	a professional worker inside the organization

Recruitment / Selection

reproc		Recruitment procedure
read		Recruitment advertisement (how do they attract people)
	1	Central pool
	2	Advertisement in newspapers/ arbets../ other specific
	3	Adverts only in specific
	4	People known
reprocd		Recruitment procedure codified
	1	One interview: with manager
	2	Two steps interview: also with the one responsible of section
	3	Some kind of test+ interview
	4	Headhunters/ manpower"
reeduql		Education criteria for recruitment (qualitative)
reeducd		What consideration education has
	1	Education as a pre-requisite
	2	Educ. and Necessary work experience
	3	No important educ., but work experience as crucial
	4	Focus on competencies: Can do the job
	5 to 4	Taking people without education and/or qualifications
reso		Recruitment Social: do they acknowledge social skills as important
	0	No
	1	Yes
resk		Interested in skills/ subject matters/ K
	0	No
	1	Yes
reedu		Has to have specific education/ right education. Educ necessary
	0	No
	1	Yes
reser		Interested in service oriented/ treatment to customers
	0	No
	1	Yes
reage		Age as a factor
	0	No
	1	Yes
refit		It has to fit/ be loyal (?)
	0	No
	1	Yes
relearn		Be open/ interested in learning
	0	No
	1	Yes
reoth		Other
	0	No
	1	Yes

Reward system

salql		How is the salary determined? (long)
salind		Salary is determined according to each indiv. (Each person is treated differently)
	1	Individual determined
	0	No
saldem		Salary depending on demand on the market
	0	No
	1	Yes
salper		Salary depending on performance measures (BSC)
	0	No
	1	Yes
salexp		Salary depending on experienced
	0	No
	1	Yes
saluni		Salary depending on central authority or Union
	0	No
	1	Yes

Information on salary from documents

salem	Number of employees to determine the salary
salmale	Number of male employees in the salary determination
salyear	Year of the salary was recorded (latest year available)
sal	Salary (hourly bases) in SEK
salcomdo	Salary comment (from Documents)

Bonus system

bonus		Does the company offer specific bonus system?
	1	Yes
	0	No
boncd		Bonus system codified (long)
bongrp		Group bonus or not
	1 to 2	Group: Given to everybody irrespective of individual's performance
	0 to 1	Individual: give different to each individual
	2 to 3	Specific group: only shared holders, or only teams with huge performanced4
	9	No bonus
	-9	Missing
bonwhy		Why they give bonus?
	1	Performance: Based on performance measures of individual or group
	2	When profit: if there are profits/ irrespective of performance
	3	When activities: if worked more
	4	Others (no body)
bontyp		Bonus type
	1	Basic contribution: financial +
	2	*Voluntary Company Contributions*: Typical employer contributions/ expense for private retirement, life insurance, disability, medical and other voluntary employee benefit plans (including executive pensions).
	3	*Perquisites*: Annual cash value of company cars, club memberships and other perquisites that are typically provided to executives. (no one)
	4	*Long-Term Incentives*: Annual expected value of long-term incentive awards (e.g., stock options, stock grants and other awards).
	5	Others

Aspect of Information Technologies

itcare	Number of people taking care of computers

	8	Outsourced/ mother company does it
itn		Number of computers
itnlap		Number of laptops
itpemp		Number of computers per employee (itncomp / emptot2)
itfac		IT facilities (explanation)
itintra		Does it have an intranet
	1	Yes
	0	No
itinter		Does it have anccess to internet
	1	Yes
	0	No
itdb		Does it have a database?
	1	Yes
	0	No
itdbac		Who has access to the database?
	0	No database
	1	All employees to at least one part of the db
	2	rstricted access
itdbcust		Has the data base customer data?
	1	
	0	
itdbsk		Has the data base information on skills/ competencies
	1	
	0	
itdbwa		Database work activity (all work activity loaded)
	1	
	0	
it2001		Investment in IT in 2001
it2002		Investment in IT in 2002
it2003		Investment in IT in 2003
itcor02		IT expenditure as a proportion of total turnover (it2002/ turnover)
itcsrv		IT cost of the server
itcser		IT cost of services
itchar		It cost Hardware
itcsft		IT cost software

Aspects on communication

colet		Communication News letter or other type of regular update of activities within the company in printed form
	0	No
	1	Yes, newsletter
	2	Yes, news in the web
	3 to 0	Verbal information in regular basis
colet2		Communication News letter or other type of regular update of activities within the company in printed form
	0	No
	1	Yes
cofge		Communication, frequency general meetings (Measure in each month: 4 weeks month)
cofge2		Communication, frequency of general meetings Recoded (cofge recoded)
	0	Less than 1 per month
	1	Once a month
	2	Twice a month

	4	Each week
copro		Communication between professional workers / project work (in each month)
	1	When needed
	2 to 3	In regular basis different each department
	3	In regular basis, scheduled (less than 1/week)
	4	in regular basis each week
	5	meeting informally or more than 1/week
	8 to 5	8= twice a week
copro2		Communication between professional workers / project work (in each month)
	0	Informally/ when needed
	1	In regular basis
cofled		Communication frequency between leader group (in monthly basis)
cofsem		Communication, frequency of seminars (in monthly bases)
	22	2 per year
	66	6 times a year
cosem		Communication, types of seminars that the organization gives (if any)
	0	no seminar
	1	With/ for customers
	2	To share information/ deep in professional role
	3	To share info and with customers
copart		Communication, Events that the company have arranged as party and others
	0	no party arranged
	1	once a year
	2	twice a year
	3	3 times a year
	4	4 events a year
	5	More than 5 events (organization informally)
cogate		Communication gatekeeper Does the company has a gatekeeper, who is he/she?
	0 to 4	It doesn't have
	1	A specific professional worker
	2	The manager
	3	The person in charge of each project/ section
	4	Each person updates him/herself

Physical space

phdes		Physical description of the place
	1	Glass environment (offices, with usually a central hall, andthe offices around in glass)
	2	Different groups share
	3	Each person his office, concrete
	4	Only offices for some specific positions
	5	Open spaces
	6	Not applicable, a school
	7	Working with the client
phme		Number of meeting places the company has
phof		Number of offices the company has
phki		Has the company a kitchen
phempof		Number of employees per office
phemfof		Number f full-time employees per office
phempof2		Number of full-time employees per office codified
	0	Less than one
	1	One
	2	More than one

Training

Training policy

emtr		Number of employees going to training
trct2001		Training cost in 2001
trct2002		Training cost in 2002
trct2003		Training cost in 2003
deterntra		How is it determine how to go to training
trdet		Training determination: How is who goes to training detrmined, codified
	1	Determined by the managers (top-down system)
	2	Bottom up system: The employees ask and are or not approved. In teh development talks
	3	IC measures to determine
trfcon		Training, frequency of conferences (per year)
trconcd		Training conference coded
	0	No conferences
	1	With all the employees = to get everybody together
	2	Small course
	3	Some employees
trnew		What do they do with new employees
	0	No introduction
	1	Standard introduction (with a program, even exams)
	2	Hand book (or law) to be learnt or a document
trmen		Do the y have a mentor system
	1	Yes
	0	No
trunico		University connections, contacts
truni		Training with universities, what do they do?
	0	No contacts
	1	In the process
	2	Contacts (some employee teachs or is PhD student), Seminars, other contacts in terms of people connection
	3	For recruitment or the festival thing
	4	Some internships
	5 to 2	Providing courses FOR the university
	6 to 2	Seminars for clients
	7 to 2	A lot of contact
truni2		University connections, contacts recodified
	0	No contacts
	1	In the process
	2	Contacts: Providing courses for, giving course, PhDs employees, seminars for clients
	3	Recruitment or festival
	4	Internships
tric		Intellectual capital accounting
	0	NO special intellectual Capital
	1	Have a IC system
	2 to 1	in the process
	3	Base Score System
	4	Evaluation of the customers + surveys
	5	The developments talks
	6 to 5	As a feeling, in my head

	7 to 1	Competence filing (as CVs, list)
tric2		Intellectual capital accounting
	0	NO special intellectual Capital
	1	have a IC system or is in the process,
	3	Base Scored system
	4	Evaluation of the customers + surveys
	5	Development talks and a feeling

Information on training events

(Unit of analysis the company)

tryear		Years of the plan refers to the last number 1.2 means: 2001 and 2002
tryearn		Number of years the plan is for
trn		Number of training incidences
trt		Sum of training time (0 is = missing value)
saltrt		Sum of training time from information on salary
trt2		Training time (combination of both previous, if both are different different answers: Actual training if not possible to understand difference: MEAN
trtemt		Average hours of training per employee (trt2/emptot)
trnpemp		Number of training events per employee (trn/emptot)
trt0		Training time indeterminated
trtcom	to trtlead	Training tine in communication
trtcc		Training time in customer capital
trthr	to trtlead	Training time in human resources
trtlea	to trtlead	Training time in leadership
trtneg	to trtlead	Training time in negotation
trtplan	to trtlead	Training time in planning
trtpcon	to trtpro	Training time in professional consultancy
trtpoth	to trtpro	Training time in professional others (not determined)
trtsad	to trtsup	Training time in support administrative
trtsit	to trtsup	Training time in support and IT
trtsoth	to trtsup	Training time in supprot others
trtval	to trtval2	Training time in values
trtvis	to trtval2	Training time in vision
trtlead		Training time for leadership training (trtcom, trtlea, trtneg, trtplan)
trtpro		Training time in professional activities (sum trtpcon, trtpoth)
trtsup		Training time support activities (sum trtsad, trtsit, trtsoth)
trtval2		Training time in meeting everybody or creating culture (trtval, trtvis)
trpinc		Average number of participants per course ((trpsup+trppro+trpoth)/trn)
trpsup		Sum of the number of supprot staff going to training (if 3 support goes to 4 courses = 12 trpsup)
trppro		Sum of the number of professional staff going to training
trpoth		Sum of the number of other or not specified staff that goes to training
trptot		Total number of participants (trpsup+trppro+trpoth)
trpptrn		Average number of participants per event (trptot/trn)
trnpp		Average number of training event per participant (trn/trptot)
trppemp		Number of training participants per employee (trptot/emptot). Or Number of training places that each individual covers
trcosted		Sum of the cost of courses and fees and other external courses
trcostem		Sum of the cost that the employer has to pay (time spent)

trcostot	Sum of other costs such as traveling or other
trcosal	Total training cost (sum of all the costs: trcosted, trcostem, trcostot)

Information on training events (unit of analysis, the training event)

course

Objectiv	Title or explanation of the course
obj1dc	**Objective of the training**
obj2dc	**Objective of the training (codified)**

	1	Custcap: Activities directed towards improving relationships with clients, suppliers or any other agent external to the company. Includes advertising if the company is not in 744
	2	ESF: Activities within the analysis phase of the ESF Objective 3
	3	Lea: Activities directed towards improving leadership skill knowledge. It includes negotiation skills, project leading, leadership training as well as certain business administration subjects
	4	Oth: Activities that cannot be included in any of the other categories. It includes language training when it is not directed towards a foreign language teacher
	5	Procon: Training in consultancy (in the main activity of the company). If the subject is not clear and can be in another category it will go to the other category.It includes team building.
	6	Protea: Training for teachers. It applies the same than in procon. If the subject is not clear and can be in another category it will go to the other category.
	7	Supadm: Activities directed towards the training of taxes handling, wage handling or law regulations in the case that this is not the main subject in the companies. Also into account who was participating.
	8	SuplTge: Activities directed towards general IT training, not specifically explained
	9	SuplTpro: Activities directed towards training of certain computer software that is necessary for that specific sector (CAD, training in distance education, etc.)
	10	SuplTsp: Activities directed towards training of certain specific programs. office package and other similar programs. It includes wages handling programs such as Hogia. Also PowerPoint.
	11	SuplTweb: Activities directed towards training or development of the web page of the company
	12	Supoth; Activities directed towards other support activities training, it could not be classified within the others or it is presentation techniques
	13	Work: Activities directed towards the training for improving the working conditions. It includes

isced1	Theme of training as classified by ISCED97 (1 digit)
isced2	Theme of training as classified by ISCED97 (2 digits)
isced3	Theme of training as classified by ISCED97 (3 digits)
Setting	Type of course provided: seminar, an internal course, external course, conference, seminar
trt	Total training time (participants*trt of the course)
trty	Training time each year (trt/yearn)
trtcy	Training time of the course yearly (trty/trpall)
trpsup	Support staff participants
trppro	Professionals participants
trpoth	Undetermined participants
trpall	Total training participants (trpsup+trppro+trpoth)
trcted	Direct cost (trcted)
trctem	Labor cost (cost of employees time on training)
trctot	Other cost
trctal	total training cost (trcted + trctem + trctot)
Comments	General comments on training information
trpally	Total number of participants per each year (trpall/yearn)
trpsp	Spindex: Training participants per course as a proportion of all employees

		(trpally/emptot)
trpspcd		Specificity index codified
	1	From 0 to 0.49
	2	From 0.50 to 0.99
	3	1
trcttrt		total training cost per hour (trt/trctal)
trctedtr		Direct training cost per hour (trt/trctal)
trctemtr		Labor training cost per hour (trt/trctal)
trctottr		Other training cost per hour (trt/trctal)

Aspects in relation to the use of knowledge

innovcom	Comments on innovation
usinov	Number of new product released in the last 2 years
uscust	Customer base (number of customers that the company has)
usncust	Number of new customers in the last year
profit01	Profit in the year 2001
profit02	Profit in the year 2001
turnover	Total capital of the company
usp01p	Proportion of profit (profit01/ turnover)
usp02p	Proportion of profit in 2002 (profit02/turnover)
usempro	Profit per employee (profit02/emptot)
useemtur	Turnover per employee
uspncust	Proportion of new customers

Questionnaire

id1	Questionnaire ID
idcomp	Company ID
idinques	ID identifier

Section A: Background information

a1	What year were you born
male	Gender (male=1)
a2	What country were you born?
a2b	Time living in Sweden
a3	Position within the company
posit	

1 Professional
3 Project leader
4 Manager
2 Support staff (kitchen, secretary)
-9 Missing

a4	Years in the company
a5	Years working in the sector or related area?
a6	Educational attainment

1 Primary and lower secondary school
2 Upper secondary school
3 Tertiary not finalized
4 Tertiary Education, 3 years or less
5 Tertiary education, more than 3 years
-9 Missing

	99 Don't know
a6com	Comments personal

Section B: Collaborative climate

b1	Sharing of knowledge is encouraged by the organization in action and not only in words
b2	We are continuously encouraged to bring new knowledge into the organization
b3	We are encouraged to say what we think even if it means disagreeing with people we work with
b4	Open communication is characteristic of the organization as a whole
b5	I learn a lot from other staff members in this organization
b6	In the organization information sharing has increased my knowledge
b7	Most of my expertise has developed as a result of working together with colleagues in this organization
b8	Combining the knowledge among staff has resulted in many new ideas and solutions for the organization
b9	There is much I could learn from my colleagues
b10	There are some people here who prefer to work on their own
b11	I know who I have to ask for help if I have a specific problem in my work
b12	We often share work experiences informally in our unit/section
b13	We help each other to learn skills we need
b14	We keep all the team members up to date with current events and work trends
bcom	Comments B

Section C: Supervisor's role

c1	Encourages me to come up with innovative solutions to work-related problems
c2	Organizes regular meetings to share information
c3	Keeps me informed
c4	Encourages open communication in my working group
c5	Encourages - by action and not only words - sharing of knowledge
ccom	Comments C

Section D: Informal learning activities

d1	Read manuals, reference books, journals or other written materials but not as part of a course.
d2	Went on guided tours at a museum, art gallery or other such cultural facilities
d3	Used media- assisted products to learn such as computers, video, television, tapes that were NOT part of a course.
d4	Asked my colleagues for help when I have a problem in my work
d5	Learnt by watching, getting help or advice from others - but NOT from course instructors
d6	Learnt by myself trying things out, doing things for practice, trying different approaches to do things
d7	Learnt by reading job-related news on the Internet.
dcom	Comments D

Section E: Associations

e1	Visited fairs, professional conferences or congresses. Could you indicate the number you attended?

e2	Attended short lectures, seminars, workshops or special talks that were NOT part of a course. Could you estimate the number?
e3	Are you a member of any external professional network or association?
ecom	Comments E

Section F: Communication and literacy practices

f1a	Emails from other colleagues in the company
f1b	Emails from customer/clients/students?
f2a	Telephone calls from colleagues?
f2b	Telephone calls from customer /clients/students
f3a	Faxes from other colleagues
f3b	Faxes from customers
f4	Average number of papers, reports, documents related to your work you wrote during last year?
f5	Average number of papers, reports, documents related with your work you read in one week
f6	Work related trips in the last year?
fcom	Comments F

Section G: Meetings

g1a	Regular meetings
g1aint	Usefulness, regular meetings
g1b	Informal meetings
g1bint	Usefulness, informal meetings
g1c	Meetings with customers
g2a	Discussion Time planning
g2b	Discuss Problems
g2c	Discuss training possibilities
g2d	Discuss economic performance
g2e	Discuss health issues
g2f	Discuss others
g3a	Discuss informal time planning
g3b	Discuss informally problems and work in progress
g3c	Discuss informally training possibilities
g3d	Discuss informally economic performance
g3e	Discuss informally health issues
g3f	Discuss informally others

ANNEX II: INTERVIEW GUIDE

Date:

Interview Guide:
Company ID: Contact person:

PART A

Organization: How is the work organized in the company? Role of the professional in support activities. Organizational chart

Human Resources: General HR policy
         Rewards/ incentives system
         Recruitment: Selection process

How many workers did you have on your payroll in 2002 of the following types of labor:

	N
Permanent, full time	
Permanent, part time	
Temporary or casual workers on your payroll	

How many of your employees left voluntary in the past year?

	Number
Retirement	
Other jobs	
Sickness	
Death	

How many of your employees left involuntary (were fired, laid off)?   No.:
How many new employees in 2002? No.:

Sick leaves during 2002: How many days of sick leave registered in 2002?

Communication: Communication routines inside the company

Physical Space: Physical arrangement of the company

IT Infrastructure: IT equipment, databases, workstations, servers, services

How many employees in your organization have access to a PC? n.

Number of workstations:
Investment in Information Technologies last year (2002): _____ Kr
Investment in Information Technologies (2001): _____ Kr

Investment in Information Technologies planned for (2003): _____ Kr
Number of people taking care of computers at the company:

Costs Server	Approx.	Kr
Cost Services (trouble shooting, technicians to solve problems) :	Approx.	Kr
Hardware (buying computers, screens…) :	Approx.	Kr
Software/licensing (buying programs, licensing):	Approx	Kr
Others :	Approx.	Kr

PART B

Training:

Number of employees going to training (2002):
Training cost (2001): _____Kr
Training cost (2002): _____Kr
Training cost planned (2003): _____Kr

Expenses included:
Our own Teachers, facilities, books
External cost for teachers
conference fees
Travel expenses and daily allowance (food, lodging)
Wage cost for employees participating in training (lost time for production)
Other (please specify)

New employees: what is the training procedure with the new employees

R&D or University Connections

Intellectual Capital Measurement: What measurement mechanisms does the company have? (Intellectual Capital Accounting? Human Capital? HR?)

PART C

Innovation

Number of new products/ services developed (during 2002):
Number of new costumers/contracts (2002):

Performance

Balance (results) of the year (2002): _____ kr

ANNEX III: DESCRIPTIVE ANALYSIS OF THE COMPANIES

Brief description of the companies and main features of the analysis plans

Company 2: Company in architectural and engineering activities with 20 employees. It is part of a large corporation based in the United Kingdom with 13 offices in Sweden and around 50 offices in other countries. It has three sections, each one managed by a manager in charge of the unit. There are 15 full time employees. The company has an office for each employee; the offices have glass walls. The offices are distributed in two corridors, and the entrance is an open hall that provides access to the two. The interview was conducted with the CEO with the help of a translator in his own office.

Company 11: Company in technical testing and analysis with 16 employees. Part of a bigger corporation based in Sweden with 19 other offices in Sweden. The workspace is at the floor with the machinery to be tested. The business is organized in four organizational units with different services each. Each of the units has a group of two to three professionals. Certain job rotation between the different units is intended. The analysis of the business environment places communication among employees as crucial for developing a trusting and honest work environment. It acknowledges that employees that feel comfortable at the workplace lead to higher profitability. Competencies are rewarded as a way of improving quality on the service. The company has developed a measuring system to evaluate the needs of each employee and section in the large company. The interview was conducted in the CEO office.

Company 24: Company in labor recruitment sector with 30 employees. It has four organizational units dedicated to labor recruitment and also personnel training. The analysis plan emphasizes the necessity of creating routines that maintain a constant upgrading of skills and competencies. This is mainly promoted through influencing employee's values. To this end, communication and networking play an important role. The interview was conducted with one of the company owners outside the company site, and therefore it was not possible to observe the company physical arrangement.

Company 26: Private school providing pre-primary education, owned by an association of parents. It has seven full time employees and eleven on part-time bases. The school is divided in four different groups according to children's ages. In total the school has 59 children. The analysis plan emphasizes the role of the "study plan for preschools" (lpfö 98). It uses it as a guiding principle for determining how the professionals work and for determining each individual's role in the organization. The activity analysis of the company also maintains the importance of promoting trust with children's families and among employees. Competence development is seen as a necessary step for providing quality services. Special attention is paid to the need to upgrad personnel's skills on information technologies. Also of importance is to present the company in a more attractive way, improving the marketing strategy. The interview was conducted at the school site with the principal of the school.

Company 30: Company providing specialized adult and vocational training in the construction sector mainly in a specific Swedish region. Owned by the Byggmästaeförening

(Constructor's organization) of that region. The company is divided in four specific units providing different services. Each of the sections work in a semi-independent manner. The activity analysis emphasizes the role of routines and networking both with customers and competitors in order to develop employee's competences and maintain competitiveness. It also acknowledges the importance of documentation for improving and maintaining quality standards. The interview was conducted with the person in charge of the ESF project, and worked as a professional at the company.

Company 33: Private vocational school with 55 full-time employees and 20 part time permanent and temporal workers. It is part of a company with two other similar schools in Sweden. The activity analysis emphasizes the importance of working together with the students in order to provide them with skills. The school is organized in teams of 10 to 15 students that work in specific subjects for 2 months. A teacher is responsible for each team and works together with the other teachers. The analysis also emphasizes the importance of networking with the surrounding society. The interview was conducted with the former CEO and one of the founders of the school.

Company 49: Company providing consultancy services in marketing and communication with 11 employees. The activity analysis places a major emphasis on the importance of routines and the clarification of the working roles of each employee in order to provide quality services. Networking is also acknowledged as important for maintaining competitiveness and customer's trust. The interview was conducted at the company site with the secretary.

Company 55: Private "folkhöskolan" with 24 employees providing services to 140 students in Stockholm region. The activity analysis plan is mainly focused on developing a system for distance education and marketing. The school is interested in developing routines for sharing knowledge. The analysis also acknowledges the importance of recruiting people from cultural backgrounds other than Swedish in order to promote multiculturalism within the personnel. The interview was conducted with the rector of the school at her office.

Company 58: A credit market corporation owned by the foundation of counties and "landsting". It has 27 employees that work in an open space in an old building. With high ceilings and different small rooms used for meetings. Their activity analysis is mainly focused on promoting continuous learning, using both formal meetings but also each other in the company. There is also an intention of improving the use of information technologies and the physical work conditions. The interview was conducted with the person responsible for human resources.

Company 68: Educational enterprise focused in the IT/media sector. It provides educational services at the high school level (Gymnasium) (from 15 to 18) and two year programs for post-secondary studies. It has around 30 full time employees and around 25 occasional workers depending on course needs. The activity analysis emphasizes the importance for the company to have employees with updated knowledge in the fields of technology and new media. It also acknowledges that training can be used as a motivator for employees. The importance of sharing knowledge among employees and experts in the different areas is also mentioned. The interview was conducted with the two directors of the school.

Company 71: Primary private school with financial support from the state. It has eighteen employees. Each teacher is in charge of one group of kids. The school has a Waldorf pedagogy approach. In the activity analysis, this is very much stressed. In this way, the plan is mainly focused on achieving the vision of instructing students to become creative individuals. The professional role of the teacher is re-evaluated; for this school the teacher has to engaged in understanding the personal situation of each student. The importance of promoting a democratic model of the school is also presented. The interview was carried out with the director of the school with eventual help of the secretary.

Company 82: Company providing marketing services. The physical space presents three main working spaces that all employees share. The company is organized by projects, where cross-functional teams are created depending on the needs of the clients. The activity analysis is focused on the importance of meeting and adapting to the clients needs. It also aims at organizing the everyday activities in a way that will promote learning. The use of information technologies and new media is also stressed. The interview was conducted with the founder of the company, retired five years ago, but still active with some clients.

Company 83: Company providing services in marketing and advertising. The company works with cross-functional teams adapting to the needs of the clients. The activity analysis emphasizes the importance of creativity in order to provide quality services. Employees are seen as the most important resource in the company. Their constant education is necessary in order to provide them with more updated knowledge that in turn will increase their authority and their responsibilities. The importance of listening and developing a dialogue among employees is also acknowledge. The interview was conducted with the person in charge of human resources.

Company 87: Company that provides services in leadership, business and IT consultancy. The company has ten employees that work at the clients site. The activity analysis emphasizes that the company has to work as a unit, where all employees share a similar culture and language. It acknowledge the importance of acquiring new knowledge and how this knowledge has to be shared among employees. Competence development is seen as a way of attracting valuable employees in the company. The company was carried out with the main support member of the company.

Company 94: Company providing law services. The company works in groups of one to three persons depending on the client. Each group is specialized in a specific area. The activity analysis mainly focused on the necessity of providing more responsibility to the employees and a higher degree of delegation. In order to do this, an identification of the main company's processes was carried out. Then, new conditions were developed in order to strengthen the company's competitiveness. The plan is very concerned with the idea of remaining a leader in an increasing competitive market. The interview was carried out with one professional.

Company 98: Company providing architecture consultancy. It has 28 employees. The company is organized in projects assigned to specific teams depending on clients needs. It has other offices in Sweden. The activity analysis emphasizes the importance of good collaborative climate in order to foster continuous learning as well as the learning nature of the project work. It mainly focused on widening the professional competencies of employees in order to improve the company's competitiveness. The interview was conducted with the CEO of the organizational unit and another professional.

Company 106: Company providing graphical products for advertising, information and documentation. It is organized in cross-functional teams depending on the client's needs. The emphasis of the activity analysis is on the necessity of providing a wider variety of services and in increasing the customer base. The competence development is acknowledged as a way of improving the quality of the services provided. It is mainly focused on developing skills for new information technologies. The interview was carried out with the two managers of the company.

Company 110: Company providing environmental consultancy. The work is organized in projects with one senior consultant in charge of a cross-functional group of two or three junior consultants. The activity analysis places a major emphasis on the creation and maintenance of networks, with other companies as well as with universities. Competence development is regarded as a strategy to provide high level of competencies in the area of expertise. Interview was carried out with the manager director.

Summary tables

Table III.1: Number of employees per company and contract arrangements

idcomp	Activity (Nace rev.1)	Manager or owner in charge of HR	Number of employees in 2001*	% of women (2001)	Total number of employees in 2003	Number of full time employees (2003)	Number of part time employees (2003)	Number of temporally workers (2003)	% of full time emp. (2003)
CONSULTANCY			205	0.40	243	214	15	14	0.87
58	741	Professional worker	21	0.67	27	27	0	0	1.00
87	741	Manager	12	0.25	12	10	1	1	0.83
94	741	yes	31	0.48	27	25	2	0	0.93
2	742	Manager	21	0.24	20	15	2	3	0.75
98	742	Manager	24	0.17	28	28	0	0	1.00
110	742	Manager	15	0.40	17	16	1	0	0.94
11	743	Manager	15*	0.13	16	15	1	0	0.94
49	744	Manager	10	0.60	9	6	3	0	0.67
82	744	Manager	17	0.35	18	18	0	0	1.00
83	744	..	24	0.54	29	25	0	4	0.86
106	744	Manager	10	0.40	10	9	1	0	0.90
24	745	..	20	0.25	30	20	4	6	0.67
EDUCATION			111	0.59	215	104	28	38	0.64
26	801	Manager	18	1.00	21	7	11	3	0.33
71	801	Manager	11	1.00	20	..	..	..	..
33	802	..	14*	0.43	75	55	10	10	0.73
30	804	Manager	21	0.14	12	12	0	0	1.00
55	804	Manager	25	0.60	25	..	..	..	..
68	804	Manager	36	0.28	62	30	7	25	0.48
ALL			316	0.47	458	318	43	52	0.81

* Data in Company 11 and 33 refers to 2002

Table III.2: Number of employees per company and type of professional role (Professional, support, or leader)

idcomp	Activity	Total number of employees in 2003	Number of full time employees	Number of employees in support role	Number of employees in Professional role	Number of employees in leadership positions	Number of employees in management positions	Number of employees with unknown position	% of professionals (as a % of all employees)
CONSULTANCY		**243**	**214**	**28**	**209**	**30**	**17**	**0**	**0.86**
58	741	27	27	6	21	..	..		0.78
87	741	12	10	2	10	..	..		0.83
94	741	27	25	4	21	..	3		0.78
2	742	20	15	2	18	9	4		0.90
98	742	28	28	2	26	..	1		0.93
110	742	17	16	1	15	5	1		0.88
11	743	16	15	2	11	3	1		0.69
49	744	9	6	1	8	3	3		0.89
82	744	18	18	3	15	4	1		0.83
83	744	29	25	0	29	4	1		1.00
106	744	10	9	1	9	2	2		0.90
24	745	30	20	4	26	..	..		0.87
EDUCATION		**215**	**104**	**31**	**129**	**15**	**9**	**40**	**0.78**
26	801	21	7	1	20	3	1		0.95
71	801	20	..	3	16	0	1		0.80
33	802	75	55	10	45	4	5	11	0.70
30	804	12	12	1	11	3	2		0.92
55	804	25	..	7	17	..	..	1	0.71
68	804	62	30	9	20	5	..	28	0.59
ALL		**458**	**318**	**59**	**338**	**45**	**26**	**40**	**0.83**

Table III.3: Human resource characteristics

idcomp	SNI3	Cases: n. of quest	Respondents as a (a1d) Proportion of total of employees	(a1d) av. Age	(a1)range years (oldest-youngest)	(a2a)Number of foreigners	Men (%)	(a4) Average number of years in the company	(a4) std. dev.	(a5) Average numbers of years working in related area	(a5) std. dev.
Consultancy		**106**	**0.48**	**41**	**28**	**5**	**0.57**	**7**	**5**	**12**	**9**
58	741	12	0.44	36	35	3	0.25	5	4	8	7
87	741	5	0.42	38	17	0	0.60	3	1	10	4
94	741	13	0.48	41	32	0	0.46	8	7	11	9
2	742	7	0.35	40	24	0	0.57	12	7	17	10
98	742	15	0.54	46	35	0	0.87	3	1	18	14
110	742	7	0.41	44	33	0	0.57	8	4	17	14
11	743	5	0.31	45	23	2	1.00	19	11	16	11
49	744	9	1.00	40	30	0	0.33	5	5	10	9
82	744	15	0.83	39	36	0	0.53	7	5	13	10
83	744	8	0.28	32	33	0	0.50	5	7	6	7
106	744	5	0.50	47	28	0	0.80	8	1	16	10
24	745	5	0.17	40	15	0	0.40	2	1	5	4
Education		**60**	**0.34**	**42**	**30**	**5**	**0.55**	**7**	**5**	**11**	**10**
26	801	9	0.43	38	21	0	0.00	8	4	13	5
71	801	8	0.40	42	36	1	0.38	4	4	5	8
33	802	13	0.17	40	35	1	0.77	5	5	12	12
30	804	5	0.42	43	30	0	1.00	3	1	11	16
55	804	9	0.36	51	33	0	0.56	18	12	20	13
68	804	16	0.26	37	23	3	0.56	3	3	6	5
ALL		**166**	**0.43**	**41**	**43**	**8**	**0.50**	**6**	**7**	**12**	**10**

Table III.4: Number of respondents by educational attainment as a percentage of all respondents

	Educational Attainment (ISCED97)				
	Primary and lower secondary education	Upper secondary school	Tertiary education not finalized	Tertiary education, 3 years or less	Tertiary education more than 3 years
Consultancy	**5**	**29**	**7**	**18**	**41**
58	8	25	8	8	50
87		20		20	60
94			8	8	85
98	7	53		13	27
2		50		33	17
110		29		14	57
11	20	60		20	
82	7	20	27	20	27
49	11	22		33	33
83		57		29	14
106		20	20	40	40
24					80
Education	**2**	**8**	**8**	**32**	**50**
26		22		56	22
71			13	13	75
33		8	8	38	46
30	20	40			40
55				22	78
68			19	38	44
ALL	**4**	**21**	**7**	**23**	**45**

Table III.5: Number of tiers and work organization

idcomp	SNI3	n. of employees	Having a middle manager	Organization of the work	Manager as a professional worker	Manager is an owner
Consultancy		**243**	**0,42**		**1**	**0,75**
87	741	12	no	Cross-functional teams	..	..
58	741	27	no	Teams	yes	no
94	741	27	no	Teams	yes	yes
110	742	17	yes	Cross-functional teams	yes	yes
2	742	20	yes	individual work	yes	..
98	742	28	no	Cross-functional teams	yes	..
11	743	16	yes	Teams	..	..
49	744	9	no	Cross-functional teams	yes	yes
106	744	10	no	Cross-functional teams	yes	yes
82	744	18	yes	Cross-functional teams	yes	no
83	744	29	yes	Cross-functional teams	yes	yes
24	745	30	no	Cross-functional teams	yes	yes
Education		**215**	**0,33**		**0,80**	**0,60**
71	801	20	no	individual work	yes	yes
26	801	21	no	Cross-functional teams	yes	no
33	802	75	yes	Cross-functional teams	yes	yes
30	804	12	no	Teams	..	..
55	804	25	no	..	yes	no
68	804	62	yes	Teams	no	yes
ALL		**458**	**0,39**		**0,93**	**0,69**

* Refers to percentage of companies

Table III.6: Recruitment and selection aspects

Table III.6a: Frequency of the methods for advertising available positions

Method for advertising available positions	Both sectors	%	Consultancy	%	Education	%
Unemployment office	7	0.44	3	0.25	4	1.00
Through contacts	6	0.38	6	0.50	0	0.00
Specialized papers	3	0.19	3	0.25	0	0.00
All companies with data	16		12		4	
Missing	2	0.11	0	0.00	2	0.11

Table III.6b: Frequency of method of selecting employees

Method of selecting employees	Both sectors	%	Consultancy	%	Education	%
One interview	7	0.44	4	0.36	3	0.60
Standardized test	3	0.19	2	0.18	1	0.20
Two-step interview	5	0.31	4	0.36	1	0.20
Outsource	1	0.06	1	0.09	0	0.00
All companies with data	16		11		5	
Missing	2	0.11	1	0.08	1	0.17

Table III.6c: Frequency of the different selection criteria

Selection criteria	Both sectors	%	Consultancy	%	Education	%
Social skills	12	0.75	8	0.73	4	0.80
Fits in the company	9	0.56	9	0.82	0	0.00
Experience	8	0.47	5	0.45	3	0.50
Specific of the company	8	0.50	6	0.55	2	0.40
Other criteria	8	0.50	6	0.55	2	0.40
Educational certificate	7	0.44	5	0.45	2	0.40
Service oriented	5	0.31	3	0.27	2	0.40
Work skills	3	0.19	0	0.00	3	0.60
Learning to learn	2	0.13	1	0.09	1	0.20
Age	1	0.06	1	0.09	0	0.00
All companies with data	16		11		5	
Missing	2	0.11	1	0.08	1	0.17

Table III.7: Aspects related with new recruitments

Table III.7a: Policy for new employees

Policy for new employees	Total	Tot%	Consultancy	con%	Education	ed%
No special program	10	63	8	73	2	40
Standarized program	4	25	3	27	1	20
Have a handbook	2	13	0		2	40
All companies with data	16	100	11	100	5	100
Missing	2	11	1	8	1	17

Table III.7b: Having a mentor

Mentor for a newly employed	Total	Tot%	Consultancy	Con%	Education	Ed%
Not present	8	53	6	55	2	50
Present	7	47	5	45	2	50
All companies with data	15	100	11	100	4	100
Missing	3	17	1	8	2	33

Table III.7c: Policy for newly employed

Program to be followed	Mentor for a newly employed		All companies with data	Missing
	Not present	Present		
No special program	7	3	10	0
Standarized program	0	3	3	1
Have a handbook	1	0	1	1
All companies with data	8	6	14	
Missing	0	1	1	2

Table III.8: Aspects within employee turnover

Idcompany	SNI3	Number of new employees in the last year	Number of employees that left the company	Number of employees that left voluntary because of retirement	Number of employees left the company because going to other job	Number of employees left involuntary	Number of employees in sick leave	employee turnover 2001-2002	Employee turnover 2001- 2003
Consultancy		**30**	**18**	**1**	**12**	**3**	**2**	**0.05**	**0.07**
58	741	5	1	0	1	0	0	0.15	0,22
87	741	0	2	0	2	0	0	-0.17	0
94	741	0	1	0	1	0	0	-0.04	-0,15
2	742	1	1	0	1	0	0	0.00	-0,05
98	742	0	0	0	0	0	0	0.00	0,14
110	742	4	1	1	0	0	0	0.18	0,12
11	743	..	1	0	0	1	0	.	0,06
49	744	5	1	0	1	0	0	0.44	-0,11
82	744	0	3	0	2	0	1	-0.17	0,06
83	744	4	5	0	3	2	0	-0.03	0,17
106	744	1	2	0	1	0	1	-0.10	0
24	745	10	0	0	0	0	0	0.33	0,33
Education		**13**	**19**	**2**	**8**	**6**	**3**	**-0.03**	**0.26**
26	801	1	2	1	0	0	1	-0.05	0,14
71	801	..	0	..	..	..	..	.	0,45
33	802	10	9	0	5	2	2	0.01	0,72
30	804	2	2	1	1	0	0	0.00	-0,17
55	804	..	0	..	..	..	..	.	0
68	804	0	6	0	2	4	0	-0.10	0,42
All companies with data		**43**	**37**	**3**	**20**	**9**	**5**	**0.03**	**0.13**

Table III.9: Criteria to determine salaries

IDcomp	SNI3	Salaries determined in individual basis	Salary criteria			
			Demand on the market	Performance	Experience	External authority
Consultancy		**7**	**1**	**3**	**3**	**4**
58	741	yes	..	..	..	..
87	741	yes	no	yes	no	no
94	741	no	yes	no	yes	no
2	742	..	..	..	..	yes
98	742	no	no	no	no	yes
110	742	no	no	no	yes	yes
11	743	yes	no	yes	no	yes
49	744	yes	..	..	..	..
82	744	yes	..	..	..	..
83	744	yes	..	..	..	..
106	744	..	..	..	..	..
24	745	yes	no	yes	yes	no
Education		**4**	**2**	**0**	**4**	**2**
26	801	no	no	no	no	yes
71	801	no	no	no	yes	yes
33	802	yes	yes	no	yes	no
30	804	yes	no	no	yes	no
55	804	yes	no	no	yes	no
68	804	yes	yes	no	no	no
All companies		**11**	**3**	**3**	**7**	**6**

Table III.10: Companies salary level

Id comp	SNi3	Employees at the moment of the salary stipulation	Number of employees with data on salaries	Employees with data on salaries as a proportion of all employees at the moment of the salary stipulation	Number of males with data on salaries	Year that the salary refers to	Average salary per employee (SEK/hour)	std. Dev.
Consultancy		**157**	**147**	**0.98**	**98**		**174.93**	**46.10**
58	741	21	18	0.86	8	2002	251.06	129.54
87	741	12	12	1.00	8	2002	238.00	0.00
94	741	27	20	0.74	13	2001	196.30	79.16
2	742	...	...		...	...	...	
98	742	24	22	0.92	21	2002	139.77	35.03
110	742	17	15	0.88	9	2002	172.00	49.40
11	743	16	17	1.06	15	2003	119.24	22.06
49	744	10	14	1.40	5	2002	158.36	39.95
82	744		...		...	...	...	
83	744		...		...	...	...	
106	744	10	10	1.00	6	2001	128.70	26.75
24	745	20	19	0.95	13	2001	170.95	5.86
Education		**114**	**97**	**0.84**	**41**		**143.04**	**39.86**
26	801	21	20	0.95	...	2002	112.05	15.86
71	801	20	15	0.75	4	2001	133.67	50.55
33	802		...		...	...	...	
30	804	12	10	0.83	4	2002	210.60	45.52
55	804	25	18	0.72	9	2002	143.11	18.86
68	804	36	34	0.94	24	2001	115.79	21.44
All companies		306	341	**0.93**			**163.54**	**45.26**

Table III.11: Bonus system

IDcomp	SNI3	Bonus system			
		Have bonus system in place	Reasons for bonuses	Individually or group	Type of bonus
Consultancy		9			
58	741	yes	Profit	Group	Retirement plan
87	741	yes	Profit	Specific group	Basic contribution
94	741	yes	Performance	individual	Basic contribution
2	742	no	no bonus	no bonus	no bonus
98	742	yes	Profit	Group	Basic contribution
110	742	yes	Performance	individual	Basic contribution
11	743	no	no bonus	no bonus	no bonus
49	744	..	..	..	..
82	744	yes	Performance	individual	Other
83	744	yes	..	individual	..
106	744	yes	Profit	Group	Basic contribution
24	745	yes	Profit	Group	Basic contribution
Education		2			
26	801	yes	Extra activities	individual	Basic contribution
71	801	yes	Profit	Group	Basic contribution
33	802	no	no bonus	no bonus	no bonus
30	804	no	no bonus	no bonus	no bonus
55	804	no	no bonus	no bonus	no bonus
68	804	no	no bonus	no bonus	no bonus
All companies		11			

Table III.12: Aspects within the communication activities I

Table III.12a: Number of companies by frequency of the general information meetings by sector

	Sector		Total
	Consultancy	Education	
Less that once a month	3	2	5
Once a month	1	0	1
Twice a month	0	1	1
Every week	8	2	10
All companies	12	5	17

Table III.12b: Number of companies by scheduled meetings of professional workers and sector

	Sector		Total
	Consultancy	Education	
Not scheduled meetings	7	4	11
Scheduled meetings	3	1	4
All companies	10	5	15

Table III.12c: Companies with newsletter by sector

	Sector		Total
	Consultancy	Education	
No news letter	5	2	7
News letter	4	3	7
Printed	0	1	1
IN the web	4	2	6
All companies	9	5	14

Table III.12d: Number of companies by person in the gatekeeper position and sector

	Sector		Total
	Consultancy	Education	
A specific professional worker	3	0	3
The main manager	2	3	5
The project leader	2	1	3
Individual employees	2	1	3
All companies	9	5	14

Table III. 13: Number of hour formal and informal meetings (Cells refers to percentage of respondents)

Company ID		N	Number of hours in			
			(g1a) regular meetings		(g1b) informal meetings	
			5 or less hours	6 or more hours	5 or less hours	6 or more hours
Consultancy			93	7	77	23
58	741	12	100		83	17
87	741	5	80	20	60	40
94	741	12	100		75	25
2	742	7	100		100	
98	742	15	100		93	7
110	742	7	100		71	29
11	743	3	100		100	
49	744	8	63	38	88	13
82	744	15	80	20	53	47
83	744	8	100		88	13
106	744	5	100		40	60
24	745	5	100		60	40
Education			87	13	72	28
26	801	8	100		57	43
71	801	7	50	50	88	13
33	802	11	83	17	77	23
30	804	5	100		100	
68	804	15	100		63	38
Total		148	91	9	75	25

Table III.14: Respondent's perceived usefulness of formal and informal meetings

Company ID	SNI3	N	Usefulness, regular meetings					Usefulness, informal meetings				
			Slightly useful	Neutral	Useful	Very useful	Not useful	Not useful	Slightly useful	Neutral	Useful	Very useful
Consultancy			**2**	**17**	**40**	**40**	**2**	**2**	**2**	**17**	**35**	**45**
58	741	12		33	67					17	67	17
87	741	5			40	60					80	20
94	741	12	8	8	25	58				17	17	67
2	742	7			86	14			14	43	43	
98	742	15	7	36	36	21			7	7	57	29
110	742	7			50	50				14	14	71
11	743	3		67		33				100		
49	744	8			25	75					38	63
82	744	15		20	13	67				27		73
83	744	8		13	50	38		13		13	50	25
106	744	5		25	75			20				80
24	745	5		25	40	60					40	60
Education			**0**	**21**	**38**	**40**	**2**	**2**	**0**	**17**	**33**	**48**
26	801	8		22	11	67		13		13	13	63
71	801	7			38	63				14	29	57
33	802	11		36	36	27				18	36	45
30	804	5		25	25	50				20	40	40
68	804	15		20	60	20				20	40	40
Total		**148**	**1**	**18**	**40**	**40**	**2**	**2**	**1**	**17**	**34**	**46**

Table III.15: Distribution of information (cells refer to percentage of respondents)

Company ID	SNI3	N	Emails per DAY				Telephone calls				Documents			
			From colleagues		From customers		From colleagues		From customers		WRITTEN last year		READ in a week	
			Less than 5	6 or more	Less than 5	6 or more	Less than 5	6 or more	Less than 5	6 or more	Less than 5	6 or more	Less than 5	6 or more
Consultancy		**101**	**75**	**25**	**71**	**29**	**78**	**22**	**67**	**33**	**64**	**36**	**64**	**36**
58	741	11	18	82	73	27	91	9	55	45	60	40	60	40
87	741	5	80	20	80	20	60	40	80	20	50	50	50	50
94	741	12	67	33	67	33	75	25	50	50	75	25	75	25
2	742	7	100	0	100	0	86	14	100	0	67	33	67	33
98	742	15	93	7	80	20	100	0	87	13	62	38	62	38
110	742	6	100	0	100	0	100	0	100	0	33	67	33	67
11	743	5	80	20	100	0	100	0	80	20	80	20	80	20
49	744	8	75	25	63	38	88	13	75	25	57	43	57	43
82	744	15	53	47	33	67	33	67	27	73	73	27	73	27
83	744	7	100	0	71	29	67	33	86	14	71	29	71	29
106	744	5	100	0	100	0	100	0	100	0	75	25	75	25
24	745	5	100	0	40	60	60	40	20	80	40	60	40	60
Education		**59**	**85**	**15**	**88**	**12**	**93**	**7**	**81**	**19**	**62**	**38**	**62**	**38**
26	801	9	100	0	100	0	100	0	100	0	100	0	100	0
71	801	8	100	0	88	13	75	25	63	38	50	50	50	50
33	802	12	75	25	92	8	100	0	100	0	25	75	25	75
30	804	5	100	0	80	20	100	0	40	60	75	25	75	25
55	804	9	89	11	100	0	100	0	100	0	57	43	57	43
68	804	16	69	31	71	29	88	13	67	33	73	27	73	27
All companies		**160**	**79**	**21**	**77**	**23**	**84**	**16**	**73**	**28**	**63**	**37**	**63**	**37**

Table III.16: Information technology infrastructure

Id company	SNI	Total number of employees (2003)	Number of computers	Number of computers per employee	Having or not an intranet	Access to internet	Having a database	Access to the database	Database content			Investment in IT in the year 2002(in MSEK)	IT cost as a proportion of the total monetary turnover	IT investment per employee (in SEK)
									Customers	Skills	Activity			
Consultancy			**19.55**	**1.03**	**10**	**12**	**12**		**10**	**3**	**8**	**1672**	**0.012**	**10460**
58	741	27	:	.	yes	yes	yes	..	yes	yes	yes		.	.
87	741	12	15	1.25	yes	yes	yes	unrestricted	no	no	no	100	0.008	8333
94	741	27	27	1.00	yes	yes	yes	unrestricted	yes	..	yes	200	0.008	7407
98	742	28	28	1.00	no	yes	yes	unrestricted	yes	no	no	100	0.004	3571
49	744	9	12	1.33	yes	yes	yes	restricted	..	no	yes	125	0.014	13889
106	744	10	12	1.20	..	..	yes	unrestricted	yes	no	yes	300	0.043	30000
24	745	30	30	1.00	yes	yes	yes	unrestricted	yes	no	yes	90	0.004	3000
2	742	20	23	1.15	yes	yes	yes	..	yes	yes	..	50	0.000	2500
110	742	17	17	1.00	yes	yes	yes	unrestricted	yes	no	yes	257	0.019	15118
11	743	16	12	0.75	yes	yes	yes	unrestricted	yes	yes	yes	:	..	13889
82	744	18	18	1.00	yes	yes	yes	unrestricted	yes	..	yes	250	..	13889
83	744	29	21	0.72	yes	yes	yes	unrestricted	yes	no	no	200	0.006	6897
Education			**35.67**	**0.92**	**4**	**6**	**3**		**2**	**0**	**0**	**2047**	**0.030**	**8917**
26	801	21	4	0.19	..	yes	no	..	..	..	..	19	0.004	889
71	801	20	2	0.10	no	yes	no	..	..	..	..		..	..
30	804	12	11	0.92	yes	yes	yes	..	..	..	..	50	0.004	4167
55	804	25	60	2.40	yes	yes	no	..	..	..	..	378	0.023	15120
68	804	62	37	0.60	yes	yes	yes	unrestricted	yes	..	no	1100	0.110	17742
33	802	75	100	1.33	yes	yes	yes	unrestricted	yes	no	no	500	0.008	6667
All companies			**25.23**	**0.99**	**14**	**18**	**15**		**12**	**3**	**8**	**3719**	**0.018**	**9946**

ANNEX IV: ADDITIONAL TABLES

Table IV. 1: Size indicators

Company identifier	Part of a large corporation	Number of offices in Sweden	Number of offices in other countries	Monetary turnover (in million SEK)	Number of employees in 2001	Total number of employees in 2003
Consultancy	0.25**	4[+]	4[+]	21.7[+]	205	243
58	No	0	0	49.8	21	27
87	No	0	0	12.4	12	12
94	No	3	0	25.0	31	27
2	Yes	13	50	..	21	20
98	Yes	8	0	24.0	24	28
110	No	0	0	13.3	15	17
11	Yes	19	0	..	15*	16
49	No	0	0	9.0	10	9
82	No	0	0	..	17	18
83	No	2	0	31.5	24	29
106	No	2	0	7.0	10	10
24	No	0	0	23.0	20	30
Education	0**	1[+]	0[+]	20.7[+]	111	215
26	No	0	0	5.2	18	21
71	No	0	0	..	11	20
33	No	3	0	60.0	21	75
30	No	0	0	12.0	14*	12
55	No	0	0	16.3	25	25
68	No	3	0	10.0	36	62
All companies	0.17**	0[+]	0[+]	21.3[+]	316	458

* Data refers to 2002, ** proportion of "yes" companies.
[+] It refers to the average

Table IV. 2: Bivariate Pearson correlation of binary recoded indicators within the construct size
(Above 0.4)

	Median	Belonging to a bigger organization	Other offices in Sweden	Other offices in other countries	Number of employees in 2001	Number of employees in 2003	Monetary turnover in 2002
Belonging to a bigger organization		1.00					
Other offices in Sweden	0	0.50	1.00				
Other offices in other countries	0	0.54		1.00			
Number of employees in 2001	19		0.45		1.00		
Number of employees in 2003	21				0.78	1.00	
Monetary turnover in 2002	14.8				0.87	0.75	1.00

Table IV. 3: Workforce stability indicators

	Proportion of Full time employees	Proportion of permanent employees	Proportion of permanent part-time employees of all part-time employees	Employees that left the company as a proportion of all employees	Respondent's number of years in the company
Consultancy	0.87	0.95	0.53	0.09	6.88
58	1	1	0	0.04	4.58
87	0.83	0.92	0.5	0.17	2.8
94	0.93	1	1	0.04	7.89
2	0.75	0.85	0.4	0.05	11.57
98	1	1	0	0	2.87
110	0.94	1	1	0.06	7.5
11	0.94	1	1	0.06	18.8
49	0.67	1	1	0.11	4.94
82	1	1	0	0.17	6.88
83	0.86	0.86	0	0.17	4.88
106	0.9	1	1	0.2	7.5
24	0.67	0.8	0.4	0	2.3
Education	0.64	0.83	0.38	0.12	6.59
26	0.33	0.86	0.79	0.1	7.54
71	.	.	.	.	3.62
33	0.73	0.87	0.5	0.12	4.69
30	1	1	0	0.17	3
55	.	.	.	.	18
68	0.48	0.6	0.22	0.1	2.68
All companies	0.81	0.92	0.49	0.10	6.78

Table IV. 4: Bivariate Pearson correlations of the binary recoded indicators of the stability construct in the selected companies (above 0.40).

	Median	Percentage of full-time employees	Percentage of permanent employees	Percentage of permanent part-time employees	Percentage of employees lost in the last year (inversed scale)	Respondent's number of years in the company in relation to companies starting date
Percentage of full-time employees	0.88	1.00				
Percentage of permanent employees	1.00	0.88	1.00			
Percentage of permanent part-time employees	0.45			1.00		
Percentage of employees lost in the last year (inversed scale)	0.10				1.00	
Respondent's number of years in the company in relation to companies starting date	0.43			0.50	0.50	1.00

Table IV. 5: Workforce experience indicators

Company ID	SNI3	Average respondent's age	(a5) Average numbers of years working in related area	Std. dev.	Percentage of employees with tertiary education degree (more than 3 years)
Consultancy		41	12	9	41
58	741	36	8	7	50
87	741	38	10	4	60
94	741	41	11	9	85
2	742	40	17	10	27
98	742	46	18	14	17
110	742	44	17	14	57
11	743	45	16	11	
49	744	40	10	9	27
82	744	39	13	10	33
83	744	32	6	7	14
106	744	47	16	10	40
24	745	40	5	4	80
Education		42	11	10	50
26	801	38	13	5	22
71	801	42	5	8	75
33	802	40	12	12	46
30	804	43	11	16	40
55	804	51	20	13	78
68	804	37	6	5	44
All companies		41	12	10	45

Table IV. 6: Professionalism indicators

Company ID	Having a middle manager	Organization of the work	% of professionals (as a % of all employees)	Manager as a professional worker
Consultancy	0.42*		0.86	1*
58	no	Teams	0.78	yes
87	no	Cross-functional teams	0.83	..
94	no	Teams	0.78	yes
2	yes	individual work	0.90	yes
98	no	Cross-functional teams	0.93	yes
110	yes	Cross-functional teams	0.88	yes
11	yes	Teams	0.69	..
49	no	Cross-functional teams	0.89	yes
82	yes	Cross-functional teams	0.83	yes
83	yes	Cross-functional teams	1.00	yes
106	no	Cross-functional teams	0.90	yes
24	no	Cross-functional teams	0.87	yes
Education	0.33*		0.78	0.80*
26	no	Cross-functional teams	0.95	yes
71	no	individual work	0.80	yes
33	yes	Cross-functional teams	0.70	yes
30	no	Teams	0.92	..
55	no	..	0.71	yes
68	yes	Teams	0.59	no
All companies	0.39*		0.83	0.93*

* Refers to proportion of companies with "yes".

Table IV. 7:Bivariate Pearson correlations of the binary recoded indicators of the professionalism construct in the selected companies (above 0.3)

	Median	Professional as a manager of the company	Main manager owns the company (totally or partially)	Having cross-functional teams	Having a middle manager	Specific person for human resource function	Number of professionals as a proportion of the total employees
Professional as a manager of the company		1.00					
Main manager owns the company (totally or partially)			1.00				
Having cross-functional teams		0.37		1.00			
Having a middle manager		-0.33			1.00		
Specific person for human resource function			-0.41			1.00	
Number of professionals as a proportion of the total employees	0.85			0.41			1.00

Table IV. 8: Recruitment policy indicators

	Method for advertising available positions	Method of selecting employees	Criteria for personnel selection: Social skills	Criteria for personnel selection: Fitting into the company	Having a mentor for new employees	Policy for newly employed
Consultancy						
58	Unemployment office	Outsource	0.73*	0.82*	0.45*	No special program
87	Unemployment office	Two-step interview	no	yes	no	No special program
94	Through contacts	Two-step interview	yes	yes	no	No special program
2	Through contacts	One interview	yes	no	yes	...
98	Through contacts	One interview	yes	yes	no	No special program
110	Unemployment office	Two-step interview	yes	yes	yes	Standardized program
11	Through contacts	One interview	.	.	yes	Standardized program
49	Specialized papers	Two-step interview	no	yes	yes	No special program
82	Through contacts	One interview	yes	no	yes	No special program
83	Specialized papers	Standardized test	yes	yes	no	No special program
106	Through contacts	...	yes	yes	no	No special program
24	Specialized papers	Standardized test	0.80*	0.00*	0.5*	Standardized program
Education						
26	Unemployment office	One interview	no	no	no	have a hand book
71	Unemployment office	One interview	yes	no	yes	Standardized program
33	Unemployment office	Standardized test	yes	no	yes	No special program
30	Unemployment office	Two-step interview	yes	no	...	have a hand book
55	...	...	yes	no	...	No special program
68	...	One interview	yes	no	no	No special program
All companies	...	One interview	0.75*	0.56*	0.47*	No special program

* Refers to proportion of companies

Table IV. 9: Company monetary reward system indicators

	Salaries determined in individual basis	Average salary per employee (SEK/hour)	Std. dev.	With bonus system in place
Consultancy	0.70*	175	46	0.82*
58	yes	251	130	yes
87	yes	238	0	yes
94	no	196	79	yes
2	..	..	..	no
98	no	140	35	yes
110	no	172	49	yes
11	yes	119	22	no
49	yes	158	40	..
82	yes	..	..	yes
83	yes	..	..	yes
106	..	129	27	yes
24	yes	171	6	yes
Education	0.67*	143	40	0.33*
26	no	112	16	yes
71	no	134	51	yes
33	yes	,,		no
30	yes	211	46	no
55	yes	143	19	no
68	yes	116	21	no
All companies	0.69*	164	45	0,65*

* Proportion of "yes" responses

Table IV. 10: Bivariate Pearson correlations of the binary recoded indicators of the monetary reward aspect construct in the selected companies (above, 0.4).

	Salary level	Salary determination individually	Bonus within the company
Salary level	1.00		
Salary determination individually		1.00	
Bonus within the company		-0.58	1.00

Table IV. 11: Communication patterns indicators by company

Company ID	N	Frequency of general information meetings (per month)	Frequency of meetings among professional workers (per month)	Percentage of respondent's					
				Attending more than 5...		Receiving more than 5...		...writing	...reading
				...formal meetings per week	...informal meetings per week	...emails from colleagues a day	...telephone calls from colleagues per day	6 or more documents a year	6 or more written materials per week
Consultancy	**101**			**7**	**23**	**25**	**22**	**36**	**36**
58	11	4	1	0	17	82	9	40	40
87	5	4	0	20	40	20	40	50	50
94	12	4	0	0	25	33	25	25	25
2	7	1	1	0	0	0	14	33	33
98	15	4	0	0	7	7	0	38	38
110	6	4	0	0	29	0	0	67	67
11	5	4	..			20	0	20	20
49	8	4	0	38	13	25	13	43	43
82	15	4	0	20	47	47	67	27	27
83	7	0	..		13	0	33	29	29
106	5	0	0	0	60	0	0	25	25
24	5	0	1	0	40	0	40	60	60
Education	**59**			**13**	**28**	**15**	**7**	**38**	**38**
26	9	0	1	0	43	0	0	0	0
71	8	9	0	50	13	0	0	50	50
33	12	4	0	17	23	25	25	75	75
30	5	0	0	0	0	0	0	25	25
55	9	2	0	0	0	11	0	43	43
68	16	4	..		38	31	13	27	27
All companies	**160**			**9**	**25**	**21**	**16**	**37**	**37**

Table IV. 12: Bivariate Pearson correlations of the binary recoded indicators of the communication construct in the selected companies

	Median	Percentage of respondents								
		With more than 5						Having regular meetings every week	Professionals having an scheduled meeting	Having a Newsletter
		hours in informal meetings	hours in regular meetings	work related written materials in one week	work related materials in one week	telephone calls per Day from other colleagues	emails per Day from other colleagues			
Percentage of respondents with more than 5 ...										
...hours in informal meetings	23.00	1.00								
...hours in regular meetings	0.00	-0.35	1.00							
...work related written materials in one week	15.00			1.00						
... work related materials in one week	36.00			0.56	1.00					
...telephone calls per day from colleagues	11.00		0.37			1.00				
...emails per day from colleagues	9.00			0.33			1.00			
Having regular meetings every week				0.55	0.31		0.65	1.00		
Professionals having an scheduled meeting			-0.30	-0.74				-0.41	1.00	
Having a Newsletter							0.43		-0.35	1.00

Table IV. 13: Information technology infrastructure indicators by company

Compa ny ID	ISIC	Number of computers per employee	Investment in IT in the year 2002(in MSEK)	IT cost as a proportion of the total monetary turnover	IT investment per employee (in SEK)
Consultancy		1.03	1672	0.012	10460
58	741	.		.	.
87	741	1.25	100	0.008	8333
94	741	1.00	200	0.008	7407
98	742	1.00	100	0.004	3571
49	744	1.33	125	0.014	13889
106	744	1.20	300	0.043	30000
24	745	1.00	90	0.004	3000
2	742	1.15	50	0.000	2500
110	742	1.00	257	0.019	15118
11	743	0.75	..	.	.
82	744	1.00	250	.	13889
83	744	0.72	200	0.006	6897
Education		0.92	2047	0.030	8917
26	801	0.19	19	0.004	889
71	801	0.10	..	.	.
30	804	0.92	50	0.004	4167
55	804	2.40	378	0.023	15120
68	804	0.60	1100	0.110	17742
33	802	1.33	500	0.008	6667
All companies		0.99	3719	0.018	9946

percentage of all companies with data

Table IV. 14: Bivariate Pearson correlations of the binary recoded indicators of the information technology investment binary indicators (above 0.40)

	Median	Number of computers per employee	Investment in IT per employee in 2002	Investment in IT as a percentage of the total monetary turnover, 2001	Investment in IT as a percentage of the total monetary turnover, 2002	Investment in IT as a percentage of the total monetary turnover, 2003
Number of computers per employee	1.00	1.00				
Investment in IT per employee in 2002	7407 SEK		1.00			
Investment in IT as a percentage of the total monetary turnover, 2001	7 per MSEK		1.00	1.00		
Investment in IT as a percentage of the total monetary turnover, 2002	8 per MSEK	0.58	0.86	0.77	1.00	
Investment in IT as a percentage of the total monetary turnover, 2003	6 per MSEK		0.65	0.75	0.41	1.00

Table IV. 15: ANOVA of course length by sector (consultancy and education)

	Sum of Squares	df	Mean Square	F	Sig.
Between Groups	396373.059	1	396373.059	12.743	.000
Within Groups	10824357.224	348	31104.475		
Total	11220730.282	349			

Table IV. 16: ANOVA of course training cost by sector (consultancy and education).

		Sum of Squares	df	Mean Square	F	Sig.
Total training cost per hour (trt/trctal)	Between Groups	9618424.402	1	9618424.402	35.330	.000
	Within Groups	84668558.131	311	272246.168		
	Total	94286982.533	312			
Direct training cost per hour (trt/trctal)	Between Groups	3274263.168	1	3274263.168	11.623	.001
	Within Groups	71550893.288	254	281696.430		
	Total	74825156.456	255			
Labor training cost per hour (trt/trctal)	Between Groups	102868.780	1	102868.780	20.254	.000
	Within Groups	1518576.885	299	5078.852		
	Total	1621445.666	300			
Other training cost per hour (trt/trctal)	Between Groups	51766.946	1	51766.946	6.369	.012
	Within Groups	2804150.945	345	8127.974		
	Total	2855917.890	346			

Table IV. 17: Number of training events and yearly estimated training time by purpose of training and company

ID	%of pro	Customer capital				ESF plan				Leadership training				Other training activities			
		f.	f%	h.	h%	f.	f%	h.	h%	f.	f%	h.	h%	f.	f%	h.	h%
Consultancy		14	4%	558	3%	14	4%	1202	7%	42	13%	3679	22%	18	5%	1061	6%
58	78%	4	8%	0	0%	0	0%	0	0%	7	14%	96	23%	7	14%	125	29%
87	83%	0	0%	0	0%	0	0%	0	0%	4	36%	1372	54%	2	18%	312	12%
94	78%	1	2%	150	5%	0	0%	0	0%	9	20%	576	19%	5	11%	464	15%
2	90%	1	4%		,	0	0%		,	1	4%		,	1	4%		,
98	93%	0	0%	0	0%	0	0%	0	0%	3	19%	312	19%	0	0%	0	0%
110	88%	1	3%	96	8%	1	3%	360	29%	3	9%	218	17%	0	0%	0	0%
11	69%	0	0%	0	0%	0	0%	0	0%	6	15%	216	8%	0	0%	0	0%
49	89%	1	6%	80	8%	1	6%	288	28%	1	6%	23	2%	0	0%	0	0%
82	83%	3	14%		,	0	0%		,	1	5%		,	0	0%		,
83	100%	1	4%		,	0	0%		,	1	4%		,	2	7%		,
106	90%	0	0%	0	0%	0	0%	0	0%	1	7%	162	10%	0	0%	0	0%
24	87%	2	6%	232	10%	12	39%	554	24%	5	16%	704	30%	1	3%	160	7%
Education		10	6%	796	4%	6	4%	1998	11%	16	10%	1638	9%	2	1%	40	0%
26	95%	3	8%	44	1%	0	0%	0	0%	5	13%	758	23%	2	5%	40	1%
71	80%	0	0%	0	0%	1	4%	906	29%	5	20%	469	15%	0	0%	0	0%
33	70%	2	20%	360	11%	0	0%	0	0%	0	0%	0	0%	0	0%	0	0%
30	92%	1	6%	16	2%	1	6%	388	43%	1	6%	64	7%	0	0%	0	0%
55	71%	2	4%	56	2%	4	7%	704	22%	3	5%	257	8%	0	0%	0	0%
68	59%	2	12%	320	7%	0	0%	0	0%	2	12%	90	2%	0	0%	0	0%
All Companies		24	5%	1354	4%	20	4%	3200	9%	58	12%	5317	15%	20	4%	1101	3%

Table IV.17 (Cont'd): Number of training events and yearly estimated training time by purpose of training and company

ID	%of pro	Work improvement conditions				Professional training				Support training				ALL	
		f.	f%	h.	h%	f.	f%	h.	h%	f.	f%	h.	h%	f.	h.
Consultancy		7	2%	640	4%	152	46%	6011	37%	82	25%	3253	20%	329	16404
58	0.78	0	0%	0	0%	17	35%	87	21%	14	29%	116	27%	49	424
87	0.83	0	0%	0	0%	2	18%	602	24%	3	27%	248	10%	11	2534
94	0.78	2	5%	102	3%	9	20%	544	18%	18	41%	1190	39%	44	3026
2	0.90	0	0%		,	18	69%		,	5	19%		,	26	0
98	0.93	0	0%	0	0%	10	63%	1092	68%	3	19%	208	13%	16	1612
110	0.88	0	0%	0	0%	17	53%	324	26%	10	31%	264	21%	32	1262
11	0.69	3	8%	152	6%	25	64%	2005	78%	5	13%	184	7%	39	2557
49	0.89	0	0%	0	0%	14	78%	631	60%	1	6%	22	2%	18	1044
82	0.83	0	0%		,	12	57%		,	5	24%		,	21	0
83	1.00	0	0%		,	15	56%		,	8	30%		,	27	0
106	0.90	1	7%	250	15%	6	40%	454	28%	7	47%	760	47%	15	1626
24	0.87	1	3%	136	6%	7	23%	272	12%	3	10%	261	11%	31	2319
Education		1	1%	48	0%	86	53%	10263	56%	41	25%	3619	20%	162	18402
26	0.95	1	3%	48	1%	23	61%	1915	59%	4	11%	436	13%	38	3241
71	0.80	0	0%	0	0%	16	64%	1306	41%	3	12%	477	15%	25	3158
33	0.70	0	0%	0	0%	6	60%	2560	77%	2	20%	400	12%	10	3320
30	0.92	0	0%	0	0%	2	13%	184	21%	11	69%	240	27%	16	892
55	0.71	0	0%	0	0%	34	61%	1218	39%	13	23%	912	29%	56	3147
68	0.59	0	0%	0	0%	5	29%	3080	66%	8	47%	1154	25%	17	4644
All companies		8	2%	688	2%	238	48%	16274	47%	123	25%	6872	20%	491	34806

Table IV. 18: Average scores and standard deviations of the informal learning items by company

Company ID	ISIC	N. of employees	N. of valid questionnaires	N. of respondents as a % of total n. of emp.	d1: Read manuals, reference books, journals or other written materials but not as part of a course.		d2: Went on guided tours at a museum, art gallery or other such cultural facilities		d3: Used media-assisted products to learn such as computers, video, television, tapes that were NOT part of a course.	
					Mean	Std. dev.	Mean	Std. dev.	Mean	Std. dev.
Consultancy		243	106	0.44	3.66	0.45	2.68	0.41	2.86	0.42
58	741	27	12	0.44	3.00	1.28	2.42	1.24	2.91	1.30
87	741	12	5	0.42	4.40	0.89	2.40	1.34	3.80	0.84
94	741	27	13	0.48	3.92	1.12	2.23	1.17	2.38	1.61
2	742	20	7	0.35	3.14	0.90	2.29	1.11	2.43	1.40
98	742	28	15	0.54	3.57	1.02	3.13	0.92	2.93	1.39
110	742	17	7	0.41	3.71	1.25	2.57	1.27	2.57	0.98
11	743	16	5	0.31	3.60	1.14	2.00	1.41	3.00	1.41
49	744	9	9	1.00	3.11	1.05	2.78	1.48	2.56	1.42
82	744	18	15	0.83	3.67	0.62	3.07	1.16	3.47	0.99
83	744	29	8	0.28	3.63	0.74	3.25	0.89	2.88	1.36
106	744	10	5	0.50	4.40	0.55	3.00	1.00	2.60	0.89
24	745	30	5	0.17	3.80	0.45	3.00	1.00	2.80	1.10
Education		215	59	0.27	3.94	0.31	2.82	0.58	3.50	0.61
26	801	21	9	0.43	3.38	1.06	1.89	0.93	3.00	1.50
71	801	20	8	0.40	4.00	0.53	3.13	0.83	2.63	0.92
33	802	75	13	0.17	3.92	1.04	2.69	1.60	3.46	1.13
30	804	12	5	0.42	4.00	0.71	2.80	1.48	3.60	0.89
55	804	25	9	0.36	4.33	0.87	3.67	1.00	4.22	1.09
68	804	62	16	0.26	4.00	1.07	2.73	1.33	4.07	1.10
All Companies		458	165	0.36	3.75	0.42	2.73	0.46	3.07	0.56

Table IV.18 (Cont'd): Average scores and standard deviations of the informal learning items by company

		d4: Asked my colleagues for help when I have a problem in my work		d5: Learnt by watching, getting help or advice from others - but NOT from course instructors		d6: Learnt by myself trying things out, doing things for practice, trying different approaches to do things		d7: Learnt by reading job-related news on the Internet.		d17: Average of all the informal learning activities	
		Mean	Std. dev.	Mean	Std. dev.	Mean	Std. dev.	Mean	Std. dev.	Mean	Std. dev.
Consultancy		3.68	0.37	3.41	0.33	3.84	0.53	3.07	0.54	3.31	0.26
58	741	3.75	0.75	3.33	1.07	3.92	0.67	2.92	1.51	3.10	0.67
87	741	3.00	1.22	3.00	0.71	3.80	0.45	4.00	1.00	3.49	0.36
94	741	4.08	0.76	3.23	1.30	3.69	1.11	2.92	1.38	3.21	0.81
2	742	3.86	0.38	3.00	0.82	2.86	0.90	3.14	1.07	2.96	0.47
98	742	3.60	0.99	3.07	1.07	3.50	0.85	2.60	1.35	3.10	0.76
110	742	3.86	0.69	3.57	0.79	4.29	0.49	3.29	1.70	3.41	0.64
11	743	3.00	0.71	3.20	0.84	3.00	1.22	2.20	0.84	2.86	0.47
49	744	3.44	1.13	3.50	1.20	3.89	0.78	2.67	1.12	3.13	0.65
82	744	3.80	0.56	3.47	0.83	3.87	0.52	3.40	0.91	3.53	0.38
83	744	4.13	0.64	3.75	0.89	4.63	0.52	2.50	1.20	3.54	0.56
106	744	3.60	1.14	3.80	0.84	4.20	1.10	3.40	1.14	3.57	0.60
24	745	4.00	0.71	4.00	0.71	4.40	0.55	3.80	1.64	3.69	0.49
Education		3.74	0.27	3.38	0.34	4.24	0.29	2.67	1.15	3.47	0.35
26	801	3.78	0.44	3.50	0.53	3.88	0.64	1.11	0.33	2.89	0.48
71	801	3.50	0.53	3.13	1.25	4.38	0.52	1.50	0.53	3.18	0.36
33	802	4.00	0.71	3.23	1.01	4.00	0.82	3.15	1.14	3.49	0.68
30	804	3.60	0.89	4.00	1.00	4.60	0.55	3.80	1.30	3.77	0.56
55	804	4.11	0.93	3.33	0.87	4.50	0.84	2.67	1.00	3.83	0.40
68	804	3.47	1.13	3.07	1.21	4.07	0.59	3.80	0.94	3.54	0.80
All companies		3.70	0.34	3.40	0.32	3.97	0.49	2.94	0.78	3.37	0.29

Table IV. 19: Total variance explained by the Factor analysis of the knowledge-creation indicators

Component	Initial Eigenvalues			Extraction Sums of Squared Loadings			Rotation Sums of Squared Loadings		
	Total	% of Variance	Cumulative %	Total	% of Variance	Cumulative %	Total	% of Variance	Cumulative %
1	2.60	37.20	37.20	2.60	37.20	37.20	2.60	37.16	37.16
2	1.85	26.48	63.68	1.85	26.48	63.68	1.82	25.97	63.13
3	1.58	22.57	86.25	1.58	22.57	86.25	1.62	23.12	86.25
4	0.39	5.62	91.87						
5	0.30	4.29	96.16						
6	0.26	3.73	99.89						
7	0.01	0.11	100.00						

Extraction Method: Principal Component Analysis.

Table IV. 20: Rotated component matrix from the factor analysis of the knowledge-creation

	Component		
	1.00	2.00	3.00
Yearly training time per employee (*trTemp*)	0.89	0.32	-0.09
Training cost per employee (*trCTemp*)	0.91	-0.38	-0.05
Budgeted training cost per employee (*trActemp*)	0.90	0.01	0.12
Training budgeted as a proportion of the total estimated cost in the relevant year(s) (*trActPer*)	0.31	0.84	0.09
Total training cost per hour (*trctT*)	0.30	-0.89	0.02
Number of training places per employee (*trPemp*)	0.04	0.21	0.88
d17	0.03	0.14	-0.90

Extraction Method: Principal Component Analysis.
Rotation Method: Varimax with Kaiser Normalization.
a Rotation converged in 4 iterations.

Table IV. 21: Bivariate Pearson correlation between knowledge-enabling construct and knowledge-creation indicators in each service

	Consultancy	Education	Consultancy	Education	Consultancy	Education	Consultancy	Education
	trTemp	trTemp	trPemp	trPemp	trCTemp	trCTemp	trActemp	trActemp
SIZEBSB	-0.35			-0.71	-0.41			0.41
STABSB	0.35	-0.25		1.00		-0.33	0.50	-0.33
EXPBSB						0.71	0.63	0.61
PROBSB	-0.55	0.32	0.31	-0.32	-0.41	0.63		1.00
RESB	0.48		-0.37	-0.50		-0.50	0.79	-0.41
SALBSB	0.40	0.00		0.00	-0.10	0.00		-0.48
COBSB		0.50	-0.37	-0.50				0.61
ITBSB				-0.71	0.80		-0.32	0.41
KIS all	0.35	0.00	-0.17	-0.71	0.17	0.00	0.16	0.40
CCIB	-0.35	0.00	-0.17	0.71	0.25	0.00	-0.16	-0.48

Table V.21 (Cont'd): Bivariate Pearson correlation between knowledge-enabling construct and knowledge-creation indicators in each service

	Consultancy	Education	Consultancy	Education	Consultancy	Education
	trActPer	trActPer	trctT	trctT	d17	d17
SIZEBSB	-0.77	0.67	0.45	-0.45		0.71
STABSB		-0.58	-0.48	-0.33	-0.37	-1.00
EXPBSB			-0.45	-0.45		
PROBSB		0.61				0.32
RESB			-0.33	0.63		0.50
SALBSB	0.58	0.17	-0.66	-0.45		0.32
COBSB	0.00	1.00		-0.32		0.00
ITBSB	0.50	0.67		-0.45	0.27	0.71
KIS all	0.50	0.67	-0.45	-0.45	-0.17	0.70
CCIB	0.00	-0.67	0.45	-0.45	-0.17	-0.71

www.ingramcontent.com/pod-product-compliance
Lightning Source LLC
LaVergne TN
LVHW062313060326
832902LV00013B/2201